# Wind of Change

# Wind of
# Change

## An American Journey
## in Post-Soviet Russia

## Kenneth Maher

Charleston, SC
www.PalmettoPublishing.com

*Wind of Change*

First Edition

Hardback ISBN: 979-8-88590-688-3
Paperback ISBN: 979-8-88590-689-0
eBook ISBN: 979-8-8229-0399-9

# Table of Contents

# Foreword

THE SOVIET UNION HAD DISSOLVED a year earlier, and I had received my master's degree in Russian Area Studies. Like many young Americans at the time, my only contact with actual Russians was through my professors or the few Russian exchange students fortunate enough to study in the United States during the perestroika period. For someone with my background in the late 1980s, the usual pathway was teaching Russian or perhaps working for the U.S. government. I had explored those options but found little attraction. Unfortunately, work opportunities outside of those areas were minimal.

In the summer of 1992, I found myself working a menial job in a local pharmacy in Chicago, where I had moved to accompany my future wife, who was studying law in the city. I still dreamt, however, of earning a living from my knowledge of Russian. For months, I spent my non-working hours dropping off my resume at companies I thought may have business internationally. One afternoon, I returned home from work to discover a voice message from a small local company exploring business in the former Soviet Union. I convinced the company to offer me a temporary position to help evaluate such opportunities. The work did not pay a great deal, but it opened the door to utilizing my university skills. Over the next two years, I traveled throughout Russia, trying to forge business ties between American and Russian businesses. It was an exciting time. The early post-Soviet landscape was chaotic and often reminded me of the 'wild west' in American folklore.

The old rules under communism were gone, but the rules in the 'new' Russia were still being written. Vast fortunes acquired by a new class known as 'oligarchs' contrasted sharply with an unprecedented level of poverty for most ordinary citizens. There was a pervasive atmosphere of hope shared by Russians and Americans that the hostilities of the Cold War were over, replaced by a new era of peace and cooperation. I believe we were all a bit naïve at the time, but it was a unique and tragically short-lived period in Russia. Coming of age in these changing times, I feel, even now, the lasting impact of this experience. My journey shaped the adult that I am today.

*Wind of Change* aims to give an American's perspective on Russia, emerging from decades of Communism, as it strived to become a more free society. This transition challenged many fundamental historical and cultural beliefs of Russians and Americans. There were severe obstacles hindering the eventual success of this transition. Recent Russian history has demonstrated the severity of these challenges as Russia drifted back toward authoritarianism, reminiscent of its Tsarist and Soviet legacy.

Three decades have elapsed since the events I describe took place. It is impossible to record every conversation word-for-word, and undoubtedly, subsequent life experience affects memory. Nonetheless, I have tried to stay true to the actual events as much as possible. I have changed the names of the Russians and Americans with whom I interacted to protect their privacy. Reality in the book is as I remember and understand it to offer a portal into a unique historical period. I hope the reader will garner an appreciation for a people and a culture that I continue to find fascinating.

# An Unexpected Journey

LYING ON MY SIDE, I tried to settle in for the long flight from Chicago to Khabarovsk. There was plenty of open space in the massive Ilyushin aircraft. The fabric scratched my skin, and the cheaply upholstered cushions provided little comfort. My feet felt restricted by the inflexible plastic armrest from the aisle seat, and the Walkman earpads pressed against the makeshift pillow from my winter coat pinched my ears. The cassette played soothing songs, but sleep was problematic. Thoughts of traveling to the 'new' Russia kept swirling around in my head. At twenty-four, I would be one of the youngest Americans to experience Russia since the collapse of the Soviet Union a little more than a year earlier. It was the journey of a lifetime that occurred almost by accident.

I had been living with my fiancée since finishing my graduate work in Russian studies. While western interest in the former Soviet Union was increasing, job opportunities remained elusive. For many months, I walked the streets of Chicago's business district, handing copies of my resume to scores of receptionists who likely discarded the piece of paper. On rare occasions, I managed to get a brief meeting with the human resources manager, who usually explained that, although my credentials were impressive, the company had no real need for my talents. In the meantime, I worked as a clerk stocking shelves at a local pharmacy. It was tedious work, but the salary provided money for food and rent.

One winter evening, I returned home to see the red light flashing on the answering machine. A man named Don McPherson had left a brief message stating that his firm, The Pyramid Group, was evaluating a project in Russia and wanted to speak with me about the opportunity. He mentioned that he had found my resume in the file kept by the receptionist. I immediately called back and set a time to meet the next day. I arrived at the six-story grey stone building on Michigan Avenue dressed in my only business suit. While standing in the elevator, I checked the knot in my green tie, using the reflection in the gold metal control panel. The lift stopped at the fifth floor, and I stepped into a small corridor covered with tan carpet. A set of glass doors inscribed with The Pyramid Group in large black letters stood to my right. I entered the suite and approached the reception desk, where I introduced myself.

Several minutes later, a tall, middle-aged man with sandy hair arrived from the back of the office. He wore a red and blue striped collared shirt and light tan pants held in place by a thick brown belt. After a brief introduction, I followed him through another set of glass doors near the reception area. Numerous framed photographs hung on the walls depicting high-rise buildings, golf courses, and commercial centers. Just past a conference room on the left, Don turned into an office. An imposing wood desk centered the room, behind which stood two tall bookcases overflowing with files, books, and various mementos anchored the room. The desk was similarly cluttered. Files lay sprinkled over the surface, and a small marble nameplate at the edge of the desk reminded visitors of its owner. More framed pictures adorned the walls, with a wide-framed photograph of a harbor scene on the right. I lowered myself into one of the thinly cushioned chairs in front of the desk.

Don explained that another Chicago company had approached The Pyramid Group to participate in a Russian Far East development project to design and build several commercial development plans, including a golf course.

"We have the real estate expertise but do not have anyone here at the firm who speaks Russian," Don added. "That's why I was interested in your resume since we will need documents translated. Is that something you could do for us?"

I responded yes and added that I would love to participate in the project. I tried to temper my excitement and told Don that I could begin immediately. He explained that the role received a small stipend and would be followed by a larger bonus payout after completing the project. It was not ideal, but my youthful enthusiasm for the prospect brushed away my concerns, and I agreed to work under those conditions. Don informed me that the firm was hosting a breakfast for a group of Russian officials and businessmen in Chicago in two weeks.

"The Russians are from Khabarovsk," Don said. "Have you heard of it?"

"No," I replied. My knowledge of the Russian Far East came mainly from the novels by Dostoyevsky and Solzhenitsyn describing life in Siberian penal camps.

Don spun around in his chair and grabbed a thin paper cylinder from a bookcase shelf. He slid out a rolled-up Russia map and unfurled it on his desk. I got up and stood over the map to better see the markings on the paper. Circled in red ink was Khabarovsk, a city of half a million located several hundred miles inland from the Pacific Ocean. The town sat on the northeast bank of the Amur River, which served as the border between Russia and China.

"I will read up on the city before the delegation arrives," I said.

"Good idea. I'd also like you to read up on some of the basics for real estate development to improve your understanding of what we do." Don turned to his bookcases again and selected several commercial and golf course development books.

"I'll be prepared," I said, taking the books from the director.

That evening I quit the pharmacy job. At first, I translated documents, mainly contracts and marketing materials, into Russian in preparation for the upcoming visit. The rest of my time was devoted to researching Khabarovsk's history and learning the fundamentals of real estate development. I felt ready to address the Russian delegation by the end of the second week. However, my youthful exuberance and business naïveté were to prove that I still had much to learn.

A placard reading 'Dobro Pozhalovat' (Welcome) greeted the group of men stepping out of the elevator. Several were clearly Russian, holding fur hats and mostly mismatched suits; they looked around anxiously. The group's leader appeared to be an African-American man dressed in an exquisite blue silk suit. A yellow tie and bright red handkerchief stuffed into his breast pocket completed his ensemble. In his right hand hung a brown felt fedora with an enormous white feather stuck in the headband. A short Asian man wearing a University of Illinois 'I' pin in his jacket buttonhole was standing next to another man, likely in his sixties, with a Chicago Bears ski hat.

Standing by the double glass entrance doors, I observed some smiles from the Russians when they read the placard. I approached the group leader, shook his hand, and welcomed him to The Pyramid Group. He replied that his name was Nathan Johnson, CEO of Cardinal Communications. I then turned to the rest of the group.

"Dobroe yutro and good morning," I said and continued in Russian. "I am glad that you have come. Please follow me."

I led the men into the reception area, where Don and John Gainfield, the firm's president, introduced themselves. Don invited Nathan and the rest of the delegation to accompany him to the main conference room. I trailed the group down the familiar tan hallway and through the glass partition that formed the inner wall of the conference room. Plates of fruit and pastries were scattered around the long wood table. John and Don sat together at the head of the table while I remained standing off to their right. We waited for the visitors to find seats and settle in. John then rose and addressed the delegation.

"I'd like to welcome all of you to The Pyramid Group this morning. I am John Gainfield, the CEO of the firm. We are excited to have the opportunity to...."

Translating his words into Russian, I scanned the faces of our guests. Luckily, the visitors gazed at me with expressions that indicated they understood what I was saying. I noticed one Russian, a man in his mid-thirties, was following my words more intensely than the others. He sat almost directly opposite me and appeared to verify each sentence I delivered. The man nodded in agreement for the first several minutes when I finished my translations. However, when I started to translate John's description of the firm's real estate development activities, the dark-haired Russian put down the pastry he had been eating and stood up.

"I am sorry to interrupt," the man said in fluent English. "I need to correct what Ken just said. My name is Ivan Ivanovich Volkov, the interpreter for the delegation."

I stood surprised as Ivan proceeded to restate, in Russian, what John had said. Having finished, Ivan sat back down. I made a few more attempts to translate the CEO's speech but was stopped each time by the Russian interpreter. Finally, Ivan announced that he would provide the translation for the meeting. Slightly embarrassed, I sat as a spectator for the remainder of the meeting. After John's speech, Nathan Johnson explained the structure of the proposed arrangement. The Pyramid Group would function as a sub-contractor to Cardinal Communications for any real estate plans in Khabarovsk. Nathan outlined the grand projects he envisioned for the Russian city. He also introduced the other two Americans who were part of his team and involved in work The Pyramid Group might undertake. Sporting the University of Illinois pin, Makoto Tanaka operated a consulting firm representing various Japanese interests in Chicago. Due to geographic proximity, Makoto expressed that some of his clients were interested in developments in the Russian Far East. Bob Garrett was a former oil and gas executive, now retired, who desired to look at energy investments in Russia. Nathan explained that a couple of additional American investors were working with his team. The Russian representatives consisted of two government officials, several local businessmen, and Ivan, the interpreter. One of the officials spoke eloquently about how the Khabarovsk government supported Western investment and would offer incentives and quick approvals for new projects.

As breakfast concluded, John and Don had agreed to participate as part of Cardinal Communication's team, evaluating several projects in Khabarovsk, including restaurants, a casino, and a golf course. Throughout the talks, I gazed from time to time at Don, trying to determine whether my initial failure would mean a quick end to my role at the firm. I envisioned having to return to the pharmacy and supplicant myself to get my job back.

I shook hands with everyone. After escorting the group to the elevators, I returned and poked my head inside Don's office. I apologized for the translation mix-up and added that I thought the meeting went well. Don replied that it was unfortunate that the Russian interpreter had to take over, but he did not seem angry. In response to my inquiry about further work I might perform, the director explained that he and John needed to discuss the details for the Khabarovsk trip and would contact me in the next few days. I left the office and went home, unsure about my future position with the firm. Over dinner, I explained the day's events to my girlfriend Deb, expressing my disappointment with my performance and admitting that my dream of working in Russia was just that: a dream. She tried to console me, encouraging me to stay persistent and optimistic.

The next day passed in silence while I stayed in the apartment, awaiting a call from Don. In the evening, I made plans to go to the pharmacy the following morning to see if I could regain my employment. It was a long sleepless night. My mind was full of doubts. I dreaded the thought of returning to stacking shelves and managing invoices. While in graduate school, I had turned down an opportunity to work for a government agency in Washington, D.C., and moved to Chicago to be with my girlfriend and find a job using Russian. The sensation that I had made a colossal error kept running around in my head.

In the morning, while I was putting on my winter coat to head to the pharmacy, I heard the phone ring. I picked up the receiver and heard Don's voice.

"Ken," he said. "John and I discussed the project in detail yesterday, and we would like to have you continue to help us. Are you still open to doing that?"

A massive sigh of relief left my body upon hearing those words. "Of course," I replied. "I would be delighted. Do you want me to come in today?"

"That would be great, yes. We only have a couple of weeks to prepare, and there is a lot to do. I'll expect to see you in a couple of hours?"

"For sure. I will be there as soon as I can."

I put down the receiver, and an involuntary wave of emotion swept over me. I felt like I did when scoring a touchdown in my high school and college football days. I let out a loud 'Yeah!' and jumped in the air pumping my fist upward. I scored my first victory in the business world, finally crossing the goal line after being stopped short on many occasions. I rushed into the bedroom, serving as a study area, and told Deb the big news. Seated at her tiny desk in the corner, she was engrossed in preparing a case brief for her next class. I startled her with my entrance.

"They want me to stay on!" I exclaimed. "The firm just called, and they want me to keep working on the project in Russia. I am going over there now. Forget the pharmacy!"

"That's awesome!" she said. "I'm so happy and proud of you. I have to finish prepping this brief but tell me all about it tonight."

I hugged and kissed her and then ran out of the apartment. My feet felt so light that I almost glided my way along the streets, reaching the grey stone building in record time. The receptionist detected my excitement when I entered the suite. She had a broad smile and told me that Don was waiting for me. The door was open, so I stepped into Don's office. He was on the phone but waved at me to take a seat.

"I was speaking with Nathan Johnson from Cardinal Communications," stated Don after he hung up. "The flight to Khabarovsk is only twelve days from today on the twenty-first. Do you have a passport?"

"Passport? I don't understand. I thought that I would just be preparing documents in Russian."

"Yes, you will. However, John and I decided that we want someone on the team who speaks Russian to protect our interests. Do you want to go to Khabarovsk?"

Did I want to go to Khabarovsk? I had been waiting since my undergraduate years to journey to the country that fascinated me. I had to turn down an opportunity to study at Moscow State University during my junior year in college because I lacked the financial resources to pay for the trip.

"Naturally, I want to go," I said, trying to contain my enthusiasm. "I have been dreaming of such an experience for several years. Unfortunately, I do not have a passport."

"Well, that might be a problem. I am not sure we can get you one before the trip. Let me have Cheryl (the receptionist) make some calls to check."

"OK. I think I'll also need an invitation from Russia to get a visa."

"That's correct. Nathan Johnson informed me that the Russians would secure invitations for everyone."

"That's one less problem then," I said.

"And, one more thing," added Don. "The Russian delegation is holding a kick-boxing exhibition on the twentieth with a formal farewell dinner to follow that evening. Apparently, the Russians brought a kick-boxing team as part of the official delegation. You should plan on attending both events. Do you have a tuxedo?"

My duties seemed to keep expanding. I informed Don that I would love to see the exhibition and attend the dinner. I explained that I did not own a tuxedo but would rent one for the occasion. With that, the discussion concluded, and I set to work. Near the end of the day, Don stopped by and asked to speak with me. Back in his office, he informed me that I could request a passport from the US State Department on a rush basis. He handed me the required documents and added that the firm would pay the rush fee. I, however, would have to go in the morning to submit the application.

The next day I went to the federal building in Chicago and submitted my passport documents. Before returning to the office, I found a men's clothing store, where I reserved a tuxedo for the farewell dinner. I tried on several styles and chose a classic black jacket and tie. It was the first time I had worn such formal dress, and I imagined I resembled James Bond while gazing at my reflection in the mirror.

The Pyramid Group considered sending two experienced developers, in addition to me, to Khabarovsk. However, after some follow-up discussions, Don decided that one developer could handle the site reviews. He selected Jim Mazuros, who had been with the firm for about a decade and was an expert in golf course development. He had an easy-going style and a good sense of humor, which made me feel more comfortable, given that we were going to be spending a lot of time together during the visit. I began to spend more time working with Jim to coordinate activities and prepare documents.

The evening before the farewell dinner, Don and John invited me to a small café just around the corner from the firm's office. The eatery sported a diner motif from the 1950s; pictures of Elvis and Chuck Berry adorned the walls while period music blasted in from overhead speakers. I slid into the aqua-colored bench and faced the two men across the table. I assumed the firm leaders wanted to give me last-minute instructions and advice for the upcoming trip.

"We are very pleased with your work so far," began John. "Don tells me the documents are ready and that you and Jim have a good rapport." He looked at his partner, who nodded in agreement.

"Thank you," I replied. "Yes. The contracts and other materials are translated, and Jim and I have mapped out the itinerary for the trip. I am looking forward to it."

"That's wonderful," continued the CEO. "We asked you here to let you know that you will be going on the trip alone. One of our major golf clients has had an emergency, and we need Jim to go to Georgia instead. I know that this is sudden, but Don and I feel that you will be capable of representing us."

I didn't know what to say. Two weeks ago, I was a clerk in a pharmacy, and now I was being asked to travel to Siberia to assess the potential for a golf course and other sites. Feelings of terror and excitement hit me at once. I sat motionless for several moments. I could tell that Don read what was in my mind.

"I understand that this seems like a lot," Don chimed in, "but your knowledge of Russian will be very effective." I sensed that he was attempting to boost my confidence. "You have picked up quite a bit about our business already."

"I appreciate that, but I am not sure I can tell whether a site is appropriate for a golf course or a restaurant."

"We don't expect you to do the evaluation," added John. "You will have a camera to take video of the various sites. The developers will examine the video when you get back."

The server brought our meals. I took a few bites of my chicken sandwich to give myself some time to absorb what I had just heard. While chewing, I imagined walking around Khabarovsk with my video camera filming various buildings. I wasn't sure that would not attract unwanted attention. Then, I thought about what an excellent opportunity to prove that I could be a valuable full-time employee for the firm. This trip might lead to a string of projects in Russia in which I could participate. I put down my sandwich.

"OK. I am ready to do this," I said a bit too loudly. "I will make sure I get some great footage during the trip."

"Excellent!" replied John. He reached into his coat pocket and pulled out a white envelope. "This is your official invitation to the farewell dinner."

I thanked John but did not open the envelope immediately. The meal finished, we said our goodbyes and shook hands. I watched the two men walk down Michigan Avenue before making my way back to the apartment. Thick snowflakes began to land upon my coat and hat as I strolled down East Ohio Street. Already, I pictured myself in a deep Russian forest surrounded by tall trees, the silence broken only by a sharp wind raging through the snow-covered branches. Deb interrupted my trance by brushing the white powder from my coat as I entered the apartment. I summarized the dinner conversation, and she shared my apprehension and enthusiasm. She told me that, despite the risk, I had to take this once-in-a-lifetime chance.

The kick-boxing event took place in the ballroom of a grand hotel. A four-cornered ring stood in the center of the space. I arrived about twenty minutes before the event and took a ringside seat at one of the small oval tables bordering the stage. The room was about half full. Lying on the table's surface was a limited food and drink menu flanked by a card displaying the schedule of matches. Ten bouts were listed on the card, one Russian versus one American. While reading the card, I felt a tap on my shoulder. I looked up and saw Don. He asked if he could join me, to which I readily agreed.

"Are you nervous about tomorrow? I know that we threw a lot at you last night."

"No, I'm fine," I replied. "It will be my first international flight. I am a little anxious since I'm going alone. But, it should be an interesting adventure."

"I agree. I wish I had the time to go. I'd love to see what Russia is like," added Don. "After the exhibition, you can pick up the video camera at the office. We bought a brand new model, so the footage should be good."

"Sounds great, thanks."

We ordered some drinks and snacks as the first match got underway. It was a featherweight bout; the two fighters were short and slender but showed a lot of energy. The Russian combatant was more skillful, forcing the American on the defensive for most of the match. After the third round, the referee ended the fight, and the three-judge panel declared the Russian the winner. I looked around the ballroom area, which was now almost full. I noticed several colleagues from The Pyramid Group dispersed among the tables. During the third match, Nathan Johnson briefly joined our table. Dressed in another colorful outfit, he expressed his good wishes for a successful trip, adding that he looked forward to signing several contracts by the end of the stay. Nathan shook our hands and moved off to another table, greeting as many people as he could. Next up was a heavy-weight bout.

Two tall, muscular athletes contorted themselves through the ropes and entered the white padded ring. The action was slower, but the blows from the fighters resounded throughout the room. While chewing on a chicken finger, a spat of blood landed on the table, staining the white cloth covering the surface. I jerked backward in alarm wanting to avoid any further blood splashes. Don shifted his chair a little farther away from the edge of the ring. This time, the American vanquished his Russian opponent, standing with arms raised in the center of the platform. After several more contests, the exhibition ended with evenly split results between the Russians and Americans. Don and I exited the ballroom and headed out of the hotel. We shared a taxi ride back to the office, where I retrieved the video camera. Don would not be attending the dinner, so he wished me well on the trip and shook my hand before I returned to my apartment to prepare for the evening.

"Here, let me fix this, so it looks right." I stood still as my girlfriend tightened and straightened my bow tie. "There, now you look handsome."

She helped me put on my overcoat so as not to wrinkle the tuxedo and accompanied me to the elevator. Hearing the familiar tone announcing the elevator's arrival, she smiled and gave me a soft kiss.

"Have a good time tonight," she said and added with a wink, "... make sure the other women don't get too jealous."

When I arrived, I saw a small gathering milling around the large oak bar at the restaurant. I recognized several people from the past couple of weeks: a few Cardinal Communications employees and some Russian delegation members whom I had met at our firm's breakfast. The Americans were all dressed in formal attire, while the Russians sported a variety of dress styles; most wore business suits, but a few had on sweaters. The conversation appeared sporadic. Ivan Ivanovich, the interpreter, was busy moving among groups to facilitate the discussion. Having grabbed a drink, I walked over to offer assistance.

"Dobry vyechor (good evening)," I said. "Looks like you have your hands full. Do you want any help?"

"Sure, I can handle this group, but I haven't had much time to work my way over there."

"Khorosho (OK, good)," I stated and moved towards the four people sitting near the corner of the bar. I said hello to everyone in both languages. The group, however, did not appear to need an interpreter. Several empty shot glasses lay overturned in front of each man. The effects of strong alcohol had removed any language barriers. Laughter, hand gestures, and a few backslaps sufficed to communicate. The men invited me to join in the next round, which I politely declined, wanting to keep my wits about me.

A few paces away, I observed one of the Russians standing silently in front of a painting. He was an older man, likely in his early sixties, dressed very elegantly in a dark blue suit. His greying hair was still bountiful, with a noticeable part down the left side, and his rigid stance displayed a sense of authority and gravity. I assumed he was an official of some kind. I approached the man respectfully and stood beside him. The painting he was staring at so intently depicted a lake surrounded by forest. Near the shore, people were gathered, families and couples, enjoying the bright sunny day. The artist had used an impressionist style with no clear-cut forms. I thought I had seen a similar piece during my past visits to the Chicago Art Museum.

"It's a beautiful painting," I said in Russian. "Do you enjoy lake scenes?

"Da (yes)," replied the distinguished gentleman. "The painting reminds me of the 'ozero' (lake) near my home. Your city is impressive, but I look forward to returning home."

"That's interesting," I replied. I wanted to build some friendships with the delegation. It would be personally rewarding, and I thought it might help me perform my work for The Pyramid Group. "I am looking forward to seeing your city over the next week. Are there many beautiful places like your lake?"

"Oh yes, many." I could see the man's face brighten. "I have lived there all my life. There are endless lakes, rivers, and forests."

"Wonderful. I hope that I get a chance to see some. I grew up by the ocean, and I miss waking up and being able to walk along the beach."

"Well then, young man, I will see what I can do," he stated.

"Thank you so much. My name is Ken Lvovich Maher." I used the Russian custom, known as a patronymic, of using the name of one's father to follow one's given name when making an introduction. "I am representing the real estate firm."

"Pleasure to meet you, Ken Lvovich. I am Prekrasov, Igor Semyonovich. I am the deputy governor of the Khabarovsk Krai (region)."

The leader of the Russian delegation extended his hand, which I shook forcefully. I was astonished to make such an acquaintance. I knew that influence in Russia depended mainly on personal relationships, and to have made a good impression with the deputy governor could only be advantageous. My new acquaintance and I talked more about Khabarovsk. He commented on how well I spoke Russian, adding that he had never met an American who spoke the language. I was describing my hometown of Boston when I was distracted by a hand on my elbow. I shifted my eyes to the left and saw The Pyramid Group's CEO standing next to me. John was wearing a traditional black tuxedo jacket but had added some flair with a light blue cummerbund.

"Are you ready to get seated," he said. "The dinner is about to get started."

"Of course," I answered. "I'm just finishing up my conversation with Igor Semyonovich."

I introduced John to the deputy governor. Pyramid's CEO was polite but did not show much interest in speaking with the delegation chief. I excused myself to Igor Semyonovich, explaining that I needed to accompany my boss. His smile indicated that he understood. I followed John from the bar into the dining area, weaving my way past scores of dark wood tables occupied by couples and families enjoying a quiet dinner. The dark brown parquet floor complemented the deep wood wall panels, while several immense chandeliers provided lighting. Near the back of the dining area were two tall wood doors with stained glass panels. Judging by John's movement, these doors were our destination. A male server in a white dress shirt and black bow tie stood by the doors. He opened one of the heavy doors and stepped aside when my boss and I reached the threshold.

The VIP room shared a similar décor to the main dining area. The same dark wood adorned the walls upon which hung several large gold-framed paintings. The artwork also appeared to be copies of famous pieces found in the Chicago Art Museum. Several long tables covered with white tablecloths stood in rows on the light brown parquet floor. A glance at the place settings indicated an expected group of at least thirty. Small name cards sat in front of each place setting. At the moment, slightly more than half the chairs had guests. John located his name card near the head of the middle table. I noticed my name written in tiny black cursive letters on the card directly to his right. I sat down on the thick cushion and copied my boss by placing the triangular napkin on my plate neatly in my lap. I took hold of the water goblet to my right, needing to quench my thirst after my long talk with Igor Semyonovich. While I felt the refreshing water flow into my mouth, I heard a high-pitched voice speaking to my boss.

"John, who is this delightful young man you have brought tonight?"

I put the goblet down, sat back in my chair, and noticed a dark-haired woman immediately to my right. The woman appeared to be in her early forties with a big fluffy hairstyle reminiscent of the mid-1980s. She wore a black sleeveless cocktail dress, and a string of white pearls accentuated her low neckline. A cigarette was dangling between her index and middle fingers, with the butt revealing a thin red circular outline of lipstick. Adeptness with makeup masked the crow's feet around her eyes, caused by the broad smile on her pleasant face. Her manner and movements revealed an elite upbringing. Most of the men at the table looked in her direction.

"This is Ken," replied John, speaking across me from the left. "He has recently joined the firm. He speaks Russian and will be traveling with the delegation tomorrow."

"Wow, how exciting," she said, feigning being impressed. "Privyet! (Hi!) That is all the Russian I know," she finished with a soft laugh. "I am Joanne Marshall. Where did you learn Russian?"

"I studied it in college in Boston. I recently completed my graduate degree in Russian Studies in Washington, DC."

I explained to her my unexpected journey to Chicago. She shared that she did a lot of philanthropic work in the city and had donated money to help pay for the Russian delegation's stay. She was interested to hear that this would be my first trip to Russia, asking, half-jokingly, whether I would bring her back a souvenir from the trip. I kept expecting John to interrupt the discussion, but he seemed content to speak with the other guests at the table. In response to my question about how she knew my boss, Joanne told me she had been an investor in several of Pyramid's real estate projects. However, by how she and John interacted, I got the impression that there was perhaps a prior personal element to the relationship. I was surprised that this woman was paying so much attention to me, but she had a pleasant manner of speaking, which made me feel more at ease. After finishing the lobster salad appetizer, I observed Joanne move her left hand to grab the cigarette box lying beside her plate. Her movement caused her white napkin to slide off the edge of the table and onto the floor.

"Oh my," she gasped. "How clumsy of me. Would you be a dear and get that for me?"

"Of course," I smiled and leaned down to fulfill her request.

Sitting upright again and holding the white cloth in my right palm, I extended my hand. Joanne clasped my hand in hers. I felt the soft, warm sensation of her skin while her eyes remained fixed on mine. Slowly, the woman removed the item and placed it back on the table.

"Thank you," Joanne said in a low tone. "You are such a gentleman."

She must have noticed the blood rush to my face because she smiled coyly while taking another cigarette from the box. She inhaled the first stream of smoke deeply before releasing it upward. She seemed to enjoy toying with me. I was unsure whether this woman was displaying genuine interest or simply trying to make John jealous. She spoke with other guests at the table throughout dinner but always would bring her attention back to me. While everyone was drinking coffee following dessert, Joanne leaned over and murmured in my ear.

"You know, I come to these events not solely for the good deeds. I also come to meet men."

"I understand," I said as I leaned my head in Joanne's direction. "I am sure that there are many men who would love to be with you. You are elegant and attractive. However, I have a fiancée who I will be marrying soon."

A broad smile came over her face. She appeared not to be disappointed or discouraged by my response. She gently tapped my knee.

"You're very sweet." She reached into the small black purse on her lap and removed a small white card. She handed me the card. "Here is my business card. I'd love to hear about your adventures. Give me a call when you get back from the trip."

I thanked her and put the card into my jacket pocket. The dinner was breaking up. John informed me that he was leaving and wanted to chat with me while we walked out. I got up and said farewell to Joanne, expressing my pleasure in meeting her. John and I walked side-by-side along the corridor towards the coatroom. He had a slight smirk on his face.

"I see Joanne was working you hard tonight," he said. "I saw her drop her napkin, hoping you'd pick it up."

"Was that intentional?" I asked, revealing my inexperience.

"Of course," laughed John. "She was flirting with you."

"Wow. Well, I let her know that I have a fiancée."

"That likely won't matter," my boss added. "Good thing you are leaving tomorrow, or she'd probably try to contact you."

"Do you know her well?"

"We went out for a couple of years. We met at an event like this one."

We took our coats from the attendant and headed outside the hotel. It had started snowing again as we walked along Michigan Avenue, which was awash in bright lights.

"Regarding the trip tomorrow," began my boss, "I am counting on you to bring back good information so we can decide whether we will get directly involved in this project. I can bring you on full-time if we go forward with the project. Remember that you are there to gather data. Do not sign anything."

"Understood. I will do my best," I answered.

"Good. Well, I am going to catch a cab. Good luck!"

We parted at the intersection of Michigan Avenue and East Ontario Street. I watched as a Yellow Taxi pulled up to the curb, and John got in. I turned down East Ontario Street in the direction of Lake Michigan. It was a short walk to my apartment on East Ohio Street. I related to Deb the events of the night, omitting most of the interaction with Joanne. While I had been dining, she took it upon herself to pack my bags for tomorrow's flight. I found two large suitcases standing in the middle of the living area.

"I am only going for a week, cutie," I stated upon feeling the weight of the bags.

"Well, you will be in Siberia, so I packed a lot of extra clothes. You know how you hate to be cold."

"OK. That makes sense. But, why is this bag so heavy?"

"I fit a twelve-pack of bottled water in that one," she said proudly. "You don't know if you can drink the water there."

I had to smile. She was right. I had no idea what I was going to face in Russia. Better to be overprepared, I thought. I walked over and gave her a big hug and kiss. We spent the rest of the evening quietly watching TV and cuddling under a blanket. We went to sleep just past midnight, knowing I had to be at the airport early the following day. Rest did not come easy. My anxiety grew now that I was on the verge of actually leaving. I stared at the white stucco ceiling for most of the night.

The following morning, I loaded the two suitcases into the trunk of the waiting taxi for the journey to the airport. Deb was standing on the sidewalk in her pajamas and winter coat. We shared a long embrace, and she reminded me to enjoy the adventure, stepping back after giving me a soft kiss. I waved at her as the taxi pulled off the curb. I exited the cab in front of the international terminal. Dragging the two large suitcases behind me, I entered the crowded airport and stood in front of the large electronic board indicating flight and gate information. Destinations to almost anywhere in the world blinked in small green lights. Looking up and down the board, I saw flights to Paris, London, Barcelona, Cape Town, and Moscow; Khabarovsk, however, did not appear on the list. I rechecked the list more slowly this time. I noticed a flight headed to 'Charter Flight' a few places below Canberra and Caracas. I recalled Don had told me that the Russian delegation had arrived on a private charter plane commissioned Khabarovsk government. To be sure, I headed to the information desk, and the airport official verified that the 'Private Charter' was indeed my flight to Siberia. She informed me that there was a special departure area for the flight and explained where to go. Following her directions, I arrived at a relatively deserted area of the terminal. There was a considerable group mingling near the gate.

As I approached the edge of the crowd, I saw Makoto Tanaka and Bob Garrett chatting with an African-American man I did not know. All three men wore thick winter-themed sweaters, which clashed with their dress pants and shoes; Bob had on his Bears knit cap. Makoto waved at me to join the discussion.

"Ken, good to see you," he said in his barely perceptible Japanese accent. "I'd like you to meet Scott Jennings. Scott operates several restaurant franchises in the city."

The tall black man smiled and extended his right hand. His broad smile and soft eyes, with traces of grey in his short trimmed hair, gave him the look of a man in his early forties.

"Very nice to meet you, Scott," I stated. I felt the firm grip of his handshake. "I didn't see you at the breakfast a couple of weeks ago.

"I couldn't make it, unfortunately. I've been busy making sure my restaurants are ready while I'm gone to Russia."

"Which restaurants do you run?" I asked.

"I own several franchises for one of the big fast-food chains. I have been doing it for almost twenty years, and the chance to maybe expand overseas is exciting."

"Very nice. I guess we'll be working together some. I am here to look at real estate opportunities."

"Yes," said Scott. "Location is the key, as you know."

"Ken," interjected Bob. "You should go over to the gate and check in. You need to have them register your passport since it is a charter flight.

I took Bob's advice and started towards the gate. The crowd thickened as I moved closer to the check-in podium. I used a mix of Russian and English to excuse myself, passing through the people. I noticed a few of the kick-boxers among those waiting, their facial bruises still evident. Almost everyone held several large plastic shopping bags filled with items acquired during their stay. I saw Nathan Johnson and his entourage from Cardinal Communications to the left, seated by the far wall. Standing and talking to Nathan was Igor Semyonovich, with Ivan providing the translation. When I reached the podium, the airline attendant took my passport information. She gave me a white paper boarding card and informed me that boarding would begin in twenty-five minutes.

Paper in hand, I rejoined the small American contingent. We talked about what the weather would be like; we had all lived in Chicago for some time, but we were, nonetheless, going to Siberia in winter! We had all packed multiple layers of clothing. I explained about my water in the suitcase, which solicited several laughs. Curious about the aircraft that would take us to Russia, I peeked out the terminal window. I expected to see the typical light blue letters of 'Aeroflot' on the side of a white passenger plane. To my surprise, an immense aircraft stood at the gate. Reminiscent of a military transport plane, the white behemoth bore few markings except a large gold hammer and sickle spread on an expansive red banner. This craft was an official private charter flight sanctioned by the local government, an Ilyushin, carrying its most precious cargo in the person of the deputy governor.

A few minutes later, the gate attendant announced it was time to begin boarding. A free-for-all ensued. Like a snake swallowing its larger prey, the procession of passengers squeezed its way into the gangway, straining the metal walls to a breaking point. My American companions and I watched in concern and disbelief as the rush of businessmen, officials, and kick-boxers herded themselves into the plane. We decided to wait for the chaos to subside before making our attempt. On the other side of the waiting area, I saw that Nathan and Igor Semyonovich shared our plan. THIRTY MINUTES LATER, when I finally entered the aircraft, I noticed that only about one-third of the endless rows of seats had a passenger.

Nevertheless, I had to stand in the aisle for several more minutes as many of the Russians were still engaged in trying to fit all of their plastic shopping bags in the overhead compartments or on empty seats. I eventually located an empty row of three seats near the middle of the plane, where I tossed my backpack and coat on the window seat. Finally, I lowered myself into the middle seat and exhaled a sigh of relief. The boarding process had been exhausting.

A short while later, a deep voice came over the intercom announcing in Russian that the plane was preparing to depart. I sat in my seat, waiting to hear the safety briefing from the flight attendants telling passengers about the plane's safety features and how to buckle seatbelts. No such briefing occurred. Suddenly, I felt a jolt as the aircraft pulled away from the gate. I fastened my seatbelt out of habit as we rolled down the tarmac. Some Russians were still standing in their rows as the Ilyushin lifted off. The force of the rise threw those standing back into their seats.

When I felt the plane level off half an hour later, I relaxed. The initial excitement had started to wear off, and fatigue had swept over my body. Having the entire row to myself, I unbuckled my seatbelt and positioned my body lengthwise across the seats. I repeatedly adjusted my body to find a comfortable spot on the stiff, thin seatbacks and cushions. I took my Walkman from the backpack, placed the foam earpads on my head, and sought to sleep using my coat as a pillow. Melodies and lyrics by Journey, Air Supply, and Guns and Roses flowed through my ears. The songs provided some relief, but I still could not find rest. However, there was one track on the cassette that I noticed I kept rewinding and replaying. The German band, Scorpions, had recorded a song following the fall of the Berlin Wall called 'Wind of Change'. In my mind, this song encapsulated the period's zeitgeist. It spoke of a 'magic moment' of putting the animosity of the past behind us. It cast a ray of hope that longtime enemies could see each other as 'brothers'. I listened to the lyrics over and over, imagining my journey to Russia as one of these magical moments where I could be part of burying the 'distant memories … in the past, forever'. As the song continued to play, I drifted off into a deep slumber, dreaming of the adventure to come.

# Fish Jello

"We are approaching Khabarovsk. Prepare for landing."

A few minutes later, the entire plane was jolted as the landing wheels struck the runway. The piercing screech caused by the friction of the rubber against the pavement went on and on, raising doubts about the plane's ability to reduce its speed and stop. At last, the pilot engaged the reverse thrusters providing enough force to bring the craft to a halt. That is when I heard the clapping of hands begin, softly at first, but then growing louder and accompanied by shouts of 'Urrah!' Like parkgoers after a thrill ride, the passengers congratulated the pilot for completing the landing. Having survived the experience, I took a deep breath of relief.

Exiting the aircraft was again chaotic. The law of the jungle reigned. I watched in amazement as the Russians scrambled to identify their belongings and raced to alight from the plane. I remained in my row until the wave of insanity had dissipated. When I stood up to gather my things, I saw that the remaining passengers consisted mainly of the Americans and Igor Semyonovich.

"That was like a scene from LaGuardia," I said jokingly. "All that was missing was the cursing."

"Or maybe a fistfight," added Scott.

The comments elicited several laughs as we made our way off the plane. The airport terminal was small and dated. Soviet-era posters and slogans still dotted the faded yellow walls, flanking several white, blue, and red Russian

Federation flags. Hard plastic blue, orange, and yellow chairs were scattered along the cracked grey tiled walkways. Our flight was the only one in the terminal, having landed shortly after 4:00 am. I was sure that the airport would generally have been closed if not for the arrival of the deputy governor. Makoto, Bob, Scott, and I formed a cluster standing by the far end of the baggage claim carousel while most Russians were spread out in a tight ring around its edges. We waited until a loud horn erupted, signaling that the luggage would soon appear. Some hardcover suitcases were the first to flow along the creaky metal slats. The pieces were well-worn and resembled luggage from the old '70s Samsonite commercials. Several large rectangular boxes containing televisions followed the bags, each displaying a 'Walmart Special' sticker in bright red. Other electronic devices also arrived, as did more and more TV cartons. Interspersed among the home entertainment purchases were additional pieces of luggage. All the travelers from Khabarovsk had taken full advantage of the time in Chicago to upgrade their home entertainment. My companions and I patiently waited for our bags to slide down the carousel. After witnessing another wave of Walmart specials, I finally saw my two suitcases.

I struggled to weave a path towards the terminal exit with my luggage in tow. An armada of baggage carts, teetering with plastic bags, suitcases, and TV boxes, had formed a blockade. Weighted down with their purchases, the Russians resembled wagon-train pioneers trying to navigate a river in the American West. Those less skilled saw their carts overturn, spilling their belongings along the tiled floor and causing further delays. Thankfully, customs and passport checkpoints were unmanned due to the arrival time, partially relieving the congestion. When I finally made it through the harrowing journey, I stopped in the main hall and waited for the other Americans to arrive. One by one, Bob, Scott, and Makoto emerged, looking pleased for having survived the ordeal. As a group, we headed across the main hall and through a heavy set of glass doors marked 'Vykhod' (Exit). Light snow was falling, giving the scene a somewhat magical appearance. I watched the white flakes pass through the muddy yellow lights of the streetlamps in the deserted parking lot.

"How are we getting to the hotel?" asked Bob as we stood on the narrow sidewalk. A glance at the clock above the entrance doors revealed that it was almost five in the morning.

"I don't know," I replied. "I am not sure the taxis are running yet, and I do not see a bus."

Looking to my right, I observed Nathan Johnson, donning his felt hat with feather, positioned a few paces away. I walked over to the Cardinal CEO and inquired about transportation. Nathan informed me that the Russians would provide vehicles. As on cue, two nondescript white vans pulled up in front of the terminal. Stowing the luggage in the rear, the Cardinal team got into one van while my companions and I occupied the second vehicle. Sitting directly behind the driver, I asked the Russian where we were heading. He explained that he had instructions to take us to the Intourist Hotel, which would take about forty-five minutes. I related our destination to my companions, and then I leaned back against the thick cushion to rest. We passed a sign indicating Matveyevskoe Shosse upon departing the airport. The 'shosse' or highway led from the airport into the heart of the city, where it became Karl Marx Street. The darkness that still gripped the city, despite some snowy illumination, masked its details. I would have to wait until daylight to get a better picture of this Siberian town.

The Intourist Hotel was a tall grey concrete structure. Pulling into the parking lot, I noticed yellow panels attached below the windows on the façade. A broad elevator tower bisected the front façade. Large gold letters spelling out 'Hotel Intourist' in English hung above the main entrance. The vans unloaded their passengers by the main doors. I made my way into the reception area with the others, where I saw one of the Russian businessmen and Ivan Ivanovich. A young woman with red hair, dressed in a white blouse with a red vest, awaited us at the reception desk. She tried to generate a smile at such an early hour to greet the large group.

"Dobre yutro," she said. "How can I help you?"

Ivan Ivanovich spoke with her. I could hear him explaining who the group was. She replied that the hotel had set up a special breakfast. She told the interpreter that we were to leave our bags in the storage room and go straight up to the restaurant. She would check us in while we were eating and have keys ready following the meal. While I listened to the interpreter translate the plan to my compatriots, I felt hunger growing inside. I had not eaten for almost a day, save the few snacks I had consumed on the plane. However, I was also exhausted and preferred to get some sleep. Judging by the reaction of my companions, it seemed that we all felt similarly. Nevertheless, we could not refuse the generous hospitality offered by the hotel. Thus, we handed over our bags and passports to the receptionist and followed Ivan Ivanovich to the elevator.

Situated on the hotel's top floor, the restaurant displayed an Asian décor. Dark red wallpaper surrounded the dining area, where scores of deep brown wood tables stood in neat rows separated by paper-thin partitions, or shoji, which gave the space a more authentic Japanese look. A waiter wearing the same white shirt and red vest outfit as the receptionist showed us to a tables near the exterior windows. Shiny porcelain plates with Japanese characters highlighted each place setting. The early dawn light was just beginning to brighten the sky. I sat in between Scott and Makoto. I heard the waiter tell Ivan Ivanovich that they would be bringing the food directly. While we waited, a woman appeared, balancing a large tray of tall cans. The inscription on the cans bore Japanese characters, but when the waitress placed one of the cans next to me, I noticed the word Sapporo in small English letters.

"That is good Japanese beer," said Makoto, noticing my confused facial expression.

"Beer, for breakfast?" I asked. "I'm not sure this goes with pancakes and waffles…."

"Very funny," he replied. "I'm sure they want to give us a good impression. Some of my contacts in Tokyo tell me that they have been exporting huge amounts of Sapporo and other Japanese products since Communism ended. This region is so close to Japan that many Japanese businessmen have arrived and looked to invest."

"Well, then I am curious what food will be served," I said, becoming aware that I would likely not be eating typical Western fare.

"Yeah, Ken," added Scott. "I bet a sausage biscuit would taste great right about now."

I nodded in agreement. Due to the recent opening of the region, many of Russia's Asian neighbors were flooding into the Russian Far East in search of new markets and opportunities. Not only Japanese but also Korean and Chinese merchants were the main foreign visitors. Several Japanese companies had already set up hotels and trading operations in the area. Makoto commented that the confectionary store in the lobby displayed standard Japanese products like Asahi beer, cooked eel, and Mild Seven cigarettes.

"The level of Japanese investment is driving the interest in the golf course," Makoto stated. "You know how popular golf is in Japan, but the cost to practice and play is so high. From Tokyo, Khabarovsk is only a two-hour flight, which is much closer than, say, Hawaii, where many Japanese go now to play golf."

"That makes sense," I said. "But, won't the cold and snow be a problem?"

"That is why I am here. My contacts want me to judge whether an investment would be profitable given the limited time to play each year."

While discussing the trip's details, the waiter and waitress returned with the breakfast plates. Small bowls of white rice were set down first. Next came another bowl containing sliced cucumbers and chopped vegetables. I watched the waitress gently slide a small white saucer onto the porcelain plate. Sitting on the saucer was what appeared to be a puck-shaped gelatin mold. The greenish mold oscillated slightly when placed on the plate, making an encased white pancake-shaped object visible. I had never seen anything like this before. I gently poked the outer rim of the mold with my fork, causing the mold to shake again. I was hoping that this was a dessert, that the object inside was cake or pudding. Glancing to my right, I observed that Scott also seemed to be analyzing his meal. I leaned my head down so that my nose almost touched the mold, which smelled like regular gelatin. I stabbed the mold with my fork and deposited the green and white material into my mouth. A bitter, slimy flavor quickly replaced the initial Jello taste. The white object was some type of fish, which I detested. My gut reaction was to spit the parcel onto my plate, but I swallowed the remaining pieces, not wanting to insult my hosts. Emitting a loud 'gulp' sound, I washed down the distasteful food with a swig of warm beer.

"Not a fan of the fish jelly?" humorously inquired Makoto. He must have been watching my struggle to devour the meal.

"No, not really," I retorted and explained my aversion to seafood, in general.

"Well, you are in for a long trip, my friend. Seafood will likely be the main cuisine while we're here."

At the end of the meal, the servers offered coffee accompanied by two cinnamon cookies. I greedily ate the cookies but refused the coffee, hoping to find some rest in my room. We returned to the lobby as a group; the receptionist read aloud each guest's name and handed him his room key and passport. A quick check with my companions unveiled that I was sharing a room with Makoto while Scott and Bob were roommates. My new roommate and I waited for our turn to get into the elevator. Exiting the cabin on the sixth floor, we dragged our luggage down the narrow corridor. The thick tan carpet impeded our progress, but eventually, we arrived at an egg-white-colored door. I inserted my key and pushed open the heavy wood frame.

The space was not overly welcoming but clean. Two small twin beds sat on opposite sides of the narrow room. Leaf-patterned light green comforters were neatly folded on each bed. The paneled walls and furniture were of the same yellowish wood material, contrasting sharply with the thin grey carpet. There were no pictures in the room, and the white lace curtains screened the rays of sunlight trying to penetrate the room. My roommate agreed to let me have the bed closest to the window, and I placed my suitcases by the end of the bed. Too tired to unpack, I removed my shoes and stretched out on the soft mattress, pulling the comforter over me for warmth. Neither the morning light nor Makoto's unpacking prevented me from dozing off.

A rocking motion awoke me from a deep sleep. Startled, I quickly sat up in the bed. I saw my roommate standing next to me when my eyes regained focus. He told me that we were expected in the restaurant in fifteen minutes. I put my shoes back on, patted down my clothes to remove any wrinkles, and splashed some water on my face in the bathroom. The rest of the Americans were already in the restaurant when we arrived. Makoto and I grabbed seats near the far end of the long oval table while the group, which included Ivan

Ivanovich, listened to Nathan Johnson discuss the following few days' activities. Nathan looked in my direction.

"The real estate possibilities," he started, "will begin tomorrow by visiting a riverboat casino. I have Igor here, representing the ownership of the riverboat."

A large muscular-looking man in his early forties stood up. Unkempt bushy black hair somewhat covered his prominent forehead, and the broad smile on his wide face made his Asiatic eyes look even smaller and revealed a number of gold teeth. He placed his hands on the table, uncovering a thick gold watch from under the sleeves of his red and brown turtleneck sweater.

"My name is Igor Petrovich Simyonov. I am the director of an investment business here. We recently purchased a large riverboat to transform into a casino, and we seek investors. We also own several other companies in the area."

"Ken, you will meet with Igor tomorrow morning to tour the boat," added Nathan. "Makoto will also be going."

"OK, sounds good.," I said. "I look forward to it."

Seemingly satisfied, the imposing Russian businessman sat back down. The Cardinal CEO then explained that visits to a local fast food restaurant and land for the golf course would occur later. There were likely some social events planned for the evenings and a group get-together later in the week. Nathan concluded his talk by expressing his desire to sign some contracts before returning to Chicago. The meeting adjourned, and I headed back to the room to unpack. Having already organized his things, my roommate decided to go to the lobby with Bob and Scott.

I stepped into the room and was surprised to find a young woman standing between the beds. My entrance must have frightened her. Her back toward me and dressed in a white blouse with a red vest and matching pants, she held the tiny wastepaper basket. She spun around, and upon seeing me, almost dropped the object. Putting my hand up to signal that I meant her no harm, I saw the name 'Olga' inscribed on the nametag attached to her vest. She was apparently a member of the cleaning service.

"Sorry, Olga," I said in Russian. "This is my room. I didn't mean to startle you." My use of Russian seemed to calm her. She composed herself and smiled.

"Good day, Sir," she said. "I am just cleaning the room. The door must have closed behind me. Do you want me to leave?"

The question entered my head about why she would be cleaning a room for guests who had just arrived. I was unsure whether she was there by simple mistake or engaged in something more sinister, perhaps looking to find something valuable. I decided to give her the benefit of the doubt.

"I am not sure there is much to clean. We just checked in this morning."

Her facial expression displayed confusion. "Oh, I have your room on my list for today. It must be a mistake. I will go." She turned her head back towards my bed with the disturbed comforter. "Maybe, just let me fix the beds." She quickly refolded the large blanket. I saw her notice my suitcases which had an American flag sticker.

"Are you an American?" she asked with interest.

"Yes. I live in Chicago," I replied. "Have you heard of it?"

"Of course," she said, grinning. "Chicago is for Al Capone, gangsters…."

I laughed. "Yes. That was a long time ago." I recalled that some of the Russian businessmen during their stay in Chicago had mentioned the city's reputation in Russia was closely tied to this criminal era.

"So, how old are you?" Olga asked.

"I am twenty-four," I answered. I was not accustomed to having such personal conversations with hotel staff, but I wanted to use my Russian.

"Ah, you are the same age as me," she stated. "What do you do for work? Such a young man traveling to Russia."

"I am a consultant. I am helping some companies do business here."

"I see. Very nice. If you need someone to show you around the city, maybe I can help," she said with an inquiring expression.

I thanked her for her offer and said I would think it over. I then told her that I was pretty tired from my flight and wanted to rest. She smiled and wished me a nice rest as she left the room. Feeling dirty from the long voyage, I jumped into the shower. The water was ice cold, but I braved the frigid temperature. I put on a fresh set of clothes and took the elevator down to the lobby.

I passed by the reception desk and found my companions seated in two black leather sofas just off the right. What looked like cognac glasses sat on the small oval coffee tables facing the sofas. I lowered myself onto the sofa cushion next to Bob. Scott described his early struggles as a young black man in Chicago trying to become a fast-food franchisor. He talked about his lessons in resilience as a minority businessman, where he had to deal with corporate and government obstacles. These lessons would have to serve him well again if he wanted to open his chain of restaurants in this Russian city. Bob spoke energetically about his years in the oil industry, managing several drilling and refining operations. The former oilman related how he had heard about the stories of the big western oil firms rushing into Russia to acquire rights to the country's massive reserves. Now in retirement, Bob was thinking of opportunities to invest some of his savings in a small-scale Russian petroleum refinery to realize a big financial return. My roommate stated that his contacts in Japan also had interests in energy and commerce, and the golf course would be an excellent way to attract more of his countrymen.

I decided not to mention my run-in with the cleaning woman. Instead, I proposed that we get our coats and hats and explore around the hotel, maybe even find a place to have dinner. Everyone liked the idea. Several minutes later, we gathered again in the hotel lobby. Appropriately dressed, we exited the main entrance of the hotel. Light snow again fell, creating a slippery layer of ice along the sideway. The air was cold but dry. The sun had long ago set, but the fresh snow provided sufficient illumination reflecting the pale yellow street lights.

"Which way should we go?" asked Bob, his Bears ski cap pulled down around his ears. He seemed eager for an adventure.

Standing in front of the hotel, I looked right and gazed at a giant statue beyond the parking area. The iron sculpture depicted Captain Yakov Dyachenko, celebrated as the founder of Khabarovsk in the mid-nineteenth century. The blowing tails of his military overcoat swayed behind the bearded man in uniform, peering resolutely towards the banks of the Amur River, whose waters were visible from the entrance.

"Well, it seems right leads straight to the river," I said. "Let's take our chances this way." I pointed straight across the parking lot where rows of houses and stone buildings bordered the hotel grounds.

We crossed the pavement half-filled with cars until we reached the edge of the lot. Turning left, we trudged along a tree-lined street, our boots kicking up small mounds of unshoveled snow. A small wooded park off to our right was empty; no children played on the multi-colored jungle gyms, and the benches held no watchers. We walked in silence, taking in the surroundings. The lack of sound deafened by the snow added to the eery quiet. The road bent to the right, and the blue sign on the corner building indicated Turgenev Street. We passed by several more two-story wooden structures and another park dedicated to war veterans. A pair of older women strolling arm and arm looked at us suspiciously from across the street. Turning left at the next intersection, we found ourselves on Murav'yevna – Amurskogo Street. Tall, stone commercial buildings flanked both sides of the street. About fifty yards down the sidewalk, we discovered a grocery store. The bright neon signage over the entrance read 'Super Market' in Russian letters.

"Hey guys," I exclaimed. "You want to check out a Russian grocery store?"

"Sure, that should be interesting," replied Scott. "I'd like to see what kind of food they sell."

"Yeah," added Bob. "Let's do it."

We entered the store, passing by several rows of semi-empty shelves containing dry goods such as cereals, rice, and pasta. The overhead lighting reflected brightly off the white tiled floor, and large white cold storage cases stood along the back wall. A few shoppers, mainly older women, were peering through the glass front of the containers, scrutinizing the available products. As we passed by each case, I translated the words 'Myaso' (meat), 'Ryba' (fish), and 'Moloko' (milk) to help the other Americans. All of us took a moment to visibly examine the variety and quality of fish, meat, and dairy products. Food supply had improved under the market reforms; the empty shelves and bread lines, common during the collapse of the USSR, were a remnant of the past. Still, sky-high inflation brought on by Russia's 'shock therapy' policy, which eliminated price controls, made life difficult for everyday Russians, many of whom lived on a fixed income.

"Not quite like you see in Chicago," mentioned Scott. "The items look fresh, but I don't see any nutrition information or expiration dates."

"One problem at a time," I said. "Just a few years ago, you wouldn't be able to find most of these products."

"Unreliable supply is a major challenge in my business," added Scott, looking closely at a cut of meat.

"I am surprised not to see more imported food from Japan," said Makoto. "The hotel has lots of such food but not here."

"It would be likely too expensive for the local population," I responded. "The hotel caters to many foreigners, especially Japanese, who can afford the higher prices."

Bob was standing by the milk case and holding a bottle that read 'Yogurt'. "I'd love to try this, but, as Scott said, I can't take the chance without any expiration date."

"Well, you could maybe find something on the non-refrigerated shelves. There are crackers, biscuits, and so forth," I stated.

No one seemed interested enough to buy anything. We finished our inspection by walking past the checkout area. Trying to appear friendly, I said hello to the two women seated at the cash registers. Both women wore white aprons, their blonde hair hidden beneath flower-patterned kerchiefs. One of them dryly replied, 'dobry vyechor'. Confident that the women recognized us as foreigners, I added that we were Americans visiting the city and were impressed with the store. However, I received no further response, so I led our group out of the store. I noticed that the snow was falling harder outside, and the wind had picked up. I asked my companions whether we should look for a restaurant for dinner. The intensity of the weather seemed to dampen the enthusiasm for further exploration. The decision was made to head back to the hotel and eat there. We followed the same route back to the hotel and enjoyed another meal, heavy with fish courses. Scott and Makoto suggested drinks at the bar following dinner, but I declined. Exhaustion had overtaken me again, and I wanted to feel fresh for the big day tomorrow. Bob also made it an early night, and we took the elevator up to our floor. I fell asleep as soon as my head hit the pillow and did not remember dreaming.

# KGB Kasino

"Dobroe yutro. Welcome, welcome," I heard as I exited the white van.

Standing a few paces from the vehicle, Igor Petrovich, his two front gold teeth glistening in the early morning sun, motioned me to approach. About fifty yards behind my host, I could see the bank of the Amur River encased in a thick coating of ice. The wind was gusting off the river, causing the lower strands from his fur hat to fall into his eye. The brawny Russian looked prepared for a cold and wet escapade in a thick winter jacket and knee-high rubber boots. Peering down at my hiking shoes and cargo pants, I felt somewhat underdressed for whatever my host had in store. The heavy shoulder strap of the video camera dug into my coat and altered my balance slightly, forcing me to pay close attention to where I walked. The sound of crunching gravel followed my every step as I made my way toward Igor Petrovich.

"Nice to see you again," I said. "I am looking forward to touring the boat."

"Yes. It is quite windy today, so we must be careful, especially on the outer gangways," stated Igor Petrovich.

"Where is the boat?" I asked. Only a massive white sheet of water was visible from where we stood.

"It is just around the bend there to the left," my host pointed to an old abandoned wooden structure. "It is docked behind the old cannery."

While Igor Petrovich was showing me the direction of the path, other footsteps sounded on the gravel. Makoto joined us, resembling an Intuit tribesman, his fur-lined jacket hood obscuring most of his face. His thick padded boots gave the impression he was ready for a dog-sled race. When the Russian turned around, he let out a boisterous laugh at the tiny Eskimo.

"Are you in there, my friend? Today is a rather mild day here in Khabarovsk."

It was hard to tell, but it looked like Makoto smiled at the comment. I had checked the weather forecast before leaving the hotel, and the predicted high was minus eleven degrees Fahrenheit. However, the humidity level was close to zero, which helped temper the impact on the body. Despite the strong winds, it did not feel negative eleven degrees. With higher humidity and wind chills, I had experienced much colder days walking along Michigan Avenue in Chicago.

My roommate and I trailed the Russian down to the riverbank, where I saw the narrow dirt path leading between the former cannery building and the water. The dilapidated structure extended farther along the bank than I thought. The wooden façade with peeling yellow paint and rows of broken windows looked out over the river. As we reached the far end of the building, the outline of a two-story vessel near the riverbank came into view. The blue hull of the long narrow ship was stuck in the ice and appeared to lean slightly towards the short wooden dock. The two upper decks were painted white and adorned with metal railings, while rectangular windows ran along the outer walkways. We followed Igor Petrovich up a narrow metal gangway leading from the river's edge to the ship's bow and found ourselves standing on a short metal landing. The slight tilt of the boat hindered secure footing.

"How long is the ship?" I asked.

"Almost 70 meters," responded the Russian. "It was a cruise ship but has not been used for almost two years. We bought it a few months ago to transform it into a casino."

The paint on the hull, outer walls, and gangways showed much cracking and peeling. Rust was visible on the railings, and many of the windows had cracks or needed replacement. Makoto and I glanced at each other. We shared the same thought. This project was going to require a lot of investment. Igor Petrovich invited us to walk with him along the port side of the ship. I cautiously shuffled along the icy metal walkway, grasping tightly to the rusty railing. Unable to defend myself from the frigid wind, small darts of frozen water attacked my face. Halfway down the port side, behind a metal staircase leading to the second deck, a door opened to the boat's interior. The heavy wooden door showed signs of neglect and was splintered in several places. Our host managed to push the door against the wall with some effort, allowing us to step inside.

The wind's howls were still audible as we moved towards the center of the hallway. Flanked by two white walls, an arched opening in the center of each, the metal flooring creaked under our boots. Looking through the arch on the left facing the bow, I could see rows of rotting benches where cruise passengers had sat. Traces of blue paint were visible on the deck floor, and rusted bolts secured the benches to the deck. Moisture had deformed many wooden ceiling planks, and the overhead lighting was broken. Standing in the archway, I removed the video camera from the case and began to pan the area to provide sufficient detail for the developers back in Chicago. While I filmed the space, Igor Petrovich explained his plans.

"This will be the slot machine section," he said. "Twenty-five machines should fit into this area." He used his outstretched right arm to indicate where the machines would stand.

"I have some contacts at a slot machine company in Tokyo," interjected Makoto, whose voice was more coherent now after pushing back his furry hood.

"Khorosho (good)," said our host. "But, Nathan has already promised to help obtain machines from Bally in Las Vegas." The Russian's eyes lit up by mentioning the name of the famous American entertainment mecca.

"Oh, ok," replied my roommate. "They are, of course, excellent, but the Japanese machines may be much cheaper."

"We shall see. If Nathan cannot deliver, we can talk."

I got the feeling that I was witnessing my first negotiation. To impress the Russians, Nathan appeared to have positioned himself and his company as the leading supplier of anything needed. I was sure that Nathan saw an immense opportunity to broaden his business beyond communication equipment. His plans, however, ran the risk of causing friction with the other members of the group, my firm included, who desired to strike their own deals.

Still holding the video camera in my left hand, I turned around and peered into the archway on the right. Rusty metal floors and dingy white walls similar to the prior space decorated this room, serving as the ship's kitchen. A half-rotted food counter guarded several steel sinks coated in ice. On either side of the sinks stood silver stoves, dark mounds on the frying surface likely the result of discarded grease. The exhaust vent covers had fallen off and were lying on the floor.

"In here," began Igor Petrovich, "we plan on setting up the roulette and backgammon tables. Of course, we will remove all this junk."

"So, you won't serve food?" inquired Makoto. "What happens when the customers get hungry?"

"I do not want to waste space that could be earning money," stated the Russian. "We will have several bars located around the decks to serve drinks. Russians will not come here for food."

"Yeah, I don't remember reading much about the food in Pushkin or Turgenev novels when they described gambling," I added, showing off my knowledge of Russian literature.

"Ha, ha, that is true," said our host. "We Russians have historically been dedicated gamblers."

When I had finished filming, Igor Petrovich led us through the hallway, where we exited through a door opposite the side we entered. A similar metal staircase was found just beyond the doorway. It was a treacherous climb due to the thin layer of ice which covered the railing and steps. The upper deck closely resembled the lower one in its state of disrepair. Most of the windows were missing, and the roof had partially caved due to the constant weight of heavy snow. A tall pile of snow dominated the center of the room, completely covering what was left of the ruined benches.

"This looks cozy," I said as I once again put the camera lens to my eye.

"Da. We will need to replace the roof. We will wait until spring when the weather permits this work," admitted Igor Petrovich. "But, when we are done, blackjack tables will take the place of those horrible benches."

"How many people do you think can gamble here at one time?" asked Makoto.

"We think at least seventy-five customers," replied the Russian. "We should be able to pull in quite a profit." The large man displayed a look of pride in talking about his future earnings.

Then, we moved into the opposite room. There were no kitchen appliances to remove here, but instead, an array of broken dining tables and chairs were strewn about everywhere. The ceiling was still intact, but the planks had a noticeable bow, threatening an imminent collapse.

"We will put craps tables here and maybe a few more blackjack tables if we have room."

"I can see that," I said. "This space is longer than at the bow. It will hold the long oval tables more effectively."

"Where is the captain's wheel?" questioned Makoto. "I didn't see where you will pilot the vessel."

"It's at the back end of this room," explained our host. "We will not need it since we do not intend to move the boat from the dock."

Igor Petrovich stepped into the room, inviting us to follow him. With my camera ready, I slowly entered the space. Panning both sides of the room, I nearly tripped over a wooden plank lying on the floor. I kept to the room's outer edges, wary not to be underneath the bow in the ceiling. I saw a dark wooden door with the inscription 'Authorized Personnel Only' written on the inlaid glass at the back end of the room. The door led to a narrow staircase at the top of which was a small wheelhouse. A thick, jagged crack split the window diagonally. The white leather upholstery of the captain's chair was torn, chunks and bits of the yellow cushion filler covered the floor. The control panel for the ship's navigation sat adjacent to the chair, and the metal wheel stood slightly above the panel's dials.

"As you can see, not much can be done with the space," said Igor Petrovich.

"You don't feel that gambling cruises along the river would be attractive?" I asked while descending the stairs.

"Nyet. Keeping the boat docked will allow a steady flow of customers. When some customers leave, others can arrive. If we are out on the water, we will limit how many can gamble."

I had to admit that our host's thinking seemed logical. The tour completed, we used the outer walkway on the upper deck to avoid going back through the run-down spaces. Due to the ice and wind, the walkway presented its own dangers. Using the railing for balance, I slowly made my way to the metal stairwell leading down to the first deck. My feet slipped only once or twice as I navigated the frictionless iron steps until reaching the lower deck. I hesitated momentarily, ensuring my footing was secure, before following the Russian back to the bow. The harrowing journey around the ship seemed to parallel, in my mind, the unsteady ground upon which stood my success and that of Russia's transition. The path ahead was fraught with many obstacles and required firm footing.

"So, what do you think?" asked Igor Petrovich, waiting for Makoto and me at the top of the narrow footbridge leading to the shore. He seemed anxious to hear our impression of his prize.

"The vessel is a good size to have as a casino," I began. "There is a lot of space, and I like your vision for several bars in lieu of a dining area. The interior of the ship is heavily damaged. This will be almost a total redesign."

"Da. I agree. It will look nothing like a cruise ship when we are done."

"Do you have the investment capital required?" I added, "or are you seeking a partner for that?"

Our host smiled, moving his hand above his head to swat away the flowing fur strands. "I believe that we can do the construction work here. It will be much more affordable. Nathan said that the gaming companies that supply the machines and tables could invest in the construction."

"So, you already have contracts with these companies?" asked Makoto, seeking an opportunity for his Japanese clients.

"Yesho nyet (not yet). Nathan is working with them while the project develops. I think (Igor Petrovich looked at me) your firm can perform the design of the casino."

"Well, I took enough video to give our people a good idea of how much work needs to be done," I said. "Would your company pay for the design work?"

"Da. We have funds ready to start the process."

I got the impression that Igor Petrovich wanted me to give him a firm commitment to agree to the project. Appearing satisfied with our responses, our host started down the footbridge. My companion and I swiftly followed and headed back to the gravel area. The three of us huddled near the van, and I thanked our host for the tour. I expressed my hope to see each other again during our stay.

"Oh, we will see each other very soon," said Igor Petrovich in an almost jovial tone. "I have a little outing set up for the group this afternoon, and tonight you are all invited to my house for dinner and drinks."

With that, we all shook hands and parted. We arrived back at the hotel near lunchtime and found Bob and Scott sitting in the lobby area. The restauranteur and retiree had also recently returned from their morning appointments. I learned from Bob that we were to gather in the lobby at 2:00 pm, prepared to leave for the adventure. Scott proposed eating lunch in the hotel restaurant to fill the downtime before departure. I was famished from the morning tour, and I agreed to go despite the risk of another meal consisting of fish. The hostess asked to wait several minutes for a table to become free. Apparently, we had arrived at the busiest time of day.

"Scott, did you look at a restaurant this morning?" I asked as we found open high-top chairs at the bar.

"No, not today," replied the franchisor. "They took me to visit this massive farm outside the city. They called it a former... hmm, what was the term, oh yeah, a 'collective farm.' There was this long structure in which had to be at least a thousand cows all packed together. Then, I went to look at this other area where they grew cabbage, lettuce, and such. Another immense operation."

I gave Scott a brief explanation of the policy of collectivization that started under Stalin, explaining the rationale for the approach and the disadvantages for efficiency. I added that many of these farms had, under perestroika, transformed into cooperatives but still employed the traditional methods under collectivization.

Scott nodded. "I went to see the farm as a potential supplier for a restaurant. The size of the operation is impressive. However, from what I saw, there would be many quality and delivery consistency issues. I have strict corporate food quality standards to which I must adhere, so an alternative may be needed."

The hostess called to us to tell us that a table had opened up. She stopped at a small table tucked into a dark corner of the restaurant. She invited us to sit and handed us all menus. A quick peruse indicated that the 'plat du jour' was again a fish dish. Determined to avoid eating more fish, I ordered two servings of rice and found a side dish of 'gyoza' or pork dumplings. A warm glass of Coca-Cola accompanied my meal. I did not want a Sapporo beer, unsure about the upcoming activity. The conversation over lunch centered on our initial impressions of the trip. Everyone was welcoming and helpful, but there seemed to be lofty expectations on the part of our hosts. I commented to the group on what Igor Petrovich had said on the boat about Cardinal's CEO having made a lot of promises to the Russians regarding closing deals. None of us were yet confident that our projects could be realized, and the unfulfillment of these expectations could lead to profound disappointment for the Russians.

After lunch, we returned to the lobby to await the arrival of our hosts. Shortly before 2:00 pm, I noticed Igor Petrovich stroll through the main entrance flanked by the translator Ivan Ivanovich and another man I did not recognize. We got up from the black leather couches.

"Dobry den!" exclaimed Igor Petrovich. "Is everyone ready to go?"

We provided a mixture of 'da' and 'yes', which pleased the Russian businessman.

"Excellent," said our host. "Please follow me into the van outside. It is about a thirty-minute ride." He turned immediately and exited the hotel.

"Ivan," I said, trying to catch the interpreter before he exited. "Do you know where we are going?"

"Da." He replied coyly without adding anything.

The now-familiar white van stood waiting by the hotel entrance. We piled into the back of the vehicle alongside Ivan Ivanovich. Igor Petrovich sat upfront with the driver and instructed him to get moving. Our northeasterly route took us past the downtown area with its multi-colored governmental and commercial buildings. Traffic was light, and we soon entered residential sections of the city where rows of tall concrete community housing complexes spread out before us. Most of the city's population dwelled in this Soviet-era construction dating from the '60s and '70s. Ivan Ivanovich pointed out that he had grown up in one of these buildings and that his parents still owned an apartment there.

"How did you find your own place?" I asked him, knowing the difficulty of securing housing even in the new Russia. It was still common for multiple generations to occupy a small apartment, usually assigned to a grandparent.

"My work as an interpreter for the deputy governor allowed me to get assistance in acquiring an apartment."

The landscape shifted from urban to rural as we moved away from the tightly packed grey communal highrises. Snow-covered fields began to dominate the scenery. Pristine layers of snow bordered the road, occasionally sullied by abandoned farm equipment that sat in hibernation until the first spring thaw. Scattered along the way were villages comprising small groups of wooden structures with farm animals or packs of dogs visible running down the uneven dirt roads.

"Are those log cabins pretty typical for the region?" asked Bob.

"Yes," responded Ivan Ivanovich. "We call them 'izbas'. Peasant huts in the past; the design has not changed much over the centuries."

"The people are mostly farmers?" added Scott, looking away from the partially frosted window.

"The inhabitants, mostly older people, work the land, yes. Many also make small crafts that they sell," said the interpreter. "Some are owned by city people who use them as a 'dacha' or vacation house."

"The younger people have left for the city, where jobs and pay are better," I said.

A short while later, the van turned into a heavily wooded area. Magnificent tall white birch trees lined the path into the forest, with clumps of snow hanging precipitously from the bare branches. The ranks of trees extended to the horizon, giving us a feeling of insignificance compared to this powerful display of nature. Following a sharp bend in the road, we arrived at a small crescent-shaped clearing where tire tracks from previous visitors were perceptible in the snow. Our vehicle stopped next to a low wooden fence that barricaded the clearing from the dense cluster of trees.

"We are here!" announced Igor Petrovich. "Before you get out, I have something for you."

Our host exited the front side passenger seat and walked around to the back of the van. Opening the back door, the Russian pulled out a sizeable circular carton. Holding the box under his arm, he returned and slid open the side door. The burst of frozen air that invaded the warm interior fogged up the windows and blocked the sunlight. The Russian then placed the carton on the snowy ground, flipped open the lid, and pulled out a dark brown object covered in a matted material.

"I got one for each of you," expressed Igor Petrovich. "These are genuine 'shapki' made right here in Khabarovsk."

The Russian businessman leaned into the van and handed the object to Makoto, who was closest to the door. My roommate unfolded the thing to reveal a fur hat similar to the one worn by our host. Makoto removed his hood and ski cap. A little too large for his head, the fur hat glided smoothly onto his head but leaned a bit to one side. Nevertheless, a broad smile stuck to the Japanese's face.

"Hey, you look like a real Russian!" exclaimed Igor Petrovich, laughing. He distributed the rest of the fur hats and waited for his guests' reactions. I removed my blue ski cap and pulled open the folded sides of the shapka. I felt the soft, woven interior slide easily over my ears while loose strands of fur around the edges tickled my skin. I gently stroked the hat's top and sides, examining the soft hair. The warmth generated by the fur was immediately noticeable. After a few minutes, beads of sweat started forming under the lining. I took off the hat until we prepared to leave the van. Judging by the facial expressions of my companions, everyone was impressed by the effectiveness of the shapki.

"Spasibo bolshoe (thanks a lot)," I said. "This is a very kind gift. I no longer have to worry about the cold now."

"You are most welcome," cheerfully replied our host. "Now, please step out. I think you will also like the next surprise."

Standing in the snow with our new hats, we looked like a gathering of locals. Our host had placed himself in the center of our semi-circle with his back to the forest.

"How many of you grew up in the countryside?" inquired Igor Petrovich.

No one responded. My compatriots and I glanced at each other; it seemed we had all experienced urban life as children.

"I lived near a beach," I blurted out, trying to end the silence. "Does that count?"

The imposing Russian gave out a boisterous laugh. "OK, so this should be a fun new experience for all of you."

At that moment, a man appeared from our right. Unseen from the vehicle, there was an opening in the fence large enough for a man and an animal. The man led a massive horse from the wooded area into the clearing. The horse, whose black coat was topped by a mangy yellow mane, stood at least seven feet high at its saddle. Its hooves, visible above the snow line, were covered by thick fur almost up to its knees. The horse would have fit in nicely pulling the Budweiser beer wagon. As the intimidating beast came closer, my companions and I took a step back toward the van.

"Don't be afraid," said Igor Petrovich. "She is quite gentle. She pulls plows in the fields in the spring and summer, but she is a great riding horse in winter. Simeon, bring her over here,"

Simeon brought the horse only a few paces from us. A thick musty scent emanated from the animal. Our host stepped over and began to pat the horse on its neck and nose, speaking kind words to her. He took out a carrot hidden away in his jacket, and the horse greedily devoured the treat.

"OK, who wants to go first?" Our host's eyes rotated back and forth, seeking to find the bravest. I had never ridden a horse and imagined something much less imposing for my first time. The others also remained motionless. "Come on!" chided Igor Pavlovich, "Where is that American spirit?"

Having found no volunteers, the burly Russian let out a 'bah' and leaped up into the saddle. With ease, he turned the horse around and sped off, kicking up snow and dirt through the opening in the fence. Heavy thuds echoed from the hooves pounding into the earth rapidly. Igor Pertrovich quickly disappeared from sight among the mass of white birch. We all stood fixated on the small breach in the fencing expecting the return of our host. Ivan Ivanovich and Simeon joined in our perplexity as the minutes dragged on.

"Is he coming back?" I finally blurted out. The cold had begun to seep into my feet and hands, causing me to shuffle in place; only my head was toasty.

"I'm sure he is enjoying the ride," stated Simeon, his long red hair hanging almost to his shoulders. "He doesn't get to ride much in the winter and has been so busy lately." Simeon's clear blue eyes were the most noticeable feature on his pock-marked face. He pointed his left arm towards the right. "Here he comes. I can feel the ground vibrate."

The features of a horse and man became visible through the forest. The horseman nimbly maneuvered the immense beast among the narrow gaps in the trees. Igor Petrovich slowed the horse to a trot before regaining the clearing. The joyous facial expression reminded me of a young boy who had been sick and bedridden, getting to go back outside to play with his friends. Our host dismounted after bringing the animal to a stop. He patted the horse firmly on the neck and returned the reins to Simeon. The exhilaration from watching the Russian glide through the air boosted our confidence. We all were ready to give the horse a try. Scott agreed to be the first to mount the animal. He took advantage of his six-foot-five frame to easily place himself in the saddle. With Simeon keeping one hand on the reins, the tall black man slowly started to move in a circular pattern. The restaurateur completed a few rotations and signaled to Simeon that he desired to get off. The red-headed Russian brought the horse to a stop and held firm to the reins allowing Scott to dismount safely.

"That was fun," exclaimed Scott. "I am a big guy, but you feel vulnerable on the back of such a powerful animal."

Next to go was Makoto. Given his short stature, my roommate required a boost from Igor Petrovich to make it into the saddle. Once seated, however, the Japanese showed no fear and took hold of the reins from Simeon. Staying in the clearing area, Makoto led the horse into a trot and increased the pace to near cantor-speed after a couple of passes. Fearful of an accident, Simeon ran after the horse and, with some effort, managed to grab hold of the reins to slow the pace. Makoto was led back to the group, where our host assisted him in dismounting.

"Way to go, Makoto!" I said. "Were you scared going so fast?"

"Nah," replied my roommate. "I love speed. It makes you feel free. You have to feel the wind hit your face."

I looked at Bob to see if he wanted to go ahead of me. He indicated that he didn't want to risk it, given his bad back. Igor Petrovich made a welcoming motion with his arm, inviting me to climb onto the animal. Being slightly taller than Makoto, I attempted to mount the horse without aid. Stretching my left leg forward as far as possible, I placed my boot into the stirrup. I reached up with my left hand to grasp the knob on the saddle and, feeling that I had a tight grip, thrust my right leg up to put it over the saddle. I must have lost momentum halfway up because my right leg faltered and came crashing down. The force tore my left boot from the stirrup, and I landed on my back. Luckily, the thick snow cushioned my fall. Staring directly into the sky, I noticed Igor Petrovich's face come into view as he leaned over me.

"Are you OK?" he inquired. I saw a brief grin on his face. Snowflakes landed in my eyes, having fallen from his fur hat. "That was quite a tumble. Again?"

I wiped the melting snow from my eyes and face with the back of my hand. "Da," I said. "Let me give it another try."

My second attempt was no more successful than the first. Anticipating my failure, our host stood behind as I swung my right leg up and caught me when I fell back again. Frustrated but determined to make it the third time, I prepared to put my leg up when Igor Petrovich put his hand on my shoulder.

"Let me give you a lift," he suggested. "It's no shame. It's getting dark, and we have to head back soon."

Holding onto the saddle knob, I felt the added force from Igor Petrovich projecting my leg up and, this time, over the horse and into the saddle. Sitting upright on the horse's back, I understood what Scott meant. It was a bit intimidating. I could feel the beast's power under my legs and knew that I was not in control. I observed Simeon waving his hand, prompting me to make the horse move.

"I've never ridden before," I said. "What do I do?" It was a question I probably should have asked before I found myself high in the air.

The Russian shook his head and shuffled back and forth with his legs tapping the insides. "Strike him with your heels," he said.

His words brought images of the many cowboy movies I saw as a kid. The men would always utter, 'gitty up' or 'hyah', and the horse would bolt. In my nervousness, I completely forgot Simeon's advice and made a sound like I was calling a dog or cat; a guttural 'knuh, knuh, khuh' sound was what came forth. Seeing that this was ineffective, I tried pulling on the reins, which I thought would also make the animal go. Sensing my inexperience, the horse turned his head towards me with disbelief. The animal stood impassively in the same spot, refusing to budge.

"I don't know what is happening," I said, looking at Simeon and Igor Petrovich. "He doesn't seem to want to move."

The two men looked at each other and started laughing. "You are confusing him," explained Igor Pertrovich. "You are telling him to go and stop simultaneously." I furrowed my brow, not comprehending what the Russian was telling me. "Your sound encourages him to move, but you are yanking on the reins, which means stop."

"Ah, that makes more sense," I stated.

"Yes," added Simeon. "They (horses) are smart. You have to let them know who's in charge."

"Well, that's definitely not me," I said. "Should I try again?"

Igor indicated that we needed to head back. He helped me climb down from the horse. The sun had just about disappeared behind the tops of the trees. A faint orange and purple glow was receding across the clearing. We thanked Simeon for bringing the impressive horse and piled back into the van. As we drove out of the clearing, I watched Simeon lead the massive animal back into the woodline; man and beast were soon hidden under the thick forest canopy. The warmth of the van made my breathing slow; my eyes felt heavy. I fell into a deep stupor with my head leaning against the window. My mind wandered in a semi-conscious state, and I found myself gliding above the forest, my boots touching the icy tips of white birch trees. I could sense the wind push against my outstretched arms and face as I drove forward in the frosty air. A V-shaped formation of birds flew past, gazing at the strange creature in flight. At one point, I looked down and observed Simeon, his long red hair blown back, riding at full speed along a winding path through the trees. Somehow I was capable of incredible acceleration and overtook the rider and horse.

Alone again above the canopy, I noticed another wide opening in the trees. I descended, landing with a slow trot and coming to a stop on the near bank of a broad river. A thick blanket of snow covered both riverbanks. Ice had formed in places, but the current was still strong. Giant snow and ice formations floated downstream, collecting more and more debris. The snow was above my knee, but my feet did not feel cold. On the far bank, several deer approached the water and drank. The large male raised his head and stared at me. His eyes were piercing and lacked any fear. Suddenly, from behind him, a crunching sound grabbed his attention and caused him to sprint off into the woods, closely followed by the does. An enormous brown bear emerged from the woodline. The bear strolled to the riverbank with intentional steps and put his heavily clawed paw into the river. The paw was lifted from the water a few moments later, grasping a fish struggling hopelessly to free itself. Still holding the fish, the bear stood on its hind legs and fixed its gaze on the man on the other side of the river. The mighty creature stared into my eyes and closed his paw around the fish with a short, single thrust. The bear tossed the lifeless prey into the snow and turned back into the forest. I stood, unable to move, as the king of the forest disappeared into his realm. The cold of the snow had begun to penetrate my layers, sending sharp stabbing pain into my feet and legs. I tried to extricate myself and leap back into the sky but remained rooted to the spot. A sense of panic was coming over me ...

A loud crashing sound startled me from sleep. Igor Petrovich had forcefully slid open the side door of the van. Makoto, sitting next to me, put his hand on my shoulder and stated that we had arrived back at the hotel. After regaining my composure, I followed the group back into the lobby. Igor Petrovich stopped by the reception desk and informed us that the van would return at 7:00 pm to take us to his apartment for a light dinner and drinks. Back in the hotel room, I decided to take advantage of the break to freshen up and relax. I took a shower, shaved again, and then laid back on my bed to read a book. I noticed that Makoto had prepared a plastic shopping bag for the evening. Not wanting to pry, I did not ask him about the bag's contents. Perhaps, I thought, he had bought a bottle of wine or vodka, which I had neglected to do.

Punctual as usual, our host was waiting for us in the lobby at the appointed time. Our host resided in a six-story apartment building near Lenin Square. From the outside, the façade looked no different from most of the buildings in the city, with concrete floors painted in light blue, yellow, and green. A brown brick wall enclosed the building, and I noticed barbed wire strewn along the wall's top. We exited the van, trailed our host through the security gate, and entered the ground floor. A gloomy-looking man dressed in black with the words 'Okhrana' (security) tagged on his chest was sitting at a small desk by the main entrance. Upon seeing Igor Petrovich, the security guard stood to attention. Our host nodded and wished him a pleasant evening. The large man responded, thanking Igor Petrovich. The man remained in his position until we all stepped into the elevator. It was a tight fit, but we managed to all find room.

The elevator stopped at the fourth floor, and I stepped into a poorly lit hallway. Our host halted in front of a heavy black wood door while searching for his keys.

"Forgive the decorations," he said. "We have not had time to take down the New Year's tree."

We followed our host into a narrow entryway with black and white striped wallpaper. A small set of drawers was set to one side, while, on the other side, a wooden coat rack hung on the wall. Crammed together in this small space, I heard a high-pitched voice approaching from a side room down the hall.

"Papa, Papa!" A tiny girl came running down the hallway about seven or eight years old. She sprinted towards our group, wearing a bright green dress with a red bow in her blonde hair. Igor Petrovich knelt down and scooped up his tiny prize. The Russian beamed as he turned around, supporting the little girl in his thick arms. She placed a row of kisses on his reddened cheeks.

"This is my daughter," began our host. "Her name is Anna Maria. She is seven and looks just like her mother."

We responded with a collective 'hello.' The girl did not appear afraid of having so many strangers in her home. I heard the father ask his young daughter where her mother was. Igor Petrovich excused himself, saying that he was required in the kitchen. He pointed to a room off to the right and invited us to make ourselves comfortable in the living room. Seemingly familiar with the apartment, Ivan Ivanovich led the way into the room. My companions left their bags in the entryway and proceeded ahead. The space was not large but tastefully decorated. Several framed paintings hung on the white walls. Tall floor lamps provided the room with adequate lighting, as did the blinking red lights from the New Year's tree next to a faux fireplace. Scott, Bob, and Makoto sat down on the black leather couch against the far wall. I moved across the hardwood floor and descended upon one of the easy chairs surrounding a small oval coffee table.

Our host entered the room accompanied by a lovely blonde woman carrying a tray of hors d'oeuvres. Igor Petrovich introduced the woman as his wife, Svetlana, and made room on the coffee table to set the tray down. A large crystal bowl sat in the middle of the tray, flanked by a spiral of soda crackers. A black gooey substance filled the bowl, and a small butter knife was inserted into the dark mound. When his wife retreated to the kitchen, our host proudly invited us to partake of the dish.

"Please," he said. "Try some of this delicious Beluga caviar. It is native to this region and a real treat."

Ivan Ivanovich, seated next to me, was nearest to the tray. He took the butter knife, gathered some of the tiny black balls, and spread them on one of the crackers. Rather than eat the morsel, he turned and offered me the cracker.

"Vot (here)," he said. "As a guest, you should have the first bite."

I had never tasted caviar before. Given my dislike of fish, the idea of consuming fish eggs was not appealing. Nevertheless, I wanted to experience this Russian delicacy. I thanked the interpreter for his hospitality and took a small bite, holding the cracker gingerly in my hand. The eggs had an almost gelatinous consistency and required chewing effort, but the roes became smoother and easier to swallow. Having survived the initial bite, I placed the rest of the cracker in my mouth. I found it difficult to discern any particular flavor since the salt taste was overwhelming.

"So, how do you like it?" asked Ivan Ivanovich. I saw that our host and my companions were all staring at me in anticipation of my response.

"Vkusno (tasty)," I replied. I lied, but I didn't want to be rude or seem uncultured. I knew that Beluga caviar was renowned and very expensive. "May I have another, please?"

My neighbor obliged me, and I devoured the second cracker in one shot. Still chewing the jelly eggs in my mouth, I gave everyone a thumbs-up sign. After that, everyone huddled around the table to receive their portion of the delicacy. Ivan Ivanovich prepared crackers for my companions and then made one for himself. A round of 'hmmms' echoed in the room, proving that caviar was enjoyed by all. Svetlana came back into the room, placing two bottles of vodka on the table next to the tray. Igor Petrovich went into the hallway and brought back several shot glasses, which he laid out on the table. Our host popped open the first bottle and filled each glass, asking us to take one. With a drink in hand, the Russian stood in the center of the room and delivered a toast.

"To friendship and great success!" loudly exclaimed our host.

Ivan Ivanovich translated the words while everyone tried to say the toast in Russian.

"Na druzhbu i uspekha!"

We all downed the alcohol in unison. The unexpected sharpness striking the throat prompted a few coughs from the Americans. The glasses were quickly refilled, and this time, Igor Petrovich requested that one of his guests provide the toast. I turned in my chair to see whether one of my companions desired to say something. A few moments of silence ensued, which became awkward. Finally, Bob suggested that, since I spoke Russian, it might be appropriate for me to give the toast. I nodded in acquiescence and stood up. I lifted my drink high in my right arm and wished for cooperation between our two countries. Again, the glasses were drained, and I lowered myself back into my chair. Several additional rounds of vodka followed before Svetlana

returned with cold sandwiches and sliced cucumbers. The sandwiches consisted of various meats, which I savored after all the fish, placed on dark rye
bread. Mustard and salt accompanied the food. Igor Petrovich placed his chair
beside the leather sofa and was eating and conversing with his guests. Ivan
Ivanovich and I ate and chatted around the coffee table.

"How are you enjoying the trip so far?" asked the interpreter.

"It's been interesting. I toured the boat this morning with Igor Petrovich.
He wants to convert it into a casino, but a lot of work is needed. I assume he
got it for a good price."

"It was practically free," said Ivan Ivanovich. He leaned towards me and
whispered in English: "You know that he was part of the security services
under the USSR. He and some of his colleagues formed a company and are
now 'biznesmen'."

"What?" I asked in astonishment. "You mean to say he used to work for
the KGB?" I whispered.

Ivan Ivanovich lowered his head. "It is quite common nowadays. These
guys realize how much more money they can make as a biznesman rather than
a security agent."

"So, how did Igor Petrovich get the boat?"

"He and some colleagues approached the owner and expressed their desire
to obtain the boat. Who would oppose KGB agents, even now in the 'free
market'?"

"The owner just gave them the boat?" I inquired incredulously.

"I am sure they paid a small amount to avoid any problems, but they acquired other assets similarly."

"Why are you telling me this?" I said. "Is that risky for you?"

"I just want you to know with whom you are dealing. I like my job, but it
is somewhat embarrassing to see these guys just steal others' things."

Ivan Ivanovich's words put me ill at ease. I looked over at Igor Petrovich,
his gold-toothed grin, using his limited English to converse with my compatriots, and saw him now in a different light. Thoughts began to enter my
head that our host's genial disposition might be simply an act. Behind the
warm smile could be hiding a ruthless, calculating individual, looking to use

deception and violence to obtain his ends. I wondered whether I should inform my companions or keep this revelation to myself; it could be a helpful negotiating tool. I decided to keep a professional distance in dealing with Igor Petrovich and not relate any personal information to be used against me.

A short while later, Anna Maria, now dressed in her pajamas and accompanied by her mother, walked into the room. Free of the bow, the girl's blonde hair flowed down past her shoulders, partially covering the unicorn print on her pajama top. Svetlana announced that the little girl wanted to say goodnight before heading off to sleep. She ran over to Igor Petrovich and placed a kiss on his cheek. He whispered something in her ear, and then she turned and somewhat shyly curtsied to the guests.

"Good night," the young girl said in accented English. She hurried back over to her mother's side in the archway. A chorus of 'good night' followed after her.

"Wait," Bob suddenly blurted out, rising from the sofa. "Igor Petrovich, before your daughter goes to bed, we have brought some gifts for her. May we give them to her now?"

Surprised by the request, our host smiled. "You didn't have to do that. But, of course, that would be very kind of you. Sveta, is that OK?"

His wife gave her approval and sent her daughter back into the room next to her father. The three men hastily made their way back into the entryway to retrieve the bags. My companions then formed a small semi-circle around Igor Petrovich and his daughter. Holding a rather large plastic shopping bag, Bob bent over and pulled a pink box from the bag. Various small pieces of furniture and figurines were detectable through the clear plastic covering. Bob explained that these were pieces that Anna Maria could use for her dollhouse. A wide smile came over the girl's face as Bob handed her the box.

"Spasibo (thank you)," she replied and gave the box to her father, who examined it briefly and placed it to the side.

Scott's height appeared to cause Anna Maria some hesitancy when he approached, so he knelt before presenting her with several thin rectangular packages.

"These are dresses for your dolls," Scott told the girl. "I heard that you have quite a collection." Ivan Ivanovich translated the words for the daughter. The youngster closely examined each dress and collectively hugged the packages. She expressed her thanks and handed the present to her father as before.

Makoto removed two boxes from his bag. I saw the famous 'Barbie' name displayed in bright cursive letters from where I sat. Anna Maria's facial expression revealed that she immediately recognized the blonde hair, blue-eyed plastic form in the box. She happily received the boxes and did a little jump of excitement. "It's a Barbie and a Ken!" she exclaimed and held up the boxes so that her mother could see. Svetlana nodded approvingly to her daughter. The girl was reluctant to part with the dolls.

"Can I open them now, papa?" asked the girl. Her face lit up in anticipation.

Igor Petrovich pondered the request for a moment and gazed at his wife. He turned back to his daughter.

"Well, it is your bedtime, but you can play with the dolls tonight since we have guests. You can open the other presents tomorrow. Make sure you thank the man."

"Spasibo bolshoe, papa!" shouted the young girl. "Thank you!" she added in English to Makoto, who was pleased with having brought joy to the child.

Anna Maria took back the two Barbie boxes and ran back to her mother, who also thanked us and escorted her happy child to bed, and a night likely filled with splendid dreams. Igor Petrovich got up from his chair and thanked the three guests for the kind gifts. I noticed his gaze fall upon me to see whether I had anything to present. Feeling slightly embarrassed, I stood up and apologized for not having a gift since I had been unaware of the visit.

"Don't worry, Ken," said our host. "Speaking Russian is a great gift in itself. I enjoyed talking on the boat this morning."

I was unsure whether he meant his words sincerely or sarcastically, but I smiled and thanked him for understanding. I leaned back towards Ivan Ivanovich and murmured how the other men knew to bring a gift. The interpreter told me that Nathan Johnson knew about the visit back in Chicago and had told the others to get presents for Igor's daughter. I hoped that this faux pas would not negatively impact our business prospects. As the evening drew to an end, our host poured one more round of vodka and asked us to stand for one final toast.

"To Anna Maria!" stated Scott, preempting Igor Petrovich.

We all raised our glasses and repeated, "To Anna Maria!".

This unexpected act had an emotional effect on Igor Petrovich. The burly Russian held out his drink with tears in his eyes and thanked us for the kind well-wishes. We each received a warm embrace from our host before stepping into the hallway. The small toast had gone a long way to building bridges with Igor Petrovich. He waved to us as we headed to the elevator with the parting words: "Do zavtra! (see you tomorrow)". The mood in the van on the ride back to the hotel was light. It had been an enjoyable evening, and creating joy for a small child had been the topper. My companions expressed more optimism regarding the possibility of doing business in Russia, and while I generally shared their enthusiasm, my thoughts kept returning to our host's former life. I began to question how much trust to have in a man who conducted business using methods from his KGB days. I presumed that the following days would perhaps shed more insight into our potential partner.

# The Golden Fish

WE ALL GATHERED IN THE lobby to visit a popular local restaurant following breakfast. Scott was very interested in seeing what might be his main competitor in the city and expressed his eagerness to examine the quality of the product offered by the restaurant. The trip would give me a better idea of the general look and feel of the architecture in the city. I noticed Bob wearing his usual Chicago Bears ski cap as we waited by the reception area.

"Bob, I appreciate your loyalty, but where is the shapka?" I jokingly asked. "It has to be much warmer than the ski cap."

"I am sure it is," Bob responded. " It felt a little itchy, and I am so comfortable in the ski cap," Bob explained that he had meetings with two local energy companies. "If the food is good, bring me back a burger. I could use a break from the fish."

Scott, Makoto, and I stepped out onto the sidewalk in front of the hotel. The day was sunny and brisk, but the almost zero humidity made the cold manageable. A few minutes later, the white van arrived, and we all boarded the vehicle. Ivan Ivanovich would be our guide for the restaurant tour, detailing that Igor Petrovich and Nathan Johnson were not available to attend. As we left the parking area, Scott began to ask Ivan Ivanovich questions about the number of restaurants in the city, what the most popular cuisines were, and the presence of other foreign-owned eateries. Our guide answered as best he could, saying that there were many places to eat in the city, most dating from the Soviet period, but the number of new restaurants had started to grow.

"Russians," he said, "were taking advantage of the chance to own a business. There are some foreign places, primarily Japanese and Korean. You will be the first American to open a restaurant in the city."

Scott seemed intrigued by the prospect of getting into the market early. When asked about labor costs for workers, Ivan Ivanovich said that wages were meager compared to America. I added that the current high inflation made wages even cheaper in dollar terms. Scott agreed but expressed his concern about sourcing reliable high quality supplies. Multi-story commercial buildings passed by as we headed towards the central business district. Stone façades, many of them colored in blue, yellow, or green, lined the district's streets. Small parks and squares appeared wedged in between the various edifices. I observed several grandmothers watching small children scurrying and climbing on metal swing sets while we waited at a stoplight. Signs for banks, furniture stores, and groceries flew quickly past. The vehicle approached a larger square with stone pavement and dotted by tall with multi-light lamps. Several large buildings surrounded the square, including one made of red brick. Ivan Ivanovich explained this was Lenin Square and pointed to the statue of Lenin standing in front of the brick façade.

"Many cities have taken down Soviet-era monuments, especially those to Stalin and Lenin," said Ivan Ivanovich, "but we have kept this Lenin statue here. We feel it is part of our history."

The van continued along the square and pulled off onto a street diagonal to the brick building. It stopped near the end of the road. Jetting outward on the corner of the intersection was a two-story white and mauve stone building. Large horizontal rectangular windows ran along the lower story allowing passersby to view customers eating. The upper floor displayed more traditional two-pane windows with white wood shutters. Over the entrance hung a faded white sign with 'Zolotaya Ryba' (The Golden Fish) inscribed in yellow. A wooded placard was affixed to the inside of the glass front door, welcoming customers to enjoy the fresh hamburgers and french fries. We exited the van and walked toward the entrance.

"Well," I said, "looks like they can use some marketing help, a burger joint called The Golden Fish."

"Yeah, maybe that's a good omen," commented Scott, pulling the collar of his leather coat up to block the frigid wind.

"There was a traditional restaurant here for many years," added Ivan Ivanovich. "However, the place is now trendy, especially with the younger people. It is the only 'fast-food' restaurant here. The new owner is very excited to meet an American restauranteur."

We reached the front steps just as a group of teenagers were leaving the establishment. Underdressed for the cold, they laughed loudly but stopped and stared at us while we ascended the stairs. I noticed that their eyes were fixed on Scott. Ivan Ivanovich walked up to the door and pulled on the metal door handle to allow his three American guests to enter the eatery. We stopped just inside the doorway. About ten square wooden tables, occupied mainly by young people, were scattered on the white tile floor. Two large fixtures hanging from the white stucco ceiling reflected light off the floor tiles and brightened the tan walls, displaying pictures of local landmarks. Like a deli, two long glass display cases stood beyond the eating area, where employees dressed in white uniforms were engaged in taking orders and preparing food. A sign over the counters listed the available menu items. Several types of hamburgers comprised the menu, and customers had the choice of chips or french fries. Drinks consisted of tea, coffee, or Pepsi Cola. A check-out station with a metal manual cash register was located at the far end of the display cases.

I again observed all eyes following us as we made our way toward the counters. From a quick glance at the tables, I discerned that the food was served on sturdy plates with real silverware; no use of plastic or Styrofoam. Ivan Ivanovich spoke with the young woman at the register, informing her of our appointment. She politely requested that we wait a moment while she announced our arrival and scurried through a set of dark grey doors into the back of the eatery. While waiting, I peered into the glass display cases, which contained rows of various meat cuts, small boxes of lettuce and tomatoes, and several plates furnished with hamburgers and chips. Our presence had disrupted normal operations, and a small queue had formed at the payment station awaiting the woman.

Suddenly, a short, stocky man with receding black hair emerged from the double doors. His puffy round face was pleasant, almost consuming his green eyes, compressed by his broad smile. He strode quickly towards us, followed by the woman.

"Welcome!" the man shouted in thickly accented English. The greeting seemed to be his only English phrase since he retreated to Russian. "I am so glad that you have come!" He shook hands with Ivan Ivanovich. "My name is Ilya Kirillovich Kuznetsov. I am the owner of Zolotaya Ryba. As you can see (he pointed back at the dining area), my food is very popular. Please step into my office area so we can talk." He looked at the customers waiting to pay. "Maria! Look at the queue. Help these customers at once!" The young woman ran past her boss and resumed her duties.

Ilya Kirillovich waved for us to follow him through the grey double doors. The area behind the counters had red tile, and a small group of crates containing lettuce was stacked against the wall. Taking a closer look, I could see that much of the produce was brown. The décor changed dramatically behind the doors. Pea-green tiles covered the walls in the dimly lit narrow hallway. The squeaking sound from my shoes came from the rubber flooring. The owner invited us into a cramped office just to the right of the hallway. Our host stood behind a green metal desk, and we remained standing.

"So, who is the restaurant owner?" asked Ilya Kirillovich, with a profound look of anticipation. Ivan Ivanovich translated his inquiry.

"That would be me," replied Scott. "I operate several franchises in Chicago." Scott described which large American fast-food chain he represented, which made a significant impression on our host.

"Wonderful. I hope that you will be interested in our operation. I am sure that we can learn much from your experience."

"I am happy to give any advice I can, within reason, of course. We may be competitors before too long."

"Da, da," laughed Ilya Kirillovich. "I think we have plenty of room for many restaurants. I started this place from scratch. I invested most of my savings and look forward to continuing our success. Would you like to see how we make the food?"

"Yes. I am curious how you get your supplies," Scott replied.

Ilya Kirillovich led us out of the office and into another narrow hallway. As we walked, I heard Scott telling his guide about his experience at the cooperative. The owner replied that he procured much of his supplies from the cooperative and admitted certain problems but added that there was no other alternative in the area. A short distance away, long opaque plastic sheets hung from a door frame. The Russian pushed out some of the sheets, leading to a spacious area containing white tiled walls reminiscent of a bathhouse or indoor pool. Initially of diamond-shaped grey stone, the flooring had been hastily covered with ill-fitted rubber squares likely to reduce slippage from the humidity. Four thick columns, also tiled, supported the octagonal ceiling inlaid with fluorescent track lighting inadequate to illuminate the space properly. As I stood there, a strong, pungent scent invaded my nostrils.

"Please follow me," said Ilya Kirillovich waving us deeper into the area. "We inventory all our vegetables in this area." He pointed to rows of wooden crates stacked two or three high that flanked the rubber walkway.

The crates were similar to the ones behind the front counters. Mostly brown heads of lettuce filled one of the top containers. In another, I observed batches of tomatoes that appeared beyond ripe and several that were clearly rotten. I looked over at Scott to gauge his reaction. Our eyes met, and he simply shook his head. Towards the center of the room, a broad kitchen island came into view. Atop the tiled surface of the island was a square wooden block. The shiny metal blade of a big hatchet was partially inserted into the wooden block. As we moved closer to the center, I noticed dried blood stains on the hatchet's handle, and small slices of meat lay discarded along the flat area supporting the wooden wedge. Looks of amazement fell on our faces as we realized that this was where Ilya Kirillovich prepared the meat cuts for his burgers. As in western fast-food places, I had expected ground beef to be stored in a refrigeration unit until needed. Standing near the cutting block, the pungent smell of flesh and blood became almost overbearing.

"You don't use prepared cuts of meat?" asked Scott. "You chop up each burger, one at a time. That is not very efficient. We have all our meats prepared beforehand for each shift."

"Nyet," responded our host, who had moved behind the tiled island using it as a podium. "We do not have the capacity to store large amounts of meat, so we use the beef delivered that day."

"From where do you get your beef, and where do you store it?" followed up Scott.

"Here, let me show you."

Ilya Kirillovich turned and moved off to the right. Our small group followed him behind a low retaining wall. At the far end of the space stood a large white porcelain bathtub. Reclined in the tub was an enormous headless cow carcass, whose flesh was the apparent source of the noxious odor filling the room. Stunned and appalled by the sight of the exposed flesh, we all put our hands over our noses to fight off the smell. Ilya Kirillovich, seemingly unaware of his guests' discomfort, asked Scott if he wanted to sample one of the eatery's burgers.

"You have to try one of our hamburgers," proudly exclaimed the owner. "I will prepare it myself, and you will see why we are so popular."

Before the American restauranteur could decline, Ilya Kirillovich approached the tub. Grabbing the long-bladed knife hanging on a nearby hook, he leaned over the carcass to slice off a chunk of flesh. As he was slicing, my compatriots and I went back towards the central area and watched the owner perform his butchery. We stood around the island column, awaiting the return of our host.

"I am not eating anything from that tub," said Scott lowly.

"I wouldn't either," I added. "I don't want to spend a night in a local hospital."

Ilya Kirillovich emerged carrying a long, thick tranche of beef still dripping blood, tiny red spots spattering the floor. Even Makoto, who had shown an ability to digest anything, appeared squeamish at eating this meat. Scott asked Ivan Ivanovich whether he had ever eaten at this restaurant, to which the reply 'no' was quickly supplied.

"Ah, here we are, my friends," stated Ilya Kirillovich. Grasping the hatchet handle, he lifted the blade off the cutting block and placed the meat onto the well-worn wooden grooves. "I just need to trim off some of the excess."

"Whoosh!" filled the room as the heavy metal blade tore through the raw flesh. Our host brought down the hatchet several times, reducing the size of the cut considerably. With a more manageable portion in his hand, Ilya Kirillovich led us back through the grey double doors and into the area behind the counters, where two open flame stoves were busy cooking burgers. Loud grease pops exploded from the stove when the cut was laid onto the awaiting fire. More cracks of oil burst into the air each time our host pressed down on the meat with a metal spatula. We stood a few paces back to observe the cook's talent.

"He has no idea how to cook a proper burger," said Scott. "Pressing down on the meat pushes all the flavor from the meat and makes it dry."

"I hope you like it well-done," I said. "See how dark the meat is getting. He's burning it."

Ilya Kirillovich removed the cooked meat with the spatula and carried it over to where several loaves of bread were stationed. He carefully placed the sizzling meat on a thick slice of bread. Our host then tore some brown lettuce from one of the crates and sliced up an over-ripened tomato. Having placed the items on the burger, he added a second slice of bread on top, pressing it down and causing streams of grease to leak into the bread.

"Here you are," happily stated Ilya Kirillovich handing the burger to Scott. "Let me know what you think."

The Russian waited in anticipation for his American guest to try his burger. Scott held the sandwich gingerly in his hands. I could read the doubt on his face whether he should take a bite of the meat, which had been sitting in an open bathtub just a few minutes ago. Not wanting to insult Ilya Kirillovich, Scott slowly raised the sandwich to his lips and took a small bite. My companion made some exaggerated chewing motions but did not appear to swallow. Smiling, Scott nodded his head in approval at the owner, who beamed in excitement at the positive response to his product.

"Is it good?" asked Ilya Kirillovich. "Does it taste like an American burger?"

Scott could tell that the Russian wanted a verbal response, so he carefully moved the portion in his mouth over to one side, where a slight bulge arose in his left cheek.

"Yes, it's tasty," Scott said. "It's not exactly what we serve in my restaurants, but I can see why you are popular."

"Oh, thank you so much!" said our host. "That means so much from an American. Would you like to try our fries or chips?"

Scott's face almost had a look of fright. "No, thank you. The burger is more than enough."

Ivan Ivanovich explained to Ilya Kirillovich that we needed to depart and thanked him for the tour. The owner wished us well, and we all shook hands, even Scott, who still had the unfinished burger in his hand. As our host escorted us to the front door, I once again noticed that all the customers followed our movement through the dining area. We walked down the concrete steps, and once we were on the sidewalk, Scott turned and spat out the portion of the burger that he had bitten. He had kept the piece against his cheek to prevent swallowing the meat.

"That was the most rancid tasting thing I have ever chewed," said Scott as we started walking back to the vehicle. "I wasn't sure I would be able to keep from swallowing the piece when I had to talk."

"Well, at least you don't have to worry about competition," I said. "If this is considered good, your food will blow them away."

"For sure. The key problem will be securing quality supplies."

While we were walking, a growing crowd of locals trailed us a short distance away. They seemed to be fixated on our group and Scott, in particular. I asked Ivan Ivanovich why the people were so interested in our presence. He explained that there were a lot of Asian and white visitors but that Scott was one of the first black person the inhabitants had ever seen.

"They are simply curious," he continued, "and want to catch a glimpse of a real black man."

Scott overheard the conversation and was surprised. "There have never been any black people here?"

"No, not really," replied Ivan Ivanovich. "Unlike Moscow and Leningrad, where many African students go to university, cites like Khabarovsk are not common destinations. Here we have many more Chinese and North Korean students."

"Well, I should let these folks satisfy their curiosity," stated Scott. "Can I talk with some of them?"

"Sure, I am happy to translate, but we do need to be back at the hotel in a short while."

We halted our progress and turned around. With Scott at the front, we strolled toward the gathering of maybe twenty people. There was a mixture of young and old faces, men and women who seemed hesitant at our approach. Scott's height caused some restraint in the crowd, which did not respond at first to his greeting in English. The Russians warmed up after receiving a translation from Ivan Ivanovich. Scott graciously described how much he enjoyed the city and how friendly everyone was. He diplomatically answered several questions about life in America for a black man contradicting some of the propaganda from the Soviet era. One young man even asked him if he had played basketball professionally and knew Michael Jordan. The only sour taste from the experience came from the burger at The Golden Fish.

# The Snow Picnic

Fresh snow had fallen overnight, covering the entire city in a dazzling blanket of white. Sitting at breakfast that morning, picking through the usual fish and rice plate, I averted my eyes due to the intense glare reflecting off the windows. No one had a meeting or tour scheduled until later so we discussed the progress made up to that point. There were some opportunities to reach deals, but, at the same time, serious obstacles remained. Scott had a clear advantage over local competitors like The Golden Fish, but he could not secure reliable local suppliers. Bob talked about his willingness to invest in upgrading energy infrastructure but learned that, by recently passed laws, he could only be a minority partner. Makoto and my initial conversations with local officials regarding constructing a golf course also unveiled difficulties in procuring legal guarantees for foreign ownership of property. Due to lack of experience or cultural influences, the Russians, although eager to attract Western capital and know-how, appeared hesitant to provide or share information and assurances to safeguard potential investments.

Nathan Johnson arrived and said that the group was invited to a local event known as a snow picnic. The van would pick us up in an hour in the lobby. Seeing the confusion on our faces, Nathan added that we should dress warmly. Later that afternoon, after the picnic, he said that a local TV station had requested an interview with the Americans visiting the city.

We stopped eating and returned to our rooms to prepare for the outing. I pilfered through my backpack to find several nutrition bars, which I stuffed into my coat pocket, wanting to ensure that I had something I could eat. I noticed Makoto adding another layer of clothing under his sweater. Following his lead, I put on a second pair of socks and an extra undershirt. Feeling ready, we left the room and went down to the lobby, where Bob and Scott were already waiting.

"What took you guys so long?" inquired Bob.

"Had to find enough extra clothes," I replied. I had spent most of the time searching for the nutrition bars but didn't use that as my excuse, hoping to avoid jokes about my eating habits.

"My friends!" echoed through the lobby in heavily accented English. I spun around and saw the round, strong, smiling face of Igor Petrovich. The former KGB agent turned businessman burst into the area. He appeared in a jolly mood and was accompanied, as usual, by Ivan Ivanovich. "How are my favorite Americans today?"

"We missed you yesterday at The Golden Fish," responded Scott. "I could have used someone to share my burger."

"I heard about your adventure. There is a reason I only dine at the finest restaurants in the city." The hefty Russian broke out in a laugh. "You should have no trouble putting that place out of business, and we can help," he finished with a wink.

Departing the hotel parking lot, Ivan Ivanovich informed us that our destination was a campground north of the city, about a thirty-minute drive. We passed through residential areas dominated by rustic wooden houses painted in various bright colors. This area was an older part of the city, explained the interpreter, where some of the town's founding families had settled. Like most far eastern cities, the Russian army comprised some of the earliest settlers as the Tsarist empire expanded rapidly in the 18th and 19th centuries. Military force helped protect traders and merchants by establishing a permanent Russian presence. As we rode along the Voronezhskoye Shosse north of the city center, the houses became smaller and less impressive. Dilapidated log structures surrounded by leaning wooden fences dominated the scenery.

We passed through a small town called Nagornoe, after which the environs shifted to a heavily forested area. The snow-laden trees presented a spectacular view. Off to our right, I noticed a rise out of the forest. It did not appear to be a mountain but rather a rocky hill. I asked Ivan Ivanovich about the elevated spot, and he explained that this was the highest point in the area, offering great views of the forest and river.

"This area," Igor Petrovich said, "is home to many camping and hiking areas. There are special camps here for the young pioneers." The young pioneers was an official organization connected with the Communist Party. In Soviet times, many children attended these camps in the summer, engaging in outdoor activities and receiving indoctrination in Communist Party dogma.

"Are the camps still used?" I asked, aware that the young pioneers had been disbanded with the collapse of the USSR.

"In the summer, yes," replied our host. "They are run now by a private organization, and the children have to pay to attend. It's outrageous."

"The city does pay for some of the costs," added Ivan Ivanovich, " but some families can not afford the fees for their children, which is a shame."

The vehicle exited the highway and headed along a narrow road. I could feel the van glide from time to time on the icy surface, but the driver did not seem to reduce speed. The pathway was lined on either side by massive, bare white birch trees, whose branches strained to support the thick white snow that had fallen overnight. A small opening on the left held a barely legible sign broadcasting a 'Detski Lager' or Children's Camp, where an imposing metal gate blocked the entrance. We came upon a small group of vehicles standing in a small non-wooded area to our right a few miles further. Beyond this tiny oasis, a vast snowfield was guarded by thick rows of trees. Our driver parked next to a blue Saab whose inhabitants had gathered over by a green Opel several yards away. Despite the frost on the window, I identified one of the people as Nathan Johnson due to his trademark white feather. Igor Petrovich slid open the door, and we left the van. The snow was heavy, and our boots made deep chomping sounds with each step.

"Here we are!" announced Igor Petrovich. "This is a popular camping area with many hiking trails and boat slips. In winter, we still use the cooking areas for picnics."

"This looks amazing," I said. The scenery is so beautiful."

The sunlight roamed free in the cloudless sky, producing an almost blinding reflection off the snow. Shielding his eyes from the glare, Igor Petrovich explained that since cars could not navigate the deep snow, he had arranged for a more traditional mode of transport. The Russian businessman turned his head to his right and gave a loud whistle. Two sleighs emerged from the woodline on the left, each drawn by a single horse. A driver sat in the front of each black carriage carrying a short whip, which he employed readily to push the animal through the deep snow. A large gold bell hung above the horse harness and rang clearly in the cold air, marking the animal's approach. The sleighs halted a few paces from the group.

"Alright, first party get in!" commanded our host.

He motioned for Nathan Johnson and his team to board the awaiting carriage. The three men climbed into the carriage, and once sitting, the driver shouted, prompting the horse to pull away into the snowfield. The second sleigh moved into the first one's slot. This time, Igor Petrovich stared at my companions and me.

"OK. Your turn. We will follow you to the picnic area when the sleighs return."

Bob went first and needed some assistance ascending the footstep. He sat on the bench adjacent to the driver. Scott climbed in and occupied the seat next to Bob. My boot slipped slightly on the icy footpad, but I entered the carriage without assistance. I lowered myself onto the thinly padded bench, where I faced Bob. The seating was hard and uncomfortable, but I noticed a rolled-up blanket sitting to my side. Makoto took his place next to me. The compartment looked small, but we all fit easily inside. Holding his whip at the ready, the man ordered the horse to move. The jolt of the carriage lifted me off my seat, feeling I would land in Bob's lap. The thick snow hindered movement at first, and I could sense the strain as the enormous creature fought against the inertia of his burden. The driver spouted strong words of encouragement to the horse, who slowly began to find a steady rhythm. The more rapid pace strengthened the wind resistance, causing sharp icy pangs to strike my cheeks.

Accompanying the sounds of the metal bell, divets of snow, dirt, and ice torn by the heavy hooves started flying into the seating area. To keep warm and block some debris, I unfurled a blanket, placing it over my legs and waist and sharing any excess material with my roommate. I gazed to my left, focusing on the passing tall birches. The white giants seemed to be surveilling our progress across their ancestral lands. As we glided through the snowfield, depictions of troika rides by Turgenev, Pushkin, and Tolstoy poured into my mind. I imagined myself as a 19th-century Russian aristocrat heading into the vast Russian countryside to visit one of my many estates, where I was lord and master.

The trek must have lasted ten to fifteen minutes, but my face was already frozen. The sleigh made a wide arc, and I saw, off to the right, a small cluster of people standing by several tables partially covered in snow. A brick fire pit was located behind the tables, and a man was tending to the bright orange flames that jumped through the black metal grill. Our driver halted beside the first carriage, from where the other Americans had just dismounted. Their cargo unloaded, the two drivers shouted 'forward!', and the horses began their return trip to collect the remaining passengers. The snow was not as deep here, and we had less difficulty trudging toward the picnic tables. In various stages of preparation, an assortment of food and drink sat on the top wooden surface of the tables. Everyone was standing since the benches were buried under a layer of white. A group of trees surrounding the recess provided some shelter from the wind. My companions and I joined the table with the other Americans. At one table, the discussion centered around the temperature and the status of prospective deals. Bob and Scott talked about their visits with local enterprises while Makoto split off with Nathan for a private conversation. Not particularly interested in the topics, I walked over to another table where Ivan Ivanovich was chatting with two unfamiliar men. One of the men was tall, with broad shoulders. His blonde hair peeked out from beneath his shapka, and his deep blue eyes showed an unexpected kindness for such an imposing figure. A thick leather strap hung over his left shoulder, causing him to tilt slightly. The second man was roughly my height and thick and squat. His fur hat barely contained the thick brown hair, which almost reached his brown eyes. He wore a blue fur-lined coat with the scars of many years' use. I introduced myself and commented on how majestic the area looked, glistening in the sunshine.

"Yes, we are very fortunate to have access to nature like this," said Ivan Ivanovich. "We Russians cherish our strong connection with the land."

"You should come here in the summer," said the tall man, who introduced himself as Pavel Pavlovich in a booming voice. "The park is crowded with families."

"Do you all come here often in the winter?"

"It is common, yes," stated the heavyset man who Ivan Ivanovich explained was Alexandr Lvovich. "Warm temperatures are brief in the region, so we have to enjoy the outside when available. Do you not have picnics in winter in America?"

I explained that I grew up and still live in a cold region in the U.S. I was sure people gathered in winter outside but had personally never attended such a picnic. The men smiled and reached for half-filled glasses that stood on the table. Ivan Ivanovich offered me a glass of the brownish liquid. A sharp sting hit my throat when I took a small sip forcing me to cough. The Russians laughed, and Pavel Pavlovich asked me if I did not enjoy the cognac. The alcohol was strong, immediately causing a warming sensation in my chest. I replied that the drink was smoother on the way down while noticing a row of metal skewers spread out on the table. Several rolled-up sheets of newspaper lay next to the rods.

"What are you preparing?" I asked, trying to shift the focus from my cough.

"Shashlik," answered Ivan Ivanovich. He unfolded the newspaper, unveiling many chunks of raw meat about the size of golf balls. "We put the beef on the skewers and place them on the grill."

"Ah, shishkabob!" I exclaimed.

The men took the meat cubes and impaled them on the metal rods. I sipped generously on my drink; the feeling of warmth distracted me from the frigid climate. Holding three to four skewers each, the Russians approached the roaring fire and placed the metal rods on the grill. I followed closely behind and could hear the 'pops' from bits of wood exploding on the log pile in the pit. My nostrils took in the potent mixture of burning wood and meat, and I gazed at the intense black cloud of smoke searing into the open sky. Mesmerized by the dancing flames, I failed to notice the arrival of our host, whose boisterous voice interrupted the idyllic scene. I turned to see Igor Petrovich standing on top of the table, surrounded by the rest of the attendees.

"Welcome everyone to a typical winter picnic here in Khabarovsk," loudly stated our host. "Please share in the food and drinks. You will find plenty of bread, cheese, eggs, cucumbers, and sausage meats. As a special treat, we have shashlik roasting on the grill." He pointed to the fire pit where I was standing beside my Russian acquaintances. "There is, of course, plenty of vodka and cognac to keep you warm." A brief cheer of 'urrah!' erupted from the Russians.

After the speech, I remained by the fire pit and chatted with the three men, diligently watching the meat cubes turn a delicate dark brown. The pangs of hunger grew louder in my stomach the longer I listened to the sizzling juices on the grill. Ivan Ivanovich detailed to me how his parents and grandparents would take him, as a child, to such winter picnics. His father would drag him through the snow on a tiny red sleigh, bundled up tightly by his mother, afraid of her child catching cold. Pavel Pavlovich spoke of long hikes in the forest with his four brothers, which would always result in a massive snowball fight. Describing his parents as rather bookish, Alexander Lvovich explained that he rarely went outside in winter; instead, they went to the library or the theater. I talked about the harsh winters growing up in Boston, such as the famous blizzard of '78, when the snowdrifts reached my house's roof. While the adults struggled to clear paths in the snow, we children carved out massive forts from the mountains of white and engaged in house-to-house battles, pelting each other with icy projectiles. Despite the past years of hostility, we all laughed at these similar experiences, showing that Americans and Russians had much in common. My youthful exuberance gave me a sense that our two peoples could overcome our past and see each other as, if not friends, at least not adversaries.

"Ah, it looks like the first one is ready," exclaimed Pavel Pavlovich. "My American friend, would you like to try it?"

"Da, konechno (Yes, of course)," I said. I put my near-empty glass back onto the table and turned back towards the grill.

"Now, the ends may be hot, so be careful not to burn yourself," added the tall Russian, extending his hand with the skewer.

Even though it reduced the dexterity of my fingers, I kept my mittens on to use as a kind of oven mitt. I took a firm grasp of the black end of the rod and held it vertically, watching waves of steam rise from the charred meat. I blew on the top few cubes despite the frosty air before attempting to bite into one. Aware that my Russian companions were eager to see my reaction to the shashlik, I brought the tower of meat close to my face and took a small piece into my mouth. It was remarkably tender in spite of the partially blackened outer edges. I took another, bigger bite and continued to chew while display-ing a broad smile. My reaction pleased the men, and Ivan Ivanovich patted me on the shoulder.

"See, you can now say that you've had shashlik in the snow," said the inter-preter. "You have a real Russian experience to talk about back home."

"Yes. I am amazed at how you keep the meat from tasting dry."

"It's marinating it with some vodka," stated Pavel Pavlovich with a wink. "Vodka is good for everything."

Satisfied that their guest enjoyed the food, the three men grabbed their own shashlik. We ate in silence for several moments when a thrashing sound was heard in the distance. I started to ask what the noise source might be but stopped when Ivan Ivanovich made a hand signal to keep quiet. A look of concern fell over the Russians' faces, which, in turn, increased my sense of uneasiness. A few moments passed as we listened intently. Then, there was the repeated sound of movement somewhere in the treeline. Glued to my spot, I observed Pavel Pavlovich turn and slowly approach the edge of the clearing, unveiling the thick leather shoulder strap supporting a Kalashnikov assault rifle. The wooden stock and metal barrel of the AK-47 jostled slightly on the tall Russian's back as he crouched down and peered around the low bushes marking the limit of the picnic area. For a few moments, everything was still;

only the breeze winding through the dead branches broke the calm. Then, like the breaking of twigs, another sound, this time closer, reached our ears.

Pavel Pavlovich swung the rifle over his shoulder with expert precision and assumed a firing position. Not wanting to distract him, my two companions and I remained quiet. We could not see what Pavel Pavlovich was looking at, which increased our level of anxiety. I could hear voices coming from the other table, where the others appeared unaware of our situation. Suddenly, Pavel Pavlovich raised the rifle's muzzle skyward, and a shattering 'crack' erupted. Although I was staring directly at the tall Russian, the firing sound still surprised me, and I stepped quickly back into a low position. Another 'crack' burst into the air. Then Pavel Pavlovich stood up, lowered his rifle, and walked back towards us. The gunfire had gotten everyone's attention, and Igor Petrovich, Nathan Johnson, and the others had joined our table.

"What was that, Pasha?" asked Ivan Ivanovich. "An elk or deer?"

With the rifle still in his hand, Pavel Pavlovich shook his head. "I thought it might be a deer, but then I saw the large face with yellow eyes bordered by orange and black stripes."

"A tiger?" I blurted out, not able to control myself.

"Da," answered the tall blonde Russian. "It is not uncommon to have a sighting in winter when the food is more scarce. I fired to warn him, and luckily, he heeded the warning."

"Would the rifle shots have stopped him if he didn't heed the warning?" I followed up.

"Maybe, assuming I was able to get a few headshots."

"A male adult tiger can weigh over two hundred kilograms (over four hundred pounds)," added Ivan Ivanovich. "Hunters use large caliber rifles when they need to bring down such a beast."

The incident dampened the otherwise jovial mood. There were some concerns about whether we should end the picnic and head back to the hotel. Sensing the overall discontent of his guests, Igor Petrovich did his best to persuade everyone that the sighting was very rare and that it was improbable the animal would return. He encouraged us all to relax and finish our food and drink. He climbed back onto the table and proposed a toast.

"To friendship and success!" shouted our host with drink in hand.

It took a few more toasts to get most guests feeling again at ease. The conversation eventually moved away from the tiger and returned to business and cultural exchanges. Our Russian companions were very interested in American culture and were fascinated by the diversity of backgrounds and experiences deriving from our, as they described, 'country of immigrants'. The Russians eagerly absorbed stereotypical rags to riches stories, appearing surprised that someone could rise from meager means and 'legally' obtain elite social and economic status. In Russia, people assumed wealth and power were obtained through illicit resources, such as bribes or other forms of corruption. We explained that many American fortunes were also achieved in this way, but opportunities still existed to become rich through honest hard work. The Russians expressed optimism that the new market economy would offer them such chances.

As the sunlight faded, Igor Petrovich announced that it was time to wrap up and return to the city. Leaving the scraps of food and empty bottles scattered around the campsite, we walked to the sleighs. The air was colder due to the late hour, so we all bundled as best we could under the blankets. The driver arrived at the makeshift parking area a short while later and pulled the sleigh up near the vehicles. We dismounted and sat inside the van, partially opening the side door. Igor Petrovich, accompanied by the other Russians, came in the last sleigh. He jumped down from the carriage and thanked us for sharing this experience. Our host bid the others farewell and retook his place in the van, where he directed the driver to make haste. The vehicle spun and swerved onto the snowy road. Detecting our nervousness, Igor Petrovich turned around, explaining that the local TV reporter would be at the hotel in thirty minutes and that we needed to hurry. I sat back in my seat while tightening the security belt.

The driver drove skillfully, avoiding several potential accidents, and dropped us off at the hotel's main entrance. A thin man in a blue tracksuit stepped forward to greet us in the lobby. I heard the man inform Igor Petrovich that he worked for the TV station and that the reporter and her crew were set up in the conference room down the hall. We traced the man's steps across the lobby and through the east wing corridor. A small placard reading 'reserved' stood on a short pole outside the doors of the hotel conference center. Entering the tan carpeting room, I saw rows of chairs stacked against the far side wall obscuring the artwork hanging on the red and beige walls. There were two large umbrellas under which sat a set of bright lights in the room's center. Two chairs flanked by a large tripod video camera were positioned between the umbrellas. Off to the side, a woman dressed in a stylish blue business suit, her long black hair pinned up into a bun, was having a spirited conversation with a taller, heavyset man with balding hair, dressed in an untucked collared polo shirt and jeans. I assumed this was the reporter and her cameraman discussing the upcoming interview. We stood still at the entryway, unsure if we should proceed further.

"Wait here," said the man in the tracksuit, "Let me ask Natalia Borisovna if she is ready for you."

The man left us and walked towards the elegantly looking reporter. As I watched them speak, I began to feel nervous, having never participated in a TV interview before. The rush in returning from the picnic exacerbated my anxiety. The facial expressions of my companions showed that they shared my uneasiness. I tapped my hand on Igor Petrovich's shoulder.

"This feels too hurried," I said. "I thought we'd have some time to prepare. I don't know what to say."

Our host did not seem to share my apprehension. "What is the problem? She asks questions, and you give answers."

Igor Petrovich suggested that we provide positive answers to show how good the visit was. Scott, hearing my translation, asked if he should avoid talking about The Golden Fish and the farm cooperative, to which I nodded yes. I had the impression that Igor Petrovich wanted to use the interview as a marketing ploy for his business connections. Makoto mentioned that he didn't see Ivan Ivanovich and wondered who would translate. Our host stated that the reporter spoke English, so they didn't need a translator.

The tracksuit man reappeared and waved to us to follow him. As we neared the interview set, the woman approached us with a broad smile; her gray eyes twinkled as she extended her hand to grasp Igor Petrovich's.

"Thank you for coming," she said before switching to English. "My name is Natalia Borisovna Nemtsov. I am so glad that you have made time to speak with me. My audience is interested in hearing from Americans who have traveled to our region." She shook each of our hands in turn. "I look forward to learning a little about each of you."

Natalia Borisovna informed us that she would talk to us individually for about ten minutes. Yuri, her cameraman, would operate the video recorder, but we should speak directly to her. Scott asked what she would ask us, and the reporter answered that the questions would be general ones and that we should say whatever we wanted. Bob asked when the interviews were to air on television. Natalia Borisovna responded that she planned to broadcast the piece the following evening. She finished by suggesting that we simply relax and answer naturally.

'OK, let's start with you," said Natalia Borisovna pointing to my roommate. Makoto took a deep breath and sat in the chair on the right side. The reporter occupied the place directly across from him.

"Are you ready?" asked the reporter. "You seem uncomfortable."

"The lights are so hot," said Makoto, using the back of his hand to wipe some beads of sweat from his brow. "May I remove my sweater?" Receiving a nod of approval from the reporter, he stood back up and pulled the thick sweater over his head. The friction from the woolen material frayed his hair, causing much of it to point towards the ceiling. Makoto tried to mat the hair down with his hand with limited effect.

"Better?" inquired Natalia Borisovna. "Can we begin?"

"Yes. Go ahead."

The reporter asked Makoto to describe his background and interest in Khabarovsk. She connected Makoto's Japanese ancestry with the large influx of Japanese and Koreans entering the area. She followed up with questions about what type of investment he hoped to complete and what he thought of the city. My roommate straightforwardly answered the questions but was careful to avoid mentioning potential obstacles to investment. Scott went next. Natalia Borisovna asked similarly about Scott's experience in America but finished by asking about his thoughts on the local restaurant market. The franchisor was very diplomatic in his responses. He talked about the attractive prospects in the city and the variety of eating options. When asked whether he had visited any local eateries, Scott explained that he toured an impressive farm and tried a hamburger at a local restaurant. Bob described his years in the oil and gas business and hopes of finding a strong Russian investment partner. When asked about his impressions of the city, the retired oilman said that Khabarovsk was a lovely city, and everyone was friendly and welcoming. I was the last to talk.

"So, Ken," she started in English. "How has such a young man come to look for investments in Russia?"

Her face beamed when I answered in Russian.

"Ah, I forgot," she said. "You speak Russian. That is wonderful! My viewers will be astounded to hear an American respond in Russian."

We continued the rest of the interview in Russian. I talked about growing up in Boston, focusing my university studies on Russia, and mentioning the Russian history course I took at Harvard to sound more impressive. Natalia Borisova took full advantage of my inexperience and exuberance to ask me how I, describing me as an American scholar of Russia, saw current US – Russia relations. My attempt at eloquence fell flat. I meant to characterize the present state of relations as the best chance for a true partnership between the historical foes but instead used the word describing a marriage ('brak'). I immediately regretted my answer, hoping the viewers would comprehend my intent. The reporter took pity on me and wrapped up the interview with a few simple questions.

"That's it. Thank you all very much," said Natalia Borisovna returning to English. "Please try to watch the show tomorrow at 7:00 pm."

Igor Petrovich shook hands again with the reporter while they had a brief private conversation. Our host returned and let us know that we were free for the rest of the evening. As almost an afterthought, he added that we would be leaving the hotel the next morning to spend the next couple of days at a compound outside the city, where we would tour the areas for the golf course. Again confused by the sudden change of plans, I asked Igor Petrovich when we were departing and whether we would be returning to this hotel.

"Nyet," he said. "We will go straight to the airport from the compound. Please take everything with you tomorrow."

The word 'compound' made me feel a little worried. "What type of compound are we going to?"

"It was a former administration site. It's very nice. You will enjoy it there. The scenery is beautiful."

We left the conference room and went to the elevators, where Igor Petrovich took his leave. He wished us a pleasant evening and exited the hotel. Inside the elevator, I could see the nervous reflections of our faces on the metal keypad.

"The itinerary just keeps changing," I said. "Did Nathan inform you all of this?"

"Nah, this is all new to me," said Scott. "I'm just kinda going with the punches."

"A compound sounds interesting," commented Bob. "That might mean an estate-like area."

We got off, and Makoto and I made our way towards our room. Inside, I asked my roommate his thoughts. He replied that you had to be flexible in business and that he was sure everything was good. Makoto's assurance made me feel better. We ate one final group dinner in the hotel restaurant and spent the remainder of the evening preparing for the upcoming journey. I expected some new adventures awaited.

# Chunky Milk

THE FIRST LIGHT OF DAY was just peeking over the horizon when we drove away from the hotel parking lot. Shivering a little from the morning's chill, I fastened my coat as high as possible and tucked my chin into the fur lining. I fidgeted while trying to secure a comfortable position on the worn seat fabric. Today's journey would be the longest, a three-hour ride north from Khabarovsk to a secluded compound. Sitting in his usual place, Igor Petrovich explained that the complex had served as a command center during Soviet times to administer the myriad of forced labor camps in the region. The site was currently a retreat or vacation area for government officials. In response to several questions from my companions, our host added that Lenin initially established these camps, but they were greatly expanded under Stalin. The area surrounding Khabarovsk had been a critical component of the 'gulag' network, which had housed millions of Soviet citizens sentenced for political crimes. I found it surprising that a former KGB agent was so forthcoming about this repressive aspect of the Soviet system.

I rested my head against the window and attempted to relax. The coolness of the glass had a calming effect, and my thoughts began to wander. Now outside the city, the scenery became monotonous with countless trees whizzing past, their naked branches forming one continuous white blur. I tried to focus on my assignment related to the golf course, but the stories and images concerning the miserable existence in the gulags kept creeping back into my mind. I recalled the tales of suffering vividly captured in the works of Solzhenitsyn, Ginzburg, and Shalamov and wondered how the fate of so many innocent people might have been decided at this compound now serving as a place of relaxation. My enthusiasm for visiting the complex drained away as the miles rolled past.

An unexpected turn from the highway onto an unmarked road shook me from my thoughts. The narrow paved road would have been impossible to find without knowing its existence. White birch giants flanked the path extending in an endless pattern as far as the eye could see. After a slight rise in the road, the slanted rooftops of several buildings were visible. We reached the top of the incline, where three distinct structures came into view. A large rectangular two-story edifice painted in yellow with tall windows framed by white shutters sat adjacent to two smaller grey stone buildings. An imposing dark wooden fence, capped with razor wire, protected the entire area. The van stopped in front of the green metal gate that permitted entry into the compound. Igor Petrovich exited the vehicle and approached a small inter-com box next to the entrance. A heavy clicking sound soon followed, and I saw the metal barrier slowly slide across its runners. Our host jumped back into the van, and we drove into the complex. We stopped several yards past the gate, and I had a brief foreboding moment as I watched the green door close behind us. Remembering the complex's past, I wondered if I would see the outside again.

We exited the vehicle in the circular driveway, grabbed our luggage, and followed Igor Petrovich into the main building. A stone-tiled hallway stretched for several yards until reaching the base of a marble staircase with wrought-iron railings. Ornately decorated with dark wood crown molding, the foyer ceiling supported a broad glass chandelier. A chorus of clicking sounds from our baggage wheels echoed off the walls decorated with crimson wallpaper. Two wings extended from either side of the staircase leading, on the right, to a series of meeting rooms and, on the left, to a formal dining area and recreation room. Wood parquet flooring was covered by narrow red and gold throw rugs. The walls of each corridor bore yellowish paint rising towards the dark wood beam ceilings.

"The sleeping quarters are upstairs," said Igor Petrovich.

Lifting my suitcases off the floor, I followed our host up to the second floor. The wood flooring here was lighter, and a thick green carpet ran along the middle of the corridor. The walls displayed the same yellowish color, but the white ceiling reflected light from the many wall lamps. Standing on the landing, I noticed a flurry of activity. Nathan Johnson and several other people were moving in and out of several rooms, carrying luggage or bringing in blankets. The Cardinal Communications' CEO halted his movement upon seeing us.

"I believe that one room remains on the far end," he said. "Each room, unfortunately, has only two beds. Two of you will need to find another space for sleeping."

Despite Nathan's warning, we all continued along the corridor until we stood in front of the square archway of the last room. Two twin beds, pillows, and a thin folded blanket stood near the far ends of the small space.

"I guess two of us will be couching it downstairs," I said. "I am offering to go. Who wants to join me?"

"I will be fine on a couch," stated Scott after a brief hesitation. "I think Bob and Makoto will fit nicely up here."

The two men put up a short protest, but Scott's and my resistance soon convinced them to move their belongings into the room. I approached Igor Petrovich, who had remained at the landing, and asked him which rooms downstairs had the most comfortable sofas.

"Ah, Ken," the Russian said. "Don't worry. You can stay in one of the guest houses."

Igor Petrovich explained that the grey stone buildings across the courtyard served as guest houses. Each structure could house two to three men comfortably and was equipped with its own toilets and shower. Ivan Ivanovich and another Russian occupied one of the grey buildings, but Scott and I were welcome to stay in the other one. Delighted to avoid 'couch surfing', my colleague and I carried our suitcases back down the stairs. I followed Igor Petrovich out of the building and across the gravel courtyard until arriving at a bluish steel door. Our host removed a keychain from his trouser pocket and unlocked the door. The heavy metal budged with a loud creak, and we walked inside. The space consisted of two rooms separated by a smooth concrete hallway. The room on the left was sparsely furnished. Two small beds faced each other across the area with a writing desk and a small nightstand with a single chair placed in the middle. A wardrobe with no door stood to the right of the entrance. Pea-green painted walls formed around the cold cement floor, and a single bare lightbulb hung from the ceiling provided all the illumination.

"Well, this is cozy," I said. "Which bed would you prefer?"

"Um, I'll take the one on the left," Scott replied with some hesitation.

"The toilet and shower are across the hall," added Igor Petrovich, who had remained standing in the doorway. "I'll let you get settled in but remember we have a lunch meeting at 1:00 pm in the main dining room."

My wristwatch indicated it was just after 12:30 pm, so I decided to freshen up before lunch. I crossed the hallway and entered the bathroom. Covered in white tiles, the floor and walls appeared in dire need of a good scrubbing. Facing me as I stepped into the space was a porcelain pedestal washbasin above which hung a square mirror cracked in one corner. A cloth hand towel laid precariously on the side of the washbasin. An old-style toilet with a pull-string flusher sat adjacent to the pedestal. A silver showerhead jetted from the wall at the back end of the room. There was no curtain or door, just a low wooden bench upon which were stacked two thin yellow bath towels. I used the thick grayish soap bar to wash my hands and face before returning to the sleeping area. Returning to the bedroom, I described the state of the bathroom, and my roommate just shook his head.

It was now 12:55 pm, and I let Scott know we needed to go back to the main building. I left the sheets and comforter folded on the bed and unpacked several items of clothing, which I hung in the wardrobe. I felt uneasy leaving everything unsecured, but my roommate convinced me that nothing would happen since no one could enter this place. In my head, I said, "and no one could exit." We scurried across the courtyard and quickly located the dining area. The others were already seated when we arrived. Scott and I took places at the end of the long lacquered wood table. Dark inlaid wood comprised the room's walls, and a huge crystal chandelier extended down from the ceiling.

Igor Petrovich, seated at the opposite end of the table, was engaged in a lively conversation with Nathan Johnson. At the same time, the other Americans and Russians sat intermingled with Ivan Ivanovich strategically placed in the middle. The first course had already been served as a bowl of red cabbage soup, or 'borscht,' lay before me. "At least it wasn't fish," I thought and hoped the main course would be a non-fish dish.

Suddenly a set of swinging doors opened behind Igor Petrovich, and a tall, blonde woman in her early twenties entered carrying a large tray. Wearing a white blouse and close-fitted black skirt, she placed the empty bowls on the tray and worked her way around the table. When she stood next to me, she noticed that my bowl was still almost full. I could see her hesitate, trying to decide whether she should remove the bowl. I looked up and nodded to signal that I had finished. The look in her blue eyes indicated that my signal had not worked.

"Are you still eating?" she asked somewhat meekly and made a hand motion mimicking the use of a spoon.

"Nyet, I am done," I replied in Russian, which surprised and pleased her.

"OK, good. I will take your bowl so I can bring the next course."

"Yes, please," I said. "And I hope it's not fish."

The woman smiled and let out a brief laugh. Igor Petrovich had been observing the interaction.

"Irina, please finish clearing the table and go bring the next dish," our host said in a commanding voice.

The smile quickly vanished. Irina completed collecting the bowls and disappeared through the swinging doors. She returned five minutes later supporting a sizeable oval tray filled with the next course. I watched as the young woman diligently laid a plate before each guest, mindful of the sharp gaze of Igor Petrovich. Not wanting to cause her further trouble, I kept silent when she served me a plate of roasted chicken with potatoes and beans. I was thrilled to have a dish not consisting of fish but did not express my joy. The main course delivered, Igor Petrovich made a short toast and dove into a description of the main event for the afternoon. A helicopter tour over the land set aside for the golf course development was scheduled following lunch.

Makoto, Ivan Ivanovich, and I would accompany the Russian businessman on the aerial visit, which was to take about two hours.

"You will love the view," described our host. "There are vast open spaces surrounded by forests and beautiful lakes. There is as much land as you need."

"Would it also be possible to drive around the land?" I asked. "It would be helpful to see the route into the area that golfers will take and where they could stay, etc."

"It is impossible to reach the area by vehicle in winter due to the snow," explained Igor Petrovich. "In summer, we can use all-terrain transportation to navigate the fields and forest."

"There are no existing roads?" I followed up, thinking that I must have misunderstood.

"No, of course not," replied Igor Petrovich with disbelief. "It's all open country. There are thousands of kilometers available."

"So, beyond building the golf course, it will be necessary to construct the roads as well?"

"Da. Nathan explained that should not be a problem."

I looked at the Cardinal CEO, who sat proudly next to Igor Petrovich.

"Our construction man, Jimmy (he pointed to the man a few seats down), will have all the contracts for roads, etc. Your firm is here just for the course design."

"Is there any electricity or sewage that can support the project," said Makoto in a lively tone.

"That will all have to be constructed," stated our host. "As I said, there is just land."

"And lodging for the guests? I assume that will be built too," added Makoto

"That's our man, Jimmy," smiled Nathan.

I gazed closer at Jimmy, sitting smugly at the table. I tried to recall Jimmy's last name. I remembered that it was Losano or Antonelli or something close to that from his business card. He was a local Chicago contractor, having some-how gotten the exclusive bid on these projects. I began to realize a bit more of the bigger picture at play. A small communications firm like Cardinal felt it hit a goldmine of opportunity by partnering with Igor Petrovich. Cardinal looked to control all the business projects, and I was sure it received a percentage of all the construction work that Jimmy would do. From my short experience at Pyramid, I knew that the firm preferred to work with builders who they trusted. I already foresaw a significant problem with this scenario.

"There are also plans to expand the airport's size," said Igor Petrovich. "If so many golfers arrive, we will need bigger and newer facilities."

"Jimmy again?" I asked sarcastically.

"Nyet. Our government is requesting funds from Moscow, and Russians will do the work."

With lunch completed, I returned to my lodging, grabbed my coat and video camera, and headed into the courtyard, where I joined the others in one of the white vans. We exited the compound and drove for several miles until reaching a man-made clearing in the dense forest. A small helicopter was sitting in the center of the opening. The snow had been removed from the site, and I saw a pilot seated inside the cockpit. Our small group made our way into the confined space of the helicopter, and, at Igor Petrovich's command, the pilot flipped the switch to start the loud humming of the props. The small craft vibrated, and our host showed us how to fasten the security belts. The vertical liftoff proceeded slowly, the pilot mindful of the tight band of trees. One above the forest canopy, we headed southeast. The forest below whizzed by in a flash, and I saw an infinite snow-covered plain to my left. The humming and vibration inside the cabin were so loud that it was impossible to hear someone speak. I caught Igor Petrovich's motion to put on the set of headphones under the seats. The thin black device also had a microphone arm through which one could talk.

"Can you hear me now?" I heard our host's voice arrive into my earpads. The sound was scratchy, but I could understand his broken English.

Makoto and I gave the thumbs-up sign. Igor Petrovich continued in Russian, pointing out important landmarks and the boundaries of the golf course area. Ivan Ivanovich translated, which was helpful with the poor quality of sound. I listened while holding up my video camera to capture as much as possible for the developers back in Chicago. The pilot lowered the aircraft lower over the open plain, allowing me some close-up landscape footage.

Several narrow scattered lakes might make interesting water hazards or become beautification points for a proposed course.

"With whom do we work to obtain the title for the property," I inquired while still filming below.

There was silence for several moments. Finally, our host began to speak again.

"As you may know, foreigners cannot acquire title to property in Russia. We can offer a fifty-year lease on excellent terms, including tax holidays for the first ten years."

Makoto and I exchanged glances. I had read about the difficulty of buying land in Russia, but I expected some flexibility given the desire to commit to the project.

"It may be challenging to find investors for such a large undertaking without the land title," I said. "You are asking for millions of dollars in financing from banks or investors who will not have the land as collateral."

"My contacts in Japan will also be wary of such an arrangement," added Makoto.

More moments of silence ensued, followed by our host's explanation that the government, by law, could not sell the land to a foreign entity.

"Investors can form a partnership with a Russian entity for the land. The Russian side, of course, will have to be the majority owner."

"I am not sure that will solve the problem," I stated. "Let's talk about titles later. Can the construction and development costs be covered by golf and club membership fees?"

"I doubt that will be plausible," chimed in Makoto. I saw that Igor Petrovich had no answers to the business projections. "With just climate alone," continued Makoto, "play will be limited to five or six months of the year before it is too cold and snowy to play."

"We could use orange balls," I retorted in jest. My companion gave me a severe look.

"Even if we can sell memberships, which cost millions like in Japan, the volume of players will likely be too low to generate sufficient revenue annually to pay for all the development and infrastructure expenses. I expected we would build the course in a more developed area with minimal infrastructure needs. Here we have virgin land."

The Russians had no viable answers to these questions. We continued the tour for another half an hour before heading back to the landing pad. It was a quiet ride back to the compound. Igor Petrovich informed us that dinner would be served at 7:00 pm and that there would be a special guest for the evening. Armed with that information, I stepped into the gray building, where I found Scott lying on his bed. He was reading what looked like a restaurant trade magazine. I put my camera back into its case, removed my boots, and fell into the bed.

"How was the tour? Scott asked.

"The land is stunning. You just can't own it. At least, if you are non-Russian."

"Yeah, that will be an issue for me as well. They are offering me a long-term lease but owning the property is where the money is for fast food."

"Well, we see where this goes. I can't see serious money invested for the golf course and infrastructure without land ownership."

"Did you hear about dinner tonight?"

"Yeah, Igor Petrovich told us when we got out of the van. Any idea who the special guest is?"

"No clue. I just hope she is pretty," added Scott with a short chuckle.

I needed a shower after the hot, close-quarters experience on the helicopter. Scott told me that he had taken a shower earlier and quickly ran out of hot water.

"How long ago was the shower?" I asked, my eyes still closed.

"About an hour or so. The tank might have reheated the water by now."

"Agh, I guess I should go and get it over with."

I grabbed some fresh underwear from my suitcase and shuffled into the bathroom. Standing next to the wooden bench, I removed my socks, and sharp cold jabs penetrated my bare feet from the tiled floor. I rapidly finished undressing and, shivering, stepped towards the rusty showerhead and turned the dial counterclockwise. I took an immediate step back, expecting the powerful stream of water to come gushing forth. My caution was premature. A slow trickle of water deposited large droplets on the tile. I could feel the goosebumps pulsating on my skin as I put my hand up to the trickle to test its temperature. I took a deep breath, grabbed the tiny bar of soap from the bench, and moved under the dribble of water. The droplets hitting my head felt like a brain freeze from drinking something cold too quickly. I sparingly used the soap to limit my exposure time to the water. Rocking on my feet to maintain blood flow, I rinsed off and employed as much of the thin towel's surface area to dry and cover skin. I dressed promptly and returned to the bedroom.

"Any hot water?" asked Scott without taking his eyes from his magazine.

"Ha. There was barely any water, and the slow drip I had to endure was freezing," I said. "I'll need a tall glass of cognac tonight to warm up."

"Well, I'm sure there will be plenty of that. Have you noticed how much booze gets drunk around here?"

"Yeah, it's a cultural and historical problem, a way to escape, in my opinion, from living under conditions where you have little control. Life expectancy for Russian men is one of the lowest in Europe due to the drinking."

"I can see that," said Scott. "Well, I can take advantage of it for a few days; it shouldn't have any permanent damage."

We bumped into Ivan Ivanovich in the courtyard on our way to dinner. Staying loyal to his boss, the Russian would not disclose who was the surprise guest for the evening. I asked him several times on the way, but he refused to tell and would only say that it was an honor to have this guest dine with us.

The main dining room was decorated for the occasion. Fine white china and crystal wine goblets sat at each place setting. About half of the attendees had already arrived with no sign of Igor Petrovich, Nathan Johnson, or the special guest. I had not spoken with Bob since we came to the compound, so I stood by his chair and asked how things were going. The former oil executive told me that he had spent a lot of time with Nathan, discussing proposed contract terms that Cardinal's CEO wanted to lock in his 'finder's fee'. Bob warned me that I was likely to see similar pressure sometime during the trip and be careful about signing anything. While I was thanking him for the advice, I heard a commotion in the room. I turned to see our host enter accompanied by Nathan and a tall and distinguished-looking man dressed in a light grey suit, his thick white hair expertly coiffed. With looks of deference, the Russians stepped forward to greet the man. Igor Petrovich escorted the man to the head of the table.

"I am honored to welcome our guest this evening," said Igor Petrovich. "I think most of you know our deputy governor, Igor Semyonovich Prekrasov."

The deputy governor I had conversed with about lakes back in Chicago was now standing before us. Used to giving speeches, Igor Semyonovich delivered an eloquent address, translated by Ivan Ivanovich, telling of the new era of cooperation between old foes and the vital role of businessmen, such as ourselves, in fostering closer ties. I thought I detected some hints of emotion in his words, especially when describing the Siberian landscape. He ended by raising a toast 'to success!' to which everyone replied in kind.

The swinging doors in the back flew open as if on cue, and Irina appeared with the first course. Due to the occasion, the blonde woman was dressed more formally, wearing a red velvet waistcoat over her white blouse and matching red skirt. A red and yellow scarf hung loosely around her neck. The meal was presented flawlessly, and I again appreciated the non-fish dishes consisting of cold cuts, roast duck, and soup. The lively conversation was interrupted from time to time by toast requests, mainly from our Russian hosts. Feeling a little tipsy, I welcomed the cup of coffee offered with dessert.

"Alright, everyone. Let's retire to the recreation room," announced Igor Petrovich. He rose and accompanied Igor Semyonovich from the dining area. The rest of the attendees followed suit.

"An evening of pool?" I asked Scott as we strolled down the hallway.

"That would be great," responded Scott with a smirk. "I could hustle up some rubles."

The centerpiece of the recreation area was the pool table supported on finely carved wooden legs, flanked by a rack holding numerous pool cues on the paneled wall. Numerous leather easy chairs stood in various spots around the room, with several concentrated in front of the roaring brick fireplace. Our host and guest of honor flanked the long buffet against the back wall displaying a menage of spirits. The space more closely resembled a traditional British cigar room than a typical American-style recreation area.

"Please," said Igor Petrovich, "make yourselves comfortable. There are billiards, but house rules are no money wagers. We all want to remain friends. The bar is fully stocked, and Irina will be happy to prepare whatever drink you desire."

I had not noticed Irina enter the room. After clearing away the dining table, she must have returned for double duty as the bartender. I watched as Scott and a Russian arranged the billiard balls for play while most of the other guests moved around in search of a cozy place to sit. Makoto invited me to sit with him by the fireplace next to Ivan Ivanovich and several others. I soon, however, rose to get a drink. I passed close by the deputy governor near the buffet, chatting with Igor Petrovich. I intentionally glanced in their direction, hoping to attract our honored guest's attention. I observed a smile come over Igor Semyonovich when he recognized my face.

"Good evening, Ken Lvovich," stated the deputy governor. I was impressed that he had remembered my patronymic. "It is a pleasure to see you again. How are you enjoying Khabarovsk?"

I stopped and replied, "The city is remarkable and the people very welcoming. And, as you described in Chicago, the land is simply stunning. The plains and lakes I have seen while driving and flying have been spectacular."

Igor Petrovich's facial expression was inquisitive, wondering how I was acquainted with the deputy governor. The bright smile on Igor Semyonovich's face was undeniable. He enjoyed talking about his homeland. We shook hands heartily.

"It's wonderful that you are getting a chance to experience my Siberia. Its winter splendor is only superseded by its summertime beauty."

"Well, I hope I will have an opportunity to return and see it for myself," I said, gazing briefly at Igor Petrovich.

"Da, da," said our host. "The trip is going very well, and I anticipate seeing you and your countrymen back here soon."

I took my leave and walked over to the buffet, where Irina was busy pouring a drink for Jimmy. The contractor had asked for a double whiskey and left content with his tall glass of brown liquor.

"Dobry vyechor, Irina," I said. "I'll have a cognac, please."

A long queue had quickly formed behind me, barring me from a more extended conversation. I received my drink, said thank you, and made my way back to the fireplace. When I sat down on the soft leather, I could feel the heat of the flames stroking my cheeks. Ivan Ivanovich was telling Makoto about Japanese soldiers captured in the region during World War II. The interpreter explained how many locals treated the Japanese prisoners kindly in a camp outside the city.

"Even though they were technically our enemy," explained Ivan Ivanovich, "the prisoners behaved well. The city residents at the time felt little animosity towards the Japanese since there were no actual major conflicts during the war. After Germany's defeat, Stalin, at the US request, had prepared an invasion plan for Japan, but the Americans (he looked at me) used the atomic bomb before Russian troops could attack."

"We have still not officially ended the war between the USSR and Japan," stated Makoto. "Your government still lays claim to the Northern Territories."

Alcohol was loosening inhibitions, and the talk of politics began to flow more freely. I remained silent and enjoyed the warming sensation of the cognac and the fire.

"Da. The Kuril Islands have multiple claimants, but I hope that, in time, a peaceful solution will be found," added Ivan Ivanovich.

Makoto nodded in agreement, and the two men clinked glasses. Wanting to steer the discussion onto something less sensitive, I asked about the lack of refrigerators in stores and private residences. I expressed my curiosity about how the inhabitants kept food cold.

"Refrigerators are rarely needed," went on Ivan Ivanovich, "because of the permafrost. Since the ground is frozen for most of the year, most people dig a basement area under their dwelling and store food there, where it stays preserved."

The overall level of intoxication in the room rose steadily during the evening. As the night wore on, the pool table fell silent due to a lack of interest or capability. Eventually, everyone gathered around the fireplace, and the volume became increasingly loud. Around midnight, I sat facing Igor Petrovich and Igor Semyonovich. The discussion now focused on the cultural experiences of Russia and America.

"In the sixties, both of our countries shared some similar interests," said Ivan Ivanovich. "There was a desire to see real change in society, to become more open and free. In America, the 'hippy' movement pushed more free expression in music and culture. There was also such a movement in the Soviet Union. In the mid-1960s, a feeling of less restrictive times seemed possible. Songs and books were written that reflected this feeling. Unfortunately, the invasion of Czechoslavakia in 1968 crushed those hopes."

"Da, I remember those times well," said Igor Petrovich. "I was in my early twenties, and my friends and I would sit around campfires singing songs forbidden years earlier."

"Yes, Igor Petrovich was a Russian 'hippy'," exclaimed Ivan Ivanovich. This comment brought a large grin to our host's face.

"The events in August 1968 changed many of our perceptions," added Igor Petrovich, his face growing darker. "A sense of pessimism and fatefulness replaced the feeling of optimism and hope." An awkward silence descended on the room for a few moments. It seemed everyone had fallen into a certain state of reverie.

Suddenly, the deputy governor, his silk tie slightly loosened, rose and began to bellow a song in a deep baritone voice. It was difficult for me to understand the phrases, but every Russian, in unison, stood and joined in the singing. The melody lasted for several minutes. My compatriots and I remained fixed in amazement at the touching display of camaraderie. When Igor Semyonovich finished, he remained standing, smiling from ear to ear. He appeared winded from the exertion, his chest extending out and in.

"That was a traditional Russian folk song from Siberia," the distinguished man said after catching his breath. "I am proud to see that all my comrades (he scanned the room) still remember it."

"We learned this song from childhood," interjected Ivan Ivanovich.

"Well, that was impressive," I said. "It was quite moving."

"OK, let's hear an American folk song!" demanded Igor Semyonovich.

The request came as a total shock. I looked around and saw nothing but blank stares from my fellow Americans. Feeling a sense of embarrassment, we huddled together, trying to decide on a song. Meanwhile, perplexed by the concern caused by this simple request, the Russians waited patiently. I explained that singing folk songs was not as common in American culture due to America's diversity. We finally agreed that each of us was familiar with the folk song 'Camptown Races'. Like a football team headed to the line of scrimmage, we broke the huddle and, standing side by side, slowly at first, began to enunciate the stanzas of 'Camptown Races'. Our harmonization was poor. I was sure that we all felt a little silly singing, 'Do Dah, Do Dah', but we made it to the end. After a brief hesitation, a slow round of applause followed, led by Igor Semyonovich, who stepped toward me and gave me a heavy slap on the shoulder.

"Bravo," he said. "I have never heard such a tune before. Is it related to your country's war experiences?"

"No," I admitted. "It's more a frivolous tune just for fun, written in the mid-19th century. I guess it concerns horse betting, which was considered immoral at the time."

"Ah, ponyatno (understood)," responded the deputy governor. "Well, anyway, thank you for sharing it with us."

"Irina, another round of drinks!" shouted Igor Petrovich. I watched as the young woman came around and refilled everyone's glasses with vodka. "To further cooperation!" exclaimed our host with his arm extended.

There was a loud touching of glasses, and then everyone downed the drink. The glasses were topped off a few more times, and we were all feeling good. More songs were sung, mainly by the Russians, as the early morning hours approached. While thundering out another folk song, the deputy governor went over and lifted Makoto from his seat and danced around the room, cradling the diminutive Japanese in his thick arms. We all stood and clapped, laughing uncontrollably at the comic scene. The song finished, and Igor Semyonovich placed Makoto back onto his feet and tightly hugged him. My Japanese companion regained his balance, bowed slightly, and sank back down into his easy chair. The frivolity ended with rounds of hearty hugs and a few cheek kisses. Dawn's first rays splashed on the buildings when Scott and I walked across the courtyard. Reeking of smoke and drink, neither bothering to undress, we collapsed onto our beds.

The stale stench of dried sweat and bad breath filled the room. Opening my eyes, I grimaced, conscious of the pungent air. My wristwatch displayed ten o'clock, usually a very late start, but today indicated a short slumber of fewer than five hours. I shuffled, muscles aching, into the bathroom, where I undressed and stood beneath the showerhead, forgetful of the previous day's experience. When I turned the dial, I inhaled deeply and cringed, expecting an onslaught of arctic water. However, fate took pity on me, and a steady stream of lukewarm water struck my head and shoulders. I exhaled and cautiously returned to my full height and washed quickly, unsure how long the non-freezy mercy would last. When I returned to the bedroom, Scott was still sleeping, his snoring audible from across the hall. My roommate didn't respond to my short shove, signaling my departure for the main building and breakfast. The cold morning air filled my lungs with a freshness that energized me. More fully awake, I became aware of the intense hunger pangs in my stomach and looked forward to a hearty meal.

I sat down in a chair close to the center of the table. There was a strong smell of fried eggs and syrniki (cheese dumplings) in the dining room. Most Americans and Russians were already eating, except Igor Petrovich and the deputy governor, likely recovering from the previous night's activities. I grabbed a piece of rye bread from a tray to my right and began to nibble. The dry coarseness of the bread stuck in my mouth, prompting me to gulp my water glass. I returned the glass to the table and felt someone's presence standing over me. Turning my head, I saw strands of blonde hair dangling in the air, whose owner was looking at me with bright blue eyes.

"Dobroe yutro (good morning)," said Irina. She was back in her daytime uniform with its white blouse and black skirt. "May I get you something to eat?"

I didn't want to insult my hosts by bringing out my usual breakfast meal of two nutrition bars or a bowl of cereal. "I'll have some bliny (pancakes) if you have it; otherwise, syrniki is good."

"Of course. Would you like them with cheese?"

"Yes," I replied. "Cheese will be fine."

"Khorosho. We also have some delicious strawberry jam."

"Excellent," I said. "Please bring some."

"Would you like chai (tea) or coffee?"

I typically did not drink tea or coffee, but I had consumed a lot of both during the visit since I had not been comfortable drinking the local tap water. This morning, however, I felt like treating myself.

"I would like a glass of milk, please," I requested.

"Moloko?" asked Irina.

"Da," I replied. "I prefer to drink milk at breakfast."

"So, no tea or coffee with milk, you want only milk?" Irina looked puzzled by my request.

"Just the milk," I repeated. "Is that a problem?"

"Nyet. There is no problem. I will return soon with the milk." The young woman turned and walked off.

"What was that all about," inquired Bob, sitting across from me and finishing his helping of syrniki.

"I don't know," I answered. "I just asked for some milk. Maybe they don't have much of it."

Almost everyone was eating or drinking in silence, their head lowered and focused on the food or cup at hand. "A lot of hangovers this morning," I thought to myself. The fogginess had almost entirely lifted from my head, but my mouth was dry, and I felt sore. As the time passed and Irina had not returned, I began to feel uneasy. Perhaps the bliny was the cause of the delay, or maybe someone had to drive to a store to buy milk (but we were in the middle of a forest). "I should have simply drank the tea," I said to myself. The woman has to serve everyone, and I made her duties more complicated. Finally, after nearly twenty minutes, I heard the wooden doors swing open, and Irina reappeared, carrying a large plate and holding a glass of white liquid. She laid down a blue plate covered in several layers of bliny in front of me. I could smell the strawberry jam lying on top.

"Here is your bliny," Irina announced. "I hope you enjoy them."

"Yes, thank you," I responded. "I hope that I did not put you to any trouble."

"It's nothing," said the young woman. "And, here is your glass of milk."

I held the glass and was surprised that the outer surface felt warm. Lowering the glass below my chin level, I noticed that the liquid was off-white, and the texture was not smooth. The milk appeared 'chunky'; small pieces were floating around the top of the surface. My first thought was that perhaps Irina had put in ice cubes to make the milk taste colder. I decided to inspect more closely objects bobbing in the glass. Raising the glass nearer to my eye, I could see that the 'chunks' were not ice cubes but rather congealed pieces of milk. Squinting harder, I noticed that thin grey and black lines were swimming in the liquid, like hair follicles. Sitting in the dining room looking at the chunky white substance, I was reminded of a grammar school field trip to a local farm to experience rural life. The experience included the milking of a cow for which I had won a prize, having filled my pail the highest. I regretted now my decision to ask for milk.

"Where did you get the milk?" I asked Irina, anxious to hear the response.

"There is a barn near the edge of the compound that houses some cows. I went there and got the milk." As she spoke, the image rushed into my head of this lovely young woman, in her tight-fitted blouse and skirt, squatting over a stool with a metal pail feverishly yanking on a pair of utters.

"Well, at least I know that it is fresh," I said, making light of the situation. The young woman smiled and stared, I assumed, waiting for me to taste the milk.

The thought of drinking this milk churned my stomach and made me lose my appetite, but I couldn't insult Irina by not touching the liquid. I slowly lifted the glass to my lips. An earthy scent was noticeable. The milk texture that flowed across my tongue reminded me of creamy soup, like clam chowder. Trying not to look at the strands of cow hair, I hurridly chewed the chunks. I placed the glass on the table and put a fake smile on my face.

"That was good, thank you," I stated. "I think that I would also like a cup of chai."

"Khorosho," said Irina, laughing slightly. She knew I had lied about the milk.

A few minutes later, Irina served me a hot cup of tea with several sugar cubes. The smell of the tea helped calm my stomach, and I regained my appetite. I ate the bliny and drank the tea while ignoring the rest of the milk. When I had finished, the young blonde returned and started to clear my place setting.

"So, do you work here all week long?" I asked.

"Nyet. I am an accountant in the city. I work here only on certain weekends to help support my daughter." She seemed more willing to talk without the watchful eye of Igor Petrovich.

"Oh, how old is your daughter?"

"She is seven. We live now with my mother after I divorce my husband."

"I am sorry to hear about your divorce."

"It is OK. It is very common now after the end of the Soviet Union."

"Well, I am glad you have found a way to make more money."

She finished collecting the plates and utensils, wiped down the table cloth, and walked back through the swinging doors. Back at the grey building, I found Scott sitting on his bed, his head in his hands. He was still suffering from last night. He told me that Ivan Ivanovich had come by and said that Igor Petrovich arranged individual meetings for the afternoon to discuss contracts and that my time was scheduled for 3:00 pm.

"Hello Ken, come in," I heard Igor Petrovich say in English. I had been standing just outside the doorway to one of the meeting rooms. Bob had just exited the room and gave me a brief smile, saying, 'be careful'. After he walked past, I poked my head through the doorway and saw our host seated at a square table covered in green felt with many file folders neatly stacked to his left. Ivan Ivanovich and Nathan Johnson flanked the Russian businessman. I entered and sat down in the empty chair directly across from Igor Petrovich. The green wallpaper and dark hardwood floor poorly reflected the single floor lamp giving the area a dim hue. Our host waited until I was seated and then took the top folder from his pile, placed it before him, and flipped open the file. He perused the folder's contents for a few moments, then laid the open file on the table and pushed the beige folder toward me.

"This is our standard contract for services," announced Igor Petrovich. "Your firm will be responsible for design work related to a golf course, casino, and other sites to be named later. Of course, you will work under the direction of Cardinal Communications."

I looked down at the documents before me. There were copies in English and in Russian. I had never reviewed a business contract before and felt that the others in the room expected me to read it at that moment or perhaps, feel pressured and sign it right there. I remembered John's direction that I was not to sign anything while in Russia.

"Khorosho, I will need to review it," I said. "I'll want a professional translator to go over the contracts to make sure both copies are identical. As you know, there can be important nuances between languages."

I turned several pages of the English copy while I considered what to do next. I observed the frustration increase on Igor Petrovich's face. Nathan Johnson's behavior also appeared uncomfortable. Perhaps, I was the only American being difficult, or our host had received similar reactions from the others. Either way, I had no intention of succumbing to any pressure and jeopardizing my job prospects.

"Mr. Maher,... Ken," said Igor Petrovich. "You have visited the ship, toured the beautiful land provided for the golf course, and enjoyed our city's welcome. You should agree that these projects represent a great opportunity for your firm. I expect that you are prepared to sign the agreement."

With all eyes upon me, I had to break the bad news. "Igor Petrovich, these are indeed interesting projects. However, The Pyramid Group has not authorized me to sign any contracts. I can take the contracts back to Chicago for review by my firm's leadership."

The broad-shouldered Russian's facial expression was one of resignation. He nodded his head in capitulation. "OK, Ken," he said. "Take the contracts to Chicago, and we will await your favorable response. I must say, however, that I don't understand why your firm would send you here if you could not approve the contract."

Thanking everyone for the time, I closed the folder and placed it under my arm. I stood up and proceeded from the room, where I passed by Makoto, who was awaiting his turn in the corridor. He looked at me, trying to detect any hints of what to expect. I rolled my eyes before heading down the hallway and into the courtyard. I did not immediately return to the gray building. Instead, I strolled around the compound's grounds, looking at the bare white birch trees and listening to my footsteps interrupt the winter silence. The cool winter air invigorated me. I felt a mixture of relief and disappointment. I had survived my first high-pressure business situation but may have ruined any future chance to return to Russia since I knew my firm would not agree to the proposed contract terms.

# A Costly Departure

WE ARRIVED AT THE TERMINAL early in the morning. The airport was practically empty. Bob, Scott, Makoto, and I huddled around the security check area while Igor Petrovich and Nathan Johnson were engaged in a lively conversation with the head security guard. I could not hear what was said, but Nathan continually shook his head.

"What do you think the problem is?" asked Scott.

"I don't know," I said, "but it doesn't look promising."

"I hope it is not a passport issue," added Bob. "I got stuck once in a Chinese airport for two days because passport control had trouble reading my visa stamp."

"Well, we could always go back to the compound," I said.

"I need to get back to Chicago," added Makoto. "I have meetings tomorrow afternoon."

"This day is just going from bad to worse," said Scott, giving me a sharp look.

The return trip home had not started well. The loud buzzing of my wristwatch alarm shook me from sleep at 4:00 am that morning. Groggy and bleary-eyed, I fumbled into the bathroom to shower, where the spray of frigid water snapped me to my senses. Having washed and shaved, I returned to find Scott shuffling his way across the narrow hallway. Still not awake, I neglected to warn my roommate about the shower water. A few moments later, I was reminded of my error by a loud cry from the bathroom. I offered my belated apologies to Scott when he entered the bedroom and finished packing my bags. We left the luggage in the room and walked back to the main building for a light breakfast consisting of bread, cold cuts, and kasha that had already been laid out for each guest. I wanted a bit more sustenance for the long ride to the airport, so I decided to head back to the guest house to grab some nutrition bars.

I was startled upon entering the grey building by a noise coming from the bedroom. I slowly walked down the hallway and cautiously peeked into the sleeping area. Irina was standing over Scott's bed and folding his comforter. The young woman rose in a start upon hearing me step into the room.

"Be calm," I said. "It's just me. I didn't mean to frighten you."

Her hand on her chest, she let out a deep sigh of relief. "dobroe yutro, Ken. I didn't hear you come in."

"What are you doing here? I thought you would be serving breakfast."

"I set up breakfast already so everyone can eat without me. I wanted to get started cleaning the rooms to leave early today. I want to get home and see my daughter."

"Ah, of course. I just came back to get some food bars."

I went over to my backpack, which was sitting on the nightstand. As I rummaged through tightly packed items, I noticed two large stacks of rubles wedged into the bottom of the bag. Upon arrival in Khabarovsk, I followed Nathan's guidance to exchange two hundred dollars for rubles. Due to the high inflation in Russia at the time, this translated into a large amount of thousand rule notes, oddly enough bearing Lenin's portrait. I had not spent any of the rubles during the trip and planned on turning back them in at the airport for dollars. However, as I observed this hard-working young woman missing a weekend with her daughter to make my bed, I removed one of the stacks of rubles and stood facing her. I had not counted the bills but assumed they were the equivalent of $100, which meant about 10,000 rubles.

"Irina," I started. She stopped her work and turned toward me. "Scott and I discussed the situation with your daughter, and we would like to help you." I extended my hand with the ruble notes.

Expecting to see a smile, I was taken aback when the woman became angry. She motioned at me with her right index finger, waving it back and forth.

"What is this?" Irina said in a loud voice. "Do you think I am some kind of whore? What do you expect from me for this? I work honestly for my money and can take care of my little one just fine! I do not need your handout."

I was silent for a moment, lowering my arm to my side, not knowing how to respond. My youthful rashness had betrayed me again. I tried to apologize to Irina, explaining that I did not aim to slight her. I had not considered how an offer of several months' salary might insinuate certain things. She abruptly walked out of the room. Placing the money back into my pack, I jumped when the front door slammed, indicating that Irina had parted. I considered myself an educated person, but at that moment, I understood that I still had much to learn about the world.

The incident completely distracted me, and I forgot about going back for breakfast. Scott found me sitting on the bed, deep in thought.

"What's up with you?" Scott asked upon entering the room. "You have any idea why the server woman gave me a dirty look when I saw her in the courtyard?"

His questions shook me out of my stupor. "Yeah, that's my fault." I related to my roommate what happened.

"Why did you involve me in this? Now, she is mad at me, and I had nothing to do with it."

"I am sorry," I said. "I wasn't thinking and got caught up in the moment. I just wanted to help and thought she would find it more acceptable if both of us wanted to give the money."

That obviously didn't work, so keep me out of it next time."

Nathan and Igor Petrovich left the security guard and approached our group.

"Airport security says we each have to pay an 'exit fee' to board the plane," Nathan said. "There is some new rule requiring foreigners to pay this fee. I have never heard of it."

"I, too, have never heard of such a fee," said the Russian businessman. "We can try to appeal this, but it could take several days."

I translated Igor Petrovich's explanation while my companions and I looked at each other in amazement.

"How much is this 'fee'?" I asked.

"$100," said Nathan.

"A hundred dollars!" Scott exclaimed. "That's outrageous."

"What if we refuse to pay?" inquired Bob, his Bears ski hat tilted slightly in his head.

"If you don't pay, you don't leave," plainly stated Igor Petrovich.

"Well, I guess we pay the damn fee," said Makoto. "I am not staying here. Where do I pay it?"

Nathan explained that once we passed through passport control, there was a station near the customs area where foreigners paid the fee. We gathered up our things and proceeded through passport control. The Russian officer gazed at me sternly as he reviewed my photo and credentials. The blonde-haired officer with a heavily pockmarked face stood up in his booth and asked me for my 'other documents'. When I replied in Russian, 'kakie dokymenti? (what documents), he realized that his attempt to intimidate me would not be successful, and he stamped my passport. As I walked past the control booth, I saw another Russian officer ask a Chinese man the same question. The man did not understand Russian and became flustered and started to panic, leading to several other officers assisting him to a 'special' room for additional questioning. In the new Russia, some things had not changed.

I continued along my way until I saw a small wooden booth in front of which was a long queue, including Bob and Scott. Two officers dressed in blue shirts with red piping were seated in the booth. I walked over and joined the line, standing behind a Korean businessman. Although crowded, the line moved quickly, and soon I was facing an officer in his mid-thirties with deep serious grey eyes. His demeanor was not welcoming.

"Passport," he demanded. I complied with his request.

"American," he continued. "Fee is $100."

"Is there a different fee for non-Americans?" I asked in a somewhat flippant tone. I was upset that I had to pay this, in my mind, made-up charge.

"Fee is $100,' repeated the officer, his facial expression unchanged.

I shook my head and removed the amount from my wallet. Holding the bills in my hand, I saw the image of Irina working tirelessly. This fee would have been better served in her hands than giving it to this official, who would likely pocket some of it anyway. I handed the officer the money. He examined my passport one more time and returned the booklet to me. The sheer gall of this extortion riled me up. Instead of walking away, I turned back toward the booth.

"Vy vsyo vory! (You are all thieves)," I said.

I stood for a moment expecting some reaction, but none occurred. I took a deep breath, spun around, and strode off. Bob and Scott were seated in multi-colored hard plastic chairs in the departure area. I must have still looked upset because Bob asked me what had happened. I told him about my outburst, and he stated how lucky I was that I did not get detained. His words struck a chord in me. Yes, I had been fortunate that I was not sitting next to that Chinese man, being ruthlessly interrogated by a pack of Russian officers. I had acted foolishly, and my arrogance could have cost me much more than $100. Scott patted me on the back.

"You need to calm down, young man," he said. "Let me buy you a drink. I wanna make sure you make it back to your girlfriend."

He brought back two glasses of vodka from the airport bar. I quietly sipped my drink, allowing the alcohol to depress my nerves. A short while later, Makoto joined our trio. He described his unpleasant experience at the passport area, where the officer attempted to say that his visa had expired. Luckily, he added, a kind Russian intervened on his behalf, and the officer allowed him to pass. Envious of our beverages, the Japanese-American visited the bar, returning with a can of Sapporo beer. Having finished my drink, I felt more relaxed and decided to take stock of the trip.

"So, guys," I said, "Did anyone sign that agreement that Igor Petrovich put in front of you? I know that my firm will find it difficult to work under the proposed conditions."

"I told Igor and Nathan that this was more of a fact-finding visit for me," said Bob. "I would need a lot more trips before I'd be ready to commit to anything."

"Yeah," added Scott, "the subcontractor clause was a bit much for me. I have run a successful business for twenty years, and, as much as I like Nathan, he knows nothing about my business."

"What about the prospects for the restaurant?" I asked.

"I would easily be the best place in town," continued Scott. "As you saw, there really is no competition. Competition, however, is not the main issue. I spoke with my national headquarters, and I cannot use any food ingredients that do not meet company standards. There is no reliable local supplier, so I would have to import the ingredients from abroad, most likely from South Korea, making the business unprofitable."

"You could build your supply locally," added Makoto.

"True. But, I do not have the time or capital to invest in such an undertaking," said Scott. "I was thinking of simply opening a restaurant, but this is getting too complicated and costly."

"What is your opinion on the golf course," I asked, looking at Makoto.

"Without the ability to own the land, Japanese investors will not put up the money for the construction. Also, the lack of infrastructure to support the site will be a big hurdle to overcome."

"Did you tell that to Nathan and Igor Petrovich?" I followed up.

"Of course. Igor mentioned that maybe the government could offer better tax breaks, etc., but there seemed to be no way to acquire the property. I also told Nathan that Japanese businesses would not agree to use Jimmy as the contractor, preferring to use Japanese companies."

"Yeah, it seems that Nathan wants to make his money off these 'finder's fees' rather than doing any work," I responded.

"Sure," said Bob. "It's easy money for him, and he gets to control the business flow. I think he'll find it hard to convince many businesses to work with him this way."

The first leg of the journey home took us to Seoul, South Korea, where we would connect to San Francisco and then Chicago. The trip to Seoul required travel via Aeroflot. This flight would be my first experience flying on the Russian state airline. While we chatted, the boarding call for our flight commenced. A smiling young woman dressed in a blue uniform, the lapel of which bore the golden hammer and sickle emblem flanked by wings, greeted me. The rickety set of stairs leading to the tarmac groaned under the weight of boots and bags, where a bus waited to take us to the plane. I found my seat near the back of the aircraft and placed my backpack in the overhead compartment. Quite a few empty spots remained when the sound of the main door being shut echoed throughout the cabin. Having an entire row to myself, I spread out my book and drink bottle on the adjacent seat. I thought it strange when the aircraft began to move. There had been no safety announcement or seat belt check by the sole flight attendant on board. The pilot maneuvered the large craft quickly, soon accelerating down the runway. Take-off was abrupt, and as we ascended, the forward cabin assumed an almost vertical position.

The plane leveled off twenty minutes later, and I looked up from my book to see the flight attendant moving about the cabin. Her blonde hair pushed up under her blue pilot's hat, she carefully strolled up the aisle, checking on each passenger. I had left the aisle seat open and was sitting in the middle. As the flight attendant moved closer to my row, I could read 'Maria' on her nameplate, bordered by tiny Japanese and Korean flag pins, indicating which languages she could converse besides Russian.

"Excuse me," I said in Russian. "Is there a meal served on the flight?"

I stared at the woman awaiting her response when suddenly she sat down next to me.

"You are American, no?" she asked. The aroma of her perfume hit me like a wave, and her makeup was exquisitely done. "You speak Russian so well."

"Spasibo," I replied. "I studied it at university."

"Molodets (excellent). I have met only a few Americans. They all were rude, and none spoke Russian. What were you doing in Russia?"

I was amazed at the casual behavior of this young woman. I had never experienced a flight attendant willing to sit and chat with a passenger. I wondered if there were regulations against such actions, but I decided to play along. I did not, however, want to divulge too much information. The faint thought passed into my head that maybe she was gathering information to report later. My Cold War conditioning had not completed thawed yet.

"I was there on business," I replied. "It is a lovely area."

"Da. I grew up in Khabarovsk. I love it there, but I want to see so many other places. That's why I became a flight attendant."

"I see you speak Japanese and Korean. That is impressive."

"Spasibo bolshoe. I studied at the pedagogical institute. I plan on learning English next so I can visit America."

"Well, there should be more opportunities for that," I said.

"Are you staying in Seoul? I know many good places to eat."

"Nyet. I am going back to America today."

"Are you returning to Khabarovsk?"

"I hope so. It all depends on how business goes. Do you know why the takeoff was so steep?"

She chuckled. "Well, Andrei, like many of our pilots, still thinks he is flying Migs."

"Ah, I hope the landing goes better."

"May I see your book?" she asked.

Perplexed, I handed it to her. I figured that maybe she was curious about what Americans read. Placing the novel in her lap, she extracted a pen from her blouse pocket and began writing on the back page of the book.

"When you come back to Khabarovsk, I can take you to a nice restaurant that my uncle owns," the flight attendant said, handing me back the novel.

I did not dare to look at what she wrote. "Thank you. That is very kind of you."

She got up. "There is a small meal that I will serve in half an hour." She turned and continued several rows behind me into the crew area.

When she had disappeared from view, I picked up the book from my lap and quickly flipped to the final page. Written in wonderfully legible letters was: Fedorova, Maria Borisovna, followed by what I assumed was her phone number. Maria reappeared thirty minutes later to serve a light meal, which consisted of several slices of sausage and cheese, a hard roll with even harder butter accompanied by a small bottle of soda water. I was glad that I had my nutrition bars. As I contemplated unwrapping the meal, I heard commotion between the passenger in the next row and Maria. A dark-skinned man with jet black hair and a mustache was vehemently rejecting the plastic tray that the flight attendant handed him. I could not understand the man's language, and neither apparently did Maria, who was refusing to take back the meal tray.

"You have to take the meal," she said, "I do not have any others."

The man continued to shake his head. His eyes were aflame with something akin to fear. I thought that perhaps he was allergic to something in the meal.

"If I do not provide the meal, they will think I didn't do my job," stated Maria, almost pleading.

I unbuckled my seatbelt and stood up beside Maria. The man looked at me for help, so I asked why he did not want the food in English. I also added some hand gestures to communicate eating and taking away. He seemed to understand some combination of my English and hand movements. He reached into his trouser pocket and pulled out a small white card. Depicted on the card was a drawing of a pig's face enclosed in a circle with a diagonal line. I nodded my head and turned to Maria.

"He is likely Muslim or Hindu and can't eat pig meat," I explained. I was not sure why the man had not displayed the card earlier.

"OK. But I need to give him the tray," said the young woman.

The man continued to watch us as we talked.

"Perhaps you can remove the meat and just leave him the cheese and bread?" I suggested.

"Good idea!" exclaimed Maria.

She took back the tray, to the relief of the man, and went back into the crew area. She returned a few moments later with the tray devoid of meat. She tried once again to hand the man the meal. Hesitant at first, the man looked at the meal, smiled, and accepted the food, seeing no cold cuts. An international incident averted, I sat back in my seat.

"Thank you so much," said Maria. She leaned toward me and murmured, "These people are such pigs, yet they won't eat them."

She went back to the crew area. Her final words tarnished the otherwise friendly image she had presented. I did not see her again until preparation for landing. As we descended, I peered out of my window to view the manned guard towers surrounding the Seoul airport. The closer we got to touching down, the more I could recognize the mounted machine gun nests on the towers. The pilot executed a smoother landing than his takeoff, and we soon arrived at the gate. I gathered my belongings and headed for the exit, where Maria, standing at the door, wished me a pleasant journey home and a quick return.

The connecting flights to San Francisco and Chicago experienced no problems. I arrived back at my apartment in time to find my girlfriend busy preparing cases for her next law class. I spent the next several days recuperating from jet lag and returned to The Pyramid Group later that week. I presented all my video and other documents to Don and John, who reviewed the materials over the following few weeks. Status meetings with Cardinal Communications took place where Nathan Johnson, of course, pushed for rapid approval of the casino and golf course projects. As expected, the firm decided that there were too many risks to commit further resources to the projects. In the end, Nathan Johnson annulled the provisional agreement, informing John and Don that he would find another real estate firm to take on the development. There would be no future trips to Khabarovsk. I wondered whether Maria was waiting for my call.

# Kazan Connections

After returning from Siberia, Deb introduced me to a Russian woman attending the same law school on an exchange program. Aliya Akhmetova was from the Republic of Tatarstan, a region in the central part of Russia. She was a licensed attorney in Russia and had come to Chicago to obtain her graduate law degree. Aliya had dinner at our apartment one evening, and she was delighted to speak Russian with me. Her spoken English was passable, and she appreciated the opportunity to relax in her native tongue. Over the course of the evening, I told her about my time spent in Khabarovsk. She laughed at some of the situations I had experienced, adding that this was typical Russian culture. In talking about her career in Russia, she mentioned that her husband, Adel, was a construction manager but had recently been appointed by the local government to help attract foreign investment to Tatarstan. I explained that I might help her husband find companies interested in the Russian market in the Chicago area. She seemed intrigued by the idea and added that she would discuss the concept with her husband.

A week or so later, Deb told me that Aliya said her husband was excited about working with an American partner. With Aliya again at our apartment for lunch, I spoke with Adel over the phone. He explained that the Tatar government had instituted a program to create joint ventures and other investments with Tatar companies. Interest in working with Americans was very high. On this call and several others, we discussed how a partnership might function. About a month later, Adel suggested that I come to Kazan, the capital of Tatarstan, located about five hundred miles east of Moscow, where I could meet with local officials and businesses to assess the investment potential. I agreed to go, and Adel said he would provide the necessary invitation to obtain a visa. In the meantime, as I was still unemployed, I needed to find funding for the trip. My first call was to Makoto.

My former roommate in Siberia got in touch with me a week later. He apologized for the delay in responding, saying that he had been in Japan on business. I explained the opportunity in Tatarstan, and Makoto told me that he would be willing to finance my travels back to Russia, but on two conditions. First, I was to present a business case to justify his investment. The plan would detail my goals for the visit and include the expected costs. Second, Makoto would receive the first chance to review any potential business opportunities I uncovered during the trip. I agreed to his criteria and set to work on developing the plan. The exercise proved helpful by forcing me to reflect on what I needed to accomplish and how to achieve my objectives; it was my first time creating a strategy. A little over a week later, Makoto and I met for lunch in a café in downtown Chicago, where I talked him through my business case. He carefully reviewed the written documents I gave him and asked pointed questions to justify each expense. I felt nervous, but the Japanese-American businessman commended me on my work and confirmed his commitment to funding my journey at the end of the meal. Having secured financing, I worked with Adel to finalize the details and dates for the trip.

The itinerary for my journey to Kazan was to arrive in Moscow and stay overnight. The following day, I would meet Adel at the Kazanskii Vokzal (train station) and continue to Kazan via train. Despite being my first trip to Moscow, I decided to book a room for the night at a private apartment offered by a Russian woman. In Chicago, I had found the room via an advertisement in a copy of one of the newly independent Russian newspapers, 'Nezavisimaya Gazeta'. The ad offered a service to rent the room, including a car ride from the airport, meals, and transportation to the train station. The cost was very affordable compared to the price of a hotel stay.

When I arrived at Sheremetyevo airport, a tall man wearing a leather jacket and jeans held a card with my name. The man introduced himself as Sergei and explained that he was from 'the service' and had a car waiting for me outside. Everything seemed to be going smoothly. After loading my luggage in the car, we headed out of the airport. In the car, Sergei informed me that 'my contact' had called the service earlier in the day, telling them that I would be going directly to the other Moscow airport, Domodedovo, to board a direct flight to Kazan that afternoon. This unexpected change in plans made me feel uneasy. I had not heard from 'my contact', who I assumed was Adel. This was the first time using this service, and I was aware of foreigners being victimized by unscrupulous companies. Therefore, I informed Sergei that I wanted to go to the woman's apartment. Sergei seemed perturbed by the idea, and we argued back and forth for a bit, but, in the end, he agreed to take me to the apartment. When we arrived at the dwelling, Sergei handed me his phone number to set up a time to drive to the train station. He accompanied me up to the apartment door on the third floor, which didn't have an elevator. The apartment owner was a lovely older woman called Yelena, who warmly welcomed me. She let me know that I was the first American to stay in her apartment, and she was delighted to see such a nice young man who also spoke Russian. Sergei talked briefly with Yelena about my situation and took down her phone number.

Yelena showed me to my room. It was a small space cozily furnished with a single bed, a night table, and several small scatter rugs in traditional designs. I put down my luggage and followed Yelena into the living room adjacent to the tiled kitchen area. In Soviet times, I was sure that more than one family had occupied this apartment, but it was evident that the owner had refurbished it. Now it resembled an apartment one might find in any metropolitan city. Yelena invited me into the kitchen, where she had prepared a small meal of bliny, bread, and tea. I was rather hungry after the long flight. It was difficult to relax, feeling troubled about the proposed change to my itinerary.

I heard the phone ring. I listened to Yelena speaking in an agitated voice with whoever had called. After a few moments, Yelena returned to the kitchen and said that Sergei was on the line and that he urgently needed to speak with me. Sergei informed me that 'my contact' (Sergei had still not said the name, Adel) was calling him again, asking why I was not at Domodedovo. I asked him to let me speak with this 'contact'. Sergei held his receiver to the other receiver on which the 'contact' was talking. In this roundabout way, I heard Adel's frantic voice asking where I was and when I would be arriving at the airport. Unbeknownst to me, Adel, trying to impress his American colleague, had convinced the owner of a small, private aircraft in Moscow to reserve his plane for a flight to Kazan, thereby skipping the originally planned overnight train journey. I let Adel know that I was at the apartment in Moscow as initially planned. I did not go to the airport because I was unaware of the change of plans, and Sergei had only referred to Adel as 'your contact', which made me unsure that I could trust him.

With desperation in his voice, Adel explained that I needed to go to the airport immediately. The aircraft owner had canceled another flight that day to accommodate us, and Adel did not have the money to reimburse the owner if we failed to show up. Upon hearing this, I told Adel that I would work on getting to the airport. With Adel on one receiver, I spoke again to Sergei, who had heard much of my conversation with Adel. I informed Sergei that I needed a car to come to the apartment immediately and take me to Domodedovo to make the flight to Kazan.

"So, you need a car?" responded Sergei. I could hear the annoyance in his reply. "Well," he continued, "all of our cars are in the garage for the night, and the driver has gone home."

Confused, as it was early evening by this time, I inquired, "You must have someone who can pick me up. Didn't you hear that this is an emergency?"

Sergei stuck to his stance that there were no cars available. I guess Yelena must have heard the nervous tone of my voice. She approached me and asked me what the problem was. I informed her of my colleague's predicament at the airport and my need to get there. She took hold of the receiver from my hand and forcefully explained to Sergei that he needed to come to take me to the airport, that he was offering a service and could not leave his customer like this, that this was not the USSR anymore. I believe she used some curses that I was unfamiliar with, but to no effect; Sergei refused to provide transportation.

So, here we were: three Russians and one American speaking on two receivers trying to determine how I would get to the airport. I angrily told Sergei that if he didn't come to get me, I would never use his service again and let other Americans know not to use his service. My threat also had no effect. Yelena threw up her hands and uttered a few more obscenities to Sergei. Adel said that the aircraft owner was furious and threatened him if he did not use the flight or compensate him for the lost revenue. I told Adel that I was not sure I could make it to the airport anytime soon. Seemingly consigned to his fate, Adel said that he would try to negotiate with the owner and that he had to hang up. I told him to call me at the apartment if he succeeded in making a deal with the owner. He hung up. I said a terse goodbye to Sergei and ended our conversation.

Still unsure about my plans for the evening, I returned to the kitchen to finish the now cold bliny and bread. Yelena and I discussed the changes in business happening in Russia, and she apologized for the poor impression Sergei had made. The fact was that many Russians still did business with the Soviet mindset. It was evident that Yelena was part of the new breed in Russia. She told me that she now owned several apartments in Moscow, which she had renovated to western standards and expected to earn a lot of money. Still, she was a bit embarrassed as the host of an American who was having a difficult time.

About an hour had passed when the phone again rang. It was Adel. He let me know that he had tried to calm the aircraft owner and reach some accommodation. Unfortunately, the owner insisted that we make the flight within the next hour or he would have to cancel it; Adel would have to pay him for the cost of the flight. Given the problems of securing transportation, it seemed impossible that I would make it to the airport within an hour. I had one final discussion with Yelena on the possibility of taking a taxi or a friend's car. She convinced me that, even so, I would unlikely arrive in time. Therefore, I told Adel that I could not get there in an hour and that I planned to stay at Yelena's overnight and we would catch the train as initially planned the following morning. I could tell that Adel was not happy with the decision, but there seemed to be no alternative. He said he would explain the situation to the owner. I settled in for the night at Yelena's, unsure how tomorrow would go.

I slept, however, wonderfully. I was exhausted by the day's events, and the minute my head sank into the plush pillow and the soft comforter warmed me up, I fell into a deep sleep. When I exited my room the next morning, Yelena had laid out a European-style breakfast of toast, marmalade, fruit, and tea. I am generally not a tea-drinker, but it tasted delightful with several spoonfuls of sugar. Over breakfast, Yelena explained that it would be easier to get a taxi in the morning or, if I was adventurous, I could take a bus to the Kazanskii Vokzal.

While pondering my options, the telephone rang. Yelena answered and informed me that it was Adel. I assumed he called to tell me where to meet him at the train station. Instead, my Tatar contact was calling me from a police station.

"Why are you at the police station?" I asked.

Adel explained that he had tried to make a deal with the aircraft owner regarding his lost flight payment. The owner was incensed for canceling another flight and wanted his payment immediately. Adel told him that he didn't have the money, but his American colleague would pay him the next day. Unsatisfied, the owner contacted the police and complained that Adel had 'stolen' money from him by not paying him for the canceled flight. The police seized Adel's identity information and passport. They brought him to the police station and questioned him. He informed the police that he had reserved the flight because his American colleague was supposed to arrive and pay for the flight cost. The police allowed Adel to call Yelena's apartment, requesting that I come to the police station to pay for the flight, and then he would be released. Confusion and frustration were commonplace as the country transitioned from its Soviet experience. The old rules no longer applied but new ones were not yet clearly defined, leaving those with authority or power to determine what was acceptable. The Russian police, historically playing the role of protector of the state from the people, were not inclined to side with citizens in disputes with businesses or the government. Stunned, I told Adel that I would leave immediately.

"The police are holding Adel at the station," I said to Yelena, "they think he stole money from the airplane owner because we didn't take the flight. What is the quickest way to get there?"

"A taxi is more direct, but bus number eight might be faster," responded Yelena. She had a concerned expression on her face, making me feel even more uneasy.

"Do you think that I am in trouble?" I asked her.

"Your friend has more to worry about," she replied, "They (the police) are less likely to treat a foreigner poorly".

I decided to test my luck with the bus. Yelena accompanied me to the bus stop and told me where to get off. The ride would be my first experience with public transportation in Moscow. Being rush hour, a large crowd was waiting at the bus stop. I had to shelter my eyes in the rising morning sunlight to make out the 'Number 8' on the approaching bus. It was awkward to navigate the queue to get on the bus while pulling my rolling bag. I could see the passengers inside pressed against the bus windows as the door opened. I had grown up in a large US city, but my experience jostling for a spot on the bus or a train in America had not adequately prepared me for the struggle I now endured.

The men and women standing peacefully at the bus stop transformed, once the bus doors opened, into a group of experienced fighters, battling to the death for a place on the bus. There were no rules of etiquette. It was everyone for themselves. I found myself elbowed and shoved away by kindly-looking babushkas. Smartly dressed women showed cat-like agility in moving between and through crevices in the queue; the men gave no quarter to the older women. I, it seemed, was the only one to show some semblance of self-restraint, letting women and kids pass me onto the bus. I wasn't sure I would make it on the bus, but I squeezed myself and my bulky bag into the last space available on the top step. I received a couple of nasty looks on account of my bag, but, in the end, the bus doors closed, and we were off.

There were several stops before reaching the police station. Standing on the top stair, I had to step off the bus at each stop to let people off the bus. I had to drag my bag with me off the bus each time and then quickly scramble back on the bus ahead of the rush of new combatants entering the breach.

Each time I endured nasty looks from fellow passengers who I inevitably brushed with my bag. Finally, it came time for my stop. Uttering a few 'prosti-ties' (excuse me), I managed to shimmy my way through the crowd and get off. I let out a sigh of relief upon touching the ground, wondering how average Russians dealt with that every day.

Across the street from the bus stop, the blue-colored building with 'Politsia' written in bright yellow letters was visible. I carefully made my way on foot to the entrance of the police station, explaining to the officer at the recep-tion area that I was here to meet a Russian colleague in custody. I gave Adel's name and waited while the officer telephoned to confirm my story. I waited for some time, receiving inquisitive glances from passing police officers, won-dering why this obvious foreigner was loitering in the station reception area.

About thirty minutes later, another officer approached me and asked me to follow him. I was a bit nervous. I was brought into a small wood-paneled conference room and asked to sit down. I had expected to see Adel, but it was just the officer and me. He sat with a notepad and a pencil and asked me to explain what happened to Adel and the aircraft owner. He wanted to know whether I had reserved the plane and had made arrangements to pay for the flight and why I had not taken the flight. I went through in detail what had happened from my point of view. I stated that Adel made the reservation to save us time in getting to Kazan but that, due to some miscommunication, I was unable to make the flight in time. The officer lifted his head from his notepad and explained that they were holding my friend and, equally impor-tant, his identification documents until the aircraft owner was reimbursed. I responded that I was willing to pay for the cost of the missed flight, depend-ing on how much it was. To my relief, the amount was reasonable and payable in US dollars. The officer then spoke about an additional payment to return Adel's identification documents; the police had exerted time and resources on processing and holding my friend. I understood that this was not standard procedure, but, under the circumstances, I really didn't have much choice. To whom would I appeal? Adel was my friend, and he was my guide and sponsor in getting to Kazan. The officer and I agreed upon a fee, which I again paid in dollars. Having settled the 'administrative matters', I asked if they would release Adel with his identity papers. The officer got up and left the room, taking his notepad and the dollar notes.

I was growing more nervous as time passed. I was at the mercy of the officers. Finally, after what seemed like hours, the door handle rattled, and Adel's relieved face entered the room, followed by the officer. I asked Adel if he had everything, including his identity papers. He replied in the affirmative. Now, we just needed to make it out of the station. I tried to be as polite as possible and thanked the officer for his time and assistance. The officer escorted us out of the station, and once we made it past the station courtyard, we finally felt secure.

"That was fun," I exclaimed as we stood near the bus stop. I inquired about the plan, given that we had missed our morning train to Kazan.

"There is another train that leaves in the evening," answered Adel. "We can go to the vokzal and buy tickets for that train. It is an overnight train, so we'll have to go in a sleeping car."

We wedged onto another bus filled with mainly pensioners and men sleeping off the night's drinking and headed to Kazanskii Vokzal. At the station, Adel asked me for ticket money while I went to find a place to sit until departure. The waiting area at the station was a microcosm of Russian life. Sitting on worn, hard oak benches were a myriad of characters from students to older couples, young families, soldiers, businessmen, and foreigner visitors (mostly Asian looking), all heading east to Kazan and perhaps destinations beyond. Rolling my luggage and carrying Adel's handbag, I moved between rows of people sitting, squatting on the ground, sleeping under benches, etc. Finally, I located a space large enough for Adel and me. I relaxed for a moment to gaze at my surroundings. The high arch ceilings in the waiting area were painted in multi-shades of green. Massive chandeliers hung from the arches giving a somewhat romantic hue to the otherwise dim space. Traces of the original late 19th-century structure remained, as were the apparent renovations undertaken during the Soviet period.

Thirsty, I strolled over to one of the numerous small kiosks offering a surprising variety of drinks and snacks and purchased a bottle of carbonated water. After a short while, I looked up from my book to see an older woman holding a pair of used rubber boots in her hands, approaching other passengers in my row. As she got closer to me, I could hear her asking everyone whether they would be interested in buying one or both boots. The government reforms in Russia had been challenging economically for many, especially older Russians, living on fixed payments that had lost much of their value due to increasing inflation. At last, the woman stood before me and hesitated. I thought she would pass me by, but then she asked,

"Would you like a pair of boots, young man?" It was an awkward moment. I did not need the boots, but I wanted to help this courageous woman, desperate enough to be here. I responded, 'Spasibo, nyet' (no, thank you), but I offered her some money anyway. I explained that I didn't need the boots, but I wanted to help. She hesitated once again; I think she was slightly embarrassed by my offered charity. But, in the end, she accepted the money and moved on.

More than an hour had passed since Adel went for tickets. I looked over, and the queue in front of him was still impressive. I had guzzled down the bottle of water and needed to use the bathroom. It was risky to leave the baggage unguarded, but I had no choice and ventured into the men's room. On the back wall were a row of stalls, in the middle stood several washing stations, and on the near wall, a row of urinals. I made my way over to one of the urinals, somewhat in the middle of the row. There were no privacy dividers, unlike most western facilities, so I resolved to keep my eyes pointed straight ahead to avoid awkward moments.

Keeping focused on what I was doing, I neglected to hear some light footsteps and the odor of ammonia approaching my position. Out of the corner of my eye, I noticed what I first thought was a child or tiny man who had stepped up to the adjacent urinal. Still staring forward, I heard a loud brushing sound coming from my new neighbor. Glancing slightly to my right, I was amazed to see an older woman, a babushka, dressed in a traditional headscarf, a gray overcoat, rubber boots similar to the ones I just rejected, and holding a large water bucket. The woman was scrubbing the inside of the urinal. Apparently, this was the woman's job. After finishing her work on the adjacent urinal, the woman paid me no attention and simply walked behind me and continued her work on the urinal directly to my left. I was a bit unsure as to the proper etiquette in this situation. Should I wait for her to move farther along the row before finishing my business or stop now? Breaking protocol, I turned my head around to see what the other facility patrons were doing. The few other men seemed not to pay any attention to the woman. Thus, I finished up and turned to use the washing stations. While I washed my hands, something on the opposite wall caught my attention.

The gaze of several men focused on me from over the stalls. The stall doors came up to each man's chest, exposing his upper torso and face. My curiosity concerning this prominent design flaw prompted me to walk into one of the empty stalls. I instantaneously understood the reason for this design. Due to the station's age, modern toilets had not been installed in the stalls. Instead, a sizeable oval-shaped hole in the tiled floor with two raised narrow foot platforms on either side. The station still employed Turkish-style toilets. I stooped over the oval and squatted down on the footpads to test this design. Having closed the door, I was squatting down with my chest and face exposed. It was an odd sight. My experiment completed, I exited the bathroom. Sitting at a small table positioned to the right of the bathroom exit, I noticed the older woman who had cleaned the urinals. A bowl sat on the table with a collection of kopeck coins, apparently tips for her service. Trying to avoid her eyes but not wanting to be rude, I dropped a ruble note into the bowl as I did not have any coins. I returned to my spot in the waiting area, relieved to see that no one had taken any of our baggage.

# Moscow Nights

My first trip to Tatarstan was brief and centered on getting to know the local government officials and some influential business people. A return visit was planned and several months later, I was back in Moscow on my way again to Kazan. This time I would be traveling alone to the Tatar capital, where Adel would meet me. I took a taxi from Sheremetevo airport to the Hotel Rossiya, located directly off Red Square. It was an enormous twenty-one-story, three thousand room building with a dismal white and gray façade built during the late Khrushchev era. In truth, it was a big eyesore right in the heart of Moscow. I had decided to stay at the Rossiya due to its central location and price. I had a reservation for two nights. The next day I had plans to meet with a former Russian law student, Sergei, whom I had met in Chicago, before taking the overnight train to Kazan for meetings with government officials and business people.

The taxi dropped me off at the main entrance. Surrounded by lacquered wood-panel walls, the reception desk welcomed visitors via a large moss green carpet decorated with an enormous four-point compass emblem. The receptionist greeted me in the former Soviet-style manner, pleasant but not friendly. She had me fill out my guest registration card and leave my passport at the registration desk, as in the USSR, retrieving it whenever I wanted to leave the hotel. I did as required and received the key to my room. The elevator ascended to my floor. Stepping out of the cabin, I was met by the glance of the 'dezhurnaya' or guard. Another legacy of Soviet times, on each floor, worked a woman whose job it was to keep the guests' keys and, more importantly, to monitor their movements. Upon leaving the floor, the guest handed the key to the woman and received it upon return.

My room was typical for hotels of this period. The room was small and sparsely decorated. On the far wall of the room stood a narrow single bed covered by a thin desert-motive, multi-colored comforter. The rest of the room contained two small wood chairs with seats and backs upholstered with what looked and felt like corduroy. The chairs sat on an aged blue carpet. There was also a narrow desk back against the other wall upon which lay a rotary phone. Completing the ensemble was a small table with an ashtray placed in front of the large window with curtains displaying the same, for some reason, desert-motive color scheme. The window was the room's best feature as it gave an excellent view of Red Square.

Since it was late evening, I felt it was more convenient for my first night to eat in the hotel. I exited my room and walked toward the elevators. I caught the ever-present look of the dezhurnaya at her desk, and I asked whether I needed to hand over the key to my room if I was simply going to the hotel restaurant. She gave me a stern nod. I gave her the key, wished her a pleasant evening, and stepped into the elevator. The restaurant was located on the second level of the hotel. Entering the restaurant, I was greeted by the maître d', who showed me to a table in the middle of a large eating area. The furniture and décor of the restaurant had not changed much from its original 1960s design. The tables and chairs had a wood paneling look and feel; it reminded me of the style used in my high school auditorium. The seat I occupied was not overly comfortable and covered with the same corduroy material found in my room. The parquet floor had alternating shades of dark and light amber. Already-faded faux marble Greek columns stood along the outer areas of the space. As with my room, the most attractive feature of the restaurant was the enormous floor-to-ceiling windows through which I could see the illuminated multi-colored cupola domes of St. Basil's Cathedral with a backdrop of the Kremlin walls and Spasskaya Tower with its famous clock.

After several minutes of waiting, a server finally appeared. Dressed in a short dark waist coat and bow tie, the waiter handed me the menu. Having decided on a selection, I signaled to the server, who had been standing off to the side at a polite distance, that I was ready to order.

"I will have the chicken Kiev," I informed the server. This was one of my favorite dishes, and I was delighted to see it on the menu that evening.

"Khorosho," replied the server, and he departed. I sipped on my soda, which, as was customary, was served without ice while I was anticipating the delicious taste of the chicken cutlet. I could hear traditional Russian folk music piped in softly in the background.

The server approached me a short while later without carrying my order. "I am sorry to inform you," he explained, "but the chef says, 'we are no longer preparing that'."

"'Ponyatno" (Understood), I said.

I understood that things happen like this. I looked at the menu again. This time I chose a lamb dish. I received another 'khorosho' from the waiter and went back to observing my fellow diners. I had mostly finished my soda when I saw my server coming back to my table empty-handed again.

"I am sorry to inform you," he repeated, "but the chef says, 'we are no longer preparing that'."

Confused and now wondering if I would ever get to have supper, I put my eyes back on the menu and selected a third item. After the now customary 'khorosho', I asked my server to bring me another soda. I was pretty hungry by now, but I soothed my thoughts by enjoying the marvelous view through the windows. In my studies at university, I had only read and seen pictures of this area, and now seeing it live for the first time, I was entranced by the splendor of the sight. I started thinking about asking my friend tomorrow if we could change our plans to include a tour of the cathedral.

My annoyance began to grow as I followed the path of my server heading back to my table, once again not bearing a meal. For the third time, I listened as my server was sorry to inform me that the chef said 'we are no longer preparing that'. Remaining polite, I asked the server why items 'no longer being prepared' were on the menu. I received a blank stare. Famished and worn out, I capitulated and, in my best sarcastic tone in Russian, asked the server if he could inform me what dishes the chef was still preparing. I thought this would be a more efficient approach. I don't believe anyone had ever asked the server this question. He seemed unsure of how to answer but eventually told me he would find out. I watched him again leave, but not before ordering a glass of vodka. The server eventually returned to tell me which items were still available. I settled for a cold-cut plate; it satisfied my hunger, but it left me bitter that I was denied the tasty warm meal I had anticipated.

Exhausted, I returned to my room, stopping off first by the dezhurnaya to retrieve my room key. I had hoped for a more pleasant evening, but now I just wanted to sleep. Although the bed was narrow, it was surprisingly comfortable. The bizarre colored comforter was plusher than it looked and sleep came quickly.

"Hello, are you lonely tonight?" were the heavily-accented English words I heard. At first, I thought I was dreaming but then realized that I had the phone receiver up to my head. I must have been in a deep sleep since I didn't recall picking up the phone. Not hearing a reply, the woman on the line repeated her phrase once again, "Are you lonely tonight?" After several moments, I replied, "What?" followed by "No, thank you". I put down the receiver and turned back over to sleep. I was awoken again by a knock at my door a while later. Still groggy, I shuffled towards the door, expecting to see the dezhurnaya. Instead, three women appeared.

Perhaps in her early twenties, a young woman dressed in a shimmering white cocktail dress barely covering her shoulders stood at the threshold. Matching white earrings glimmered under her curly blonde hair. She was flanked by two older women, likely in their late thirties. One, her black hair tied in a bun, wore what looked like a bridesmaid's red velvet outfit with an enormous bird-shaped pin on her right breast. She tightly held a small black purse in her hands. The white blouse of her companion appeared to be straining under the weight of a full bosom. Her leather skirt barely concealed black fishnet stockings. The women looked like they were dressed up for a night on the town and had somehow erroneously ended up at my door. The woman in the white blouse spoke first. I recognized the voice from the telephone when she said "Hello there! We heard that you were lonely." In my sleepy state, I tried again to inform them that I was not interested, but to no use. The talkative woman walked past me into my room, quickly followed by the other two women, and sat down in one of the chairs.

"We know that men get lonely in Moscow, and we can take care of you," she began. She then went on to introduce herself and her companions. "I am Lena, and this is Vera and Angela." Vera was the woman in the red dress, and Angela was the younger one. "You can choose any one of us," added Lena. She then stated what the price would be.

I looked at the women, who all appeared to be wearing their most glamorous outfits. My head was clearing. All three ladies were smiling, but their eyes revealed a mixture of embarrassment and contempt; their presence resulted from necessity. It was evident that each lady had been compelled into this situation by difficult economic circumstances associated with their country's transition. These women were housewives and students, not professional prostitutes. I explained in my best Russian that I appreciated their offer but that I did not require their services. I even dared to ask Lena how she knew I was here and where my room was. Revealing her inexperience in this line of work, she told me that the concierge at the hotel kept track of foreign guests and wealthy Russians. He would then provide information to their manager as to the names and rooms and would receive payment for the info. There was an awkward silence. The women were not accustomed to receiving a negative reply. I finally insisted that I needed to get back to sleep and escorted them out of my room. After the ladies departed, a heavy perfume scent hung in the air as I tried to fall back asleep. I awoke in the morning with a dry throat and headache.

I met Sergei in the morning as planned. "How was your first night in Moscow?" he inquired. I explained to him the strange events of the prior evening. He was astonished by my experiences. He felt the need to apologize and promised me that this day would be more regular. The business meetings were uneventful. Sergei invited me to a new trendy restaurant, called Popular Pizza, for lunch. Many new restaurants were popping up all over the city. Western icons such as KFC and Burger King, following McDonald's entry in 1990, recently opened their first locations in Russia's capital. We walked over to the square where the restaurant was located. Sergei has not undersold the popularity of the restaurant. As we approached the eatery's courtyard, we could see a massive queue of people waiting to get inside.

"The line looks endless," I said. "We have only an hour or so before the next meeting."

"I agree. We will need to find another place," replied Sergei.

We chatted and decided we still wanted pizza, so we headed to Pizza Hut. Located about a mile from the Kremlin, this Pizza Hut had been open since 1990 and no longer had the massive lines seen at newer places like Popular Pizza. Being familiar with Pizza Hut at home, I expected a similar experience as I entered the door to the restaurant.

Instead, what I saw was vastly different from the Pizza Huts in the U.S. The restaurant was not a fast food place. It more closely resembled an upscale restaurant. The color scheme and logos were the same, but the floors and tables were immaculately clean. The staff wore pristine uniforms, and there was a sizeable full-service bar serving all the alcohol one would imagine at a high-end restaurant. There was a small line inside, and Sergei and I took our places in the queue. The menu choices, placed overhead on a large screen, were displayed in English and Russian. In my mind, I was reminded of the prior evening's debacle at the hotel restaurant and was hoping to avoid a repeat experience. I approached the employee behind the counter and ordered an individual pizza. The employee told me the price, and I handed him a 100 ruble note. The employee counted out the change and, with a broad smile and the banknotes still in his hand, said to me, "some rubles for me?" I was taken aback at first as I did not immediately understand what he meant. I put my hand out to receive the change, and he repeated, "some rubles for me?" Here was a very enterprising young man. He had grasped the concepts of capital-ism. He was trying to make extra cash by having customers leave him some of their change. Convinced that this was not part of his regular duties, I never-theless appreciated his ambition and let him keep ten rubles of my change. I was sure that he would need it when he got fired for his activities. The rest of the day did proceed normally, as did that evening. In the morning, having got-ten a full night's sleep without interruption, I headed to the Kazanskii Vokzal and boarded the overnight train to Kazan.

# Aces Wild

"Good day! Where is compartment number fifteen?" I said to the porter as I stepped up onto the train.

The porter, dressed in a dark blue uniform with a wide-brimmed cap that sported a prominent logo, reminded me of a military officer. With my second-class ticket in hand, I followed the porter down the narrow corridor of the train car. We passed several compartments, and then he stopped.

"Here is your compartment," stated the porter.

He pulled on the outside handle of the door, sliding it open to reveal another narrow space containing four sleeping berths, two each on opposite sides of the compartment. In the back of the room stood a small metallic table. Above the table was a window that looked out over the station tracks. The window glass was opaque due to its thickness, and a short row of curtains covered the bottom to mid-portion of the window. The walls of the space were of a light pea-green color. The beds bore a dark green color and were composed of a hard foam-like material, reminding me of the school bus seats. The lower beds folded up against the walls and served as benches when not used.

I had not been the first passenger to enter the compartment. Lying on both lower beds were small handbags and jackets, the owners of which must have left the cabin. Both upper berths were empty, so I decided to take the one on the upper right-hand side. Bag in hand, I used the small ladder embedded against the nearby wall to boost myself up. I seated myself up on the berth, my legs dangling over the edge. Off to my left was a small storage area that extended over the door to the compartment. I squeezed my bag into the tiny space. A seatbelt stretched across the width of the bed to prevent the passenger from falling while sleeping.

While I was busy examining my sleeping area, one of my fellow passengers must have returned as I heard 'Zdrastvyite!' from below. I looked down to see a man, perhaps in his early forties, dressed in a collared blue work shirt, faded jeans, and well-worn leather shoes. I returned his greeting and introduced myself.

"Menya zovut Ken (My name is Ken)."

"You are English?" The passenger was surprised to find a non-Russian in his compartment.

"Nyet, Amerikanyets (American)," I answered, unsure whether the man understood English.

"My name is Alexei Petrovich. You speak Russian well."

"Spasibo (thank you)," I said and explained to Alexei that I had studied Russian at university and was now doing business in Russia. The initial pleasantries concluded, he nodded and then went and sat down on his berth directly below mine.

A short while later, the second passenger arrived back in the compartment. This man noticed me but did not immediately greet me. Instead, he looked at Alexei. He looked roughly the same age as Alexei and was similarly dressed. I heard Alexei quickly explain who I was and that I spoke Russian. The man then greeted me, adding that his name was Pyotr Ivanovich.

"Ochen priyatno," or nice to meet you, I replied.

Alexei and Pyotr were traveling companions. Both men were from Moscow but worked in the Kazan region and were heading back to Kazan after a short holiday with family. Initially, I could feel a sense of awkwardness or nervousness in the cabin. The fact that I was not Russian made the men more reticent than usual. At least, that was the impression I had at the time.

The train departed in twenty minutes, so we started to settle in for the journey. Unsure whether I would be able to dine on the train, I had brought along some nutrition bars, a local brand of potato chips, and a bag of bite-sized candies to quench my sweet tooth. My companions were busy arranging their blankets and jackets to make room to sit on the benches when someone opened the compartment door. We all turned to see a rather tall, lanky younger man enter the car. He had bushy blondish hair and an aquiline nose with somewhat high cheekbones that accentuated his thicker lips. He was wearing a blue and white horizontal striped shirt and what looked like fatigues for pants. His military-style boots added to his height. The man introduced himself as Alexander but quickly said to refer to him as Sasha. Seeing that he was the fourth for the compartment, Sasha placed his bag on the upper berth opposite me. Given his height, I was not sure how his legs would squeeze into the short length of the bed.

"English?" asked Sasha, gazing up at my obvious non-Russian attire.

"Amerikanyets" followed Alexei with a nod.

"Privyet! (Hi)" I said and added that I did speak some Russian. "Do you know if there is a dining car for the trip?" I thought talking about dinner could break the ice.

The three Russian smiled broadly and started to laugh. "We must have a 'mazhor' with us, boys." Alexei referred to the young nouveau riche, who had become more prevalent in places like Moscow; young men whose fathers had made vast fortunes from questionably legal privatization sales. I had seen an impressive number of European sports cars driving through Moscow the day before. I, too, could not help but laugh.

"No such luck," I said. "I just recently finished university, so I brought my dinner with me," I added. I took out my nutrition bars and potato chips from my bag and waved them in front of my companions.

"Molodets!" chortled Sasha, "He'll be alright, boys." After that, the atmosphere of awkwardness or nervousness dissipated. My attempt at levity had made an impression.

Over the intercom came the announcement of the train's imminent departure. The porter poked his head into each compartment to make a final check. He was followed by a diminutive older woman dressed in a light gray uniform top with red piping and a matching skirt.

"Dobry vyechor! (good evening)" the woman declared as she entered the compartment. "Chai?"

The woman placed a metallic tray on the table by the window. A small silver teapot was set on the table, surrounded by four traditional Russian tea glasses set in decorative metal holders, four spoons, and a cup containing sugar cubes. The woman filled the four glasses and then withdrew from the compartment. The tea tasted wonderful with the melted flavor of several cubes of sugar. Sitting next to Alexei on what would be his bed for the night, I sipped my tea and watched my companions. Suddenly, I felt a jolt as the train began to move.

"Well, boys, is it time for dinner?" Alexei asked, so I figured it was time to climb back up to my berth to sit and eat. It was nearly 9:00 pm, and I didn't want to eat too late to get some rest during the night. I began to take out my nutrition bars and chips. The three Russians had sat around the small table by the window finishing their tea.

"Come and join us," Sasha said.

"We've all brought our food as well. Let's see what kind of a meal we can make out of it".

Joining the others, I placed my items into the communal food collection. Alexei had a partial loaf of dark rye bread, several cucumbers, salt, and cold-cut meats. Pyotr placed on the table some onion stalks, a large oval loaf of black bread, several hard-boiled eggs, and what looked like some type of small potpie, while Sasha added some more bread and cucumbers and a bottle of vodka. In comparison, my nutrition bars and chips were the least attractive choice.

"Put those back and enjoy some real Russian food," said Alexei.

I smiled. "Khorosho, spasibo", and I threw my food onto my bed.

All three Russians produced small knives and started to slice and divide the food.

"Can I help?" I inquired.

Alexei responded, "Nyet. You are our guest for the evening."

Once the food was equitably distributed using the paper bags for plates, Sasha filled the tea glasses with vodka and gave a toast.

"Na zdrovyie! (Cheers)"

We all repeated the toast to Sasha and clanked glasses. This was not my first time drinking vodka, but it was in such an amount. I took an initial swig of the vodka while I watched my three companions drink their glasses in one attempt. Alexei gave me an encouraging wink, and I finished the rest of my glass. The vodka produced a sharp sting in my throat that made me cough. The Russians found this very amusing. Alexei slapped me on the shoulder.

"There you go! By the time we reach Kazan, we'll make you a real Russian".

Heavily salted cucumber slices and bread accompanied the toast, and I devoured them. When I saw Sasha start to refill the glasses again with vodka, I put up my hand in protest, wanting to avoid getting drunk in the presence of friendly but total strangers.

"Davaite, davaite! (go on!)" exclaimed Sasha urging me to take my glass.

It seemed the more I protested, the more adamant became my companions. In the end, I smiled and downed the 'shot'. Feeling the effects of the vodka, I made sure to consume as much bread as I could. I needed to keep my wits about me.

"How about a game of cards?" interjected Pyotr, who had been mainly silent up to this point.

"Great idea!" was Alexei's response. "We can play a game of 'Durak' (fool)."

I had read many Russian novels in which card games played an important role. The famous Pushkin tale, The Queen of Spades, quickly rushed back into my head. I had, however, no actual knowledge of how to play any Russian card games.

"I have never played 'Durak'," I said. "Is it like in Pushkin's Queen of Spades?"

My comments again drew laughter. "No, you would need a 19th-century man for that game," said Alexei.

After a hearty meal and several more rounds of vodka, I noticed that the Russians were now addressing me with the familiar 'you' instead of the formal 'thou'. Alexei explained the game's basic rules: there would be 36 cards; each player would be dealt six cards. The bottom card of the deck is turned and placed face-up on the table, its suit determining the trump or rank suit for the current deal. Players attack and defend using higher suit cards. The game's goal was to discard all your cards, with the last person holding a card being the 'durak' or fool. A player didn't want to win but rather not be the loser or fool. We played individually at first, assuming that I would learn the game better as we played more. I was a great source of amusement for my companions when I played the wrong card or failed in my attack and defense. As expected, I was crowned the fool quite often in the beginning. When the play switched to playing in pairs, I teamed up with Sasha, who, being an experienced player, improved my card selections.

Since the Russians had supplied the dinner, I decided to contribute by providing dessert. Besides drinking vodka and tea, my companions had not brought any cakes or sweets. I offered my bag of sweets to repay their kindness for dinner. In hindsight, I should have purchased some high-level chocolate. All I could offer was a handful of Snickers bite-size candies. Each graciously accepted the handful of gold and brown wrapped candies nibbling on them as they sipped on the remnants of the tea. The bottle of vodka did not survive dinner.

I started to execute successful attacks with Sasha's assistance and even fended off the Seven of Clubs attack from Pyotr by throwing a Ten of Clubs, which impressed Alexei. The game was delightful, and there was much laughter. At one point, Alexei inquired about my family origin. I was still hesitant to provide too much personal information to my new acquaintances.

"My last name," I explained, "used to be spelled with an "-ovskii" at the end, but when my great-grandfather emigrated to the US, he dropped the "-ovskii" ending to make the name sound more German to find work."

This story was a fabrication. If my companions believed I had Russian ancestors, I thought they would be less likely to take advantage of me. During the evening, Alexei and Pytor discussed their jobs in a small city along the Volga River known as Zelenodolsk, where they worked as engineers. Like many in the region, their factory was experiencing difficulty adjusting to the switch to capitalism. The factory struggled to sell its products, and pay was intermittent. Management gave employees like Alexei and Pyotr extended time off to visit family. Sasha spoke about recently leaving the military and returning to his parents' home north of Kazan, where he hoped to find employment. He explained that many soldiers, sailors, etc., had become unemployed over the past few years as the Soviet and now Russian governments could no longer afford to keep a large military.

"Many of my comrades have gone into private security or protection," continued Sasha. "I want to avoid that and hope I can find an honest job."

"I am meeting a colleague in Kazan who is helping me establish opportunities for American and Russian companies to work together," I stated.

This work impressed my companions, expressing their desire for closer cooperation with their former Cold War foe.

"If most Americans are like you, we should have few problems getting along," was how Alexei put it. He shared the optimism, typical at the time, that quickly faded a few short years later.

At this point, Pyotr suggested that we should make the game more exciting and play for money. I was already fighting fatigue, and wagering money on a game that I had just learned worried me. In addition, I was sure that I was the only one in the group who had hard currency. I thanked Pytor for the offer but respectfully declined, explaining my strong desire for rest. Pyotr and Alexei appeared disappointed by my response, but luckily Sasha took my side regarding sleep. At daylight came an announcement over the intercom that the train was approaching Kazan. I had slept longer than my companions, who I noticed were already packed and ready to depart.

"Too much vodka?" Alexei asked sarcastically.

"Likely, yes," I replied with a smile.

I scrambled to gather my belongings. Assured that my wallet and passport were still in my backpack, I jumped down and followed Alexei, Pyotr, and Sasha out onto the platform at the end of the car. As the train slowed on approaching the station, I noticed that the platform in front was damp. The train halted in front of a large building whose façade displayed "Vokzal Kazan" in large white letters. The station was a two-story rectangular structure covered by red brick with trimmings in white along the rows of windows. A tall silver spire topped the central part of the building, and two adjacent symmetrical wings flanked the entrance. Each wing sported a small spire atop a slanted silver roof and what appeared to be miniature spherical adornments along the outer edges. Once inside, we said our goodbyes and wished each other well. I walked towards the main exit of that station, where I saw Adel waiting for me.

"Did you have a good trip?"

"Yes," I responded. "It was quite an experience."

Adel had a car waiting for us, and we headed off into the city's downtown area. I related my card-playing adventure to my Tatar colleague in the car, who agreed it was wise not to have wagered money. "Have you ever read a Russian gambling story that ended well?"

# Mr. Bauman

It was a short drive into downtown Kazan. We departed the station and headed south along Bukhana Shakhidi Street. We then made a left onto Tazi Gizzata Street until we reached the Bulak River, which ran through central Kazan. I looked to my left as we again headed south, and I could see off in the distance the tall green tower capped with a gold spire and red star, which symbolized the Soyembika Tower. The tower was one of the most iconic buildings in this famous Kazan landmark: the White Kremlin. The site bore its name from the white brick walls ('kremlin' means wall in Russian) that surrounded the tower and several other well-known historical buildings, some dating from the 16th century. Kazan played an important role in Russian history. Ivan the Terrible, in the mid-16th century, besieged the town and succeeded in wresting power and control from the Mongol Khanate, which stopped any further Mongol advance into western Russia. Taking a final glance in the rear-view mirror, I hoped to have a chance to visit the area in the next few days. We continued south along the river and made a left turn onto Pushkin Street. A minute or two later, Adel pulled the car into the parking area of the Hotel Tatarstan.

"This is the hotel where most businessmen and foreigners stay," Adel explained to me as he helped me carry my baggage from the car. Above the two-story-high glass arched entryway stood fifteen floors of off-white-colored concrete and glass. The building resembled typical Soviet-era construction.

Hotel Tartarstan, written in large red English letters, stood on the top of the building. There were several shops and a restaurant, also named Tartarstan, attached to the sides of the main entrance. We entered the hotel lobby with its white and gray marble floor and scattered Turkish rugs.

At the reception desk, I went through the typical process of signing the registration forms and leaving my passport. The receptionist gave me my room key, and Adel informed me that he needed to go to his house for a short while but would come back to meet me shortly.

"Khorosho," I answered and headed off to take the elevator up to my room. I had not slept great on the train, so I thought I would take advantage of the time alone to nap.

I exited the elevator and was surprised to see no guard on the floor. I continued, unaccompanied, along the narrow hallway whose white walls lacked decorations or artwork. I had some difficulty with my roller bag since the gold-trimmed red carpet on top of the white tiled floor was bunched up, causing the bag's wheels to get stuck. Having found my room, I inserted my key and entered. The room was very narrow, with white stucco walls. Along the far wall stood a typical small, twin-sized bed. To my amazement, the bed cover had the same desert-motive color as the one I had seen in Moscow. "The wonder of Soviet production," I thought. The furnishings consisted of a small wooden table and chair, and there were several tears in the green shaded carpet, which hadn't been vacuumed for a while.

I approached the large window at the back of the room beneath which the heater/cooler unit was installed. It was a pleasant day, so I thought I would open the window to breathe fresh air. I went to turn the handle on the window and saw that uncovered insulation foam was visible between the window sill and the heating unit. Walking over to the other end of the room, I forcefully pulled the closet handle only to see a cracked lower shelf and an absence of hangers.

I entered the bathroom to wash my hands and face. The bathroom had a sink and toilet adjoined by a European-style shower stall with a shower head attached to a flexible cord. However, the shower did not have a curtain or glass partition. The water would flow freely into the bathroom. There were also no bath or hand towels. Back in the living area, I bent down to pick up my backpack and noticed something like a string jetting out from under the bed. I leaned down to get a closer look and jumped back. It was the tail of a dead mouse. Lifting the bed cover slightly, I could see the deceased rodent lying on its side just under the bed. I rang the reception desk using the rotary-dial phone in the room. A woman's voice answered the call.

"Hello, how may I help you?"

"Hi, this is room 515. I have a dead mouse in my room, no towels or clothes hangers in the wardrobe, and my shower has no curtain. I'd like someone to come and remove the mouse and fix the other problems."

"Are you sure the mouse is dead?"

"I am not sure what you mean. It hasn't moved, and I will not touch it."

"Well, we don't have someone who can come up right now. Can you simply put it in the trashcan, and I will send up someone later."

"Pick it up with what? I told you that there are no towels in the room. How long do you think it will be until someone can come?"

"We are quite busy at the moment. It may be more than an hour."

"I need to rest since I have some meetings in a few hours. Could you put me in another room?"

"We are quite busy. I can maybe look for a room later this evening."

"Are you joking? There are no available rooms in the hotel?"

"As I said, we are quite busy."

"Understood…" I said and hung up.

I had been in the room for about thirty minutes but decided to change accommodations. I was not planning on staying in this hotel any longer than necessary. There had to be a better hotel in the city. I picked up the phone again and dialed the number for Adel's house. I hated calling him so quickly, but I was afraid to discover something more disturbing.

"Hello," I heard Adel answer.

"Hi, Adel, it's me. I hate to ask this, but I need to switch to another hotel."

I explained briefly to my colleague the condition of the room and the attitude of the hotel reception desk. After some brief moments of silence, I heard:

"Ladno (OK). I will come back to the hotel and pick you up. Meet me in the lobby."

I felt bad about the situation, knowing that Adel had made the reservation in hopes of taking good care of his western guest. I understood that service was still a novelty in Russia and even rarer in the provinces far from Moscow or St. Petersburg. Still, I could not spend the next week under these conditions. I watched Adel stroll into the hotel through the main entrance about fifteen minutes later. Wearing jeans, work boots, and a well-worn white dress shirt with the sleeves rolled up, he approached me to inquire whether I was ready to leave. I nodded, and we walked over to the reception desk to cancel the reservation and retrieve my passport. The woman at the reception desk appeared not to understand why someone would cancel a reservation.

"Why are you canceling?" she addressed Adel.

"How is a guest supposed to stay in a room with no towels and a dead mouse?"

The explanation did not seem to affect her, and she gave no response. Adel requested a return of his deposit as well as my passport.

"You have to fill out this form and get approval from the manager to get your deposit back."

"Yasno (clear). Give my colleague back his passport, and I will fill out the form."

She showed him the required form and reluctantly handed me my passport. Adel filled out the form, and we exited the hotel.

"I'm sorry for the poor experience once again. It is shameful for Tatars to treat a guest in such a way."

"I am sorry you have to wait to get your deposit back. I hope it was not too much."

"It's ok. I'll get it tomorrow."

"Where shall we go now?"

We had reached the car, and both sat in the front seats.

"I have a contact at another hotel nearby. It's quite a bit older, but it was once the best hotel in the city. It's called the Hotel Kazan."

The word 'contact'; was one that I would repeatedly hear during my travels in Russia. Personal relationships or 'contacts' were an essential aspect of life during Soviet times. Contacts were necessary to obtain desired goods or services within the Soviet economy, based on an intricate network of privileges. Those members of society holding high positions in the Communist Party enjoyed access to a wider variety of goods and services than average citizens. These privileges included admission to better schools, select stores that offered foreign goods not commonly available, and selective clubs and private dachas. The average Soviet citizen developed his own network of 'contacts', usually with other average Soviet citizens, to provide him access to privileges to which he would not generally be entitled. For example, suppose one needed a replacement part for an automobile, which was very difficult to obtain. A 'contact' who worked in a repair shop might locate this part in exchange for something the repairman needed. This contact network allowed the Soviet economy to function by filling in the gaps created by a state-directed production system. Even with the collapse of the Soviet Union, these contacts were still vital to economic life in 1992.

We drove away from the hotel and followed Pushkin Street towards Tukay Square, and soon turned left onto Bauman Street. Bauman Street was one of the main thoroughfares in Kazan, connecting Tukay Square, the city's main square, with the White Kremlin compound. The street was named for Nikolai Bauman, a Russian revolutionary, and was distinguished by its colored pavement, rows of three or four-story multi-colored buildings containing banks, commercial centers, and hotels. The street dated from the 15th century and had always served as one of the city's leading trading and commercial streets. Until Soviet times, the street had been known as Breach Street, which referred to the two breaches made to the White Kremlin's walls during the siege by Ivan the Terrible in the 1550s.

We drove along Bauman Street for several minutes until we approached an impressive V-shaped building stretching for more than a block. The four-story stone façade was painted in sea-foam green. A multitude of tall windows capped with a triangular faux awning and trimmed in white stretched along each story of the façade. Wrought-iron balconies jutted out from several of the windows, mainly at the vertex of the building. Sitting on the roof of the vertex was a faded brown dome with 'Gostinitsa Kazan' (Hotel Kazan) carved in a base relief just below. The hotel dated from Tsarist times and still displayed some of its old-world splendor. Running along the height of the green façade in between the windows were faux columns made of white-washed stone blocks. Like most buildings in the city, there were numerous shops on the street level.

"I have a good relationship with the hotel manager," said Adel as we entered the main lobby.

Adel informed the receptionist that he was here to see the manager. She seemed to recognize Adel and rushed off into the administrative office directly behind. A few minutes later, a woman, likely in her early forties, well-dressed with a dark blue jacket and matching skirt, appeared. The attractive features from her youth were still evident. She had a gentle smile alongside bright hazel eyes and thick, long black hair styled on top of her head.

"Adel, what a surprise! I was not expecting you today."

"Privyet, Marina! I am hosting a colleague from America, and I need a room for his stay."

"That should not be a problem. How long is your colleague planning to stay?"

"A week or so. He is here with me to meet some officials and businessmen in the area."

"Khorosho, we will find something appropriate for such a guest."

Marina then informed the receptionist which room to reserve for me.

"Mr. Maher, you will, I hope, enjoy your stay with us," added Marina after reviewing my passport. "I have given you a room for special guests."

To my surprise, the receptionist returned my passport and gave me the room key.

Marina then accompanied Adel and me down the long corridor on the left until we reached my room number. In contrast to the other hotel we just left, ornate framed mirrors decorated the white corridor walls. The floor tiles were stone and appeared to be original, although well worn. I stood facing an enormous wood door, which took an effort to pull open.

I walked into the room, followed by Marina and Adel. There was a small foyer with a parquet floor, a floor-to-ceiling mirror, and a wood portmanteau. I left my bags in the foyer and stepped to my left into a large salon. The space was vast, with twelve-foot-high ceilings ornately decorated and parquet flooring covered by several small rugs. A three-person sofa and a love seat surrounded a dark wood coffee table. There was an old-style television sitting atop a short commode. To the right, I could see the sunlight cascading through the two tall windows with lace patterned curtains, which looked out onto Bauman Street. The overall feel of the room was late 19th/early 20th century. The ornateness of the room was dampened slightly by the apparent disregard for maintenance; numerous paint cracks, chips on the parquet floor, and cracks in the crown molding.

"The room is beautiful," I exclaimed.

"I am glad you like it," smiled Marina, adding, "the bedroom is over to the right."

The bedroom was narrower than the salon and contained the typical twin bed and comforter with a small dressing table and wardrobe. It also had a window looking out onto Bauman Street. There was a small but adequate bathroom to the right of the bedroom. The suite was, by far, the most extensive and prettiest room I had seen in Russia.

"This will work just fine, thank you," I said.

"Khorosho, I will leave you to rest. If you have any problems, please come and see me."

Marina then took her leave of us. Adel and I remained in the room.

"I should hurry up and get changed. I don't want us to be late for that meeting this afternoon."

"Ah," said Adel. "I forgot to tell you that the meeting was delayed until tomorrow. The official called me while I was at my house to give his apologies."

"So, what is the plan then?"

"I still need to finish some things at home. We can meet for dinner, say around 7:00 pm?"

"Ladno." I was still feeling some fatigue from the overnight train voyage.

The plan set, Adel departed. I unpacked and decided to lay down for a bit. When I awoke, I noticed that the sun had set. "I must have been more tired than I thought," I said to myself. I went into the salon, where the clock on the coffee table indicated almost 6:00 pm. After changing clothes, I sat in the salon to read a book while waiting for Adel to arrive. A copy of "The Godfather" sat in my lap. The book's plot seemed relevant to the present situation in Russia, where many Mafiosa families had become prominent in the country. It was not hard to envision the Russian version of the Corleone family plotting its next criminal undertaking. Many media reports told of the rising influence of criminal gangs throughout the country. Legal protections were weak, and most aspiring Russians were accustomed to paying criminal gangs for protection. More sophisticated 'entrepreneurs' acquired assets such as banks and oil and gas companies, later becoming oligarchs. The rise of organized crime and official corruption created disillusionment and frustration among the general population struggling to understand the new market economy.

A knock at my door shook me out of my thoughts. I opened the door and found Adel standing there.

"Before we eat, I wanted to talk with you about something."

"Ok," I said. "What about?"

"When I was leaving earlier, Marina spoke with me about your visit. Marina is aware that the hotel needs renovation to attract foreigners and Russian businesspeople. She is very interested in finding an American partner to invest in the hotel. Would you be OK meeting with her?"

"Sure. I have worked some in the industry (recalling my time at The Pyramid Group) and would be happy to speak with her."

"Great. She would like to meet with us tonight for dinner. We can eat in the hotel restaurant."

I couldn't turn down a meeting with the woman who was nice enough to put me in this beautiful room. The restaurant was situated on the opposite side of the hotel. We retraced our journey along the corridor, passing by the reception desk again, and walked along a similar corridor until we reached two large glass wood-framed doors with 'Restaurant Kazan'. "These restaurants really could use some brand marketing help," I thought as we entered. Marina was standing next to the hostess and greeted us warmly.

"Welcome to our wonderful restaurant! I'm so glad you agreed to meet with me this evening."

"It's my pleasure," I replied.

"Please, follow me. I have reserved our best table for tonight."

We followed the hotel manager into the main dining area. The room was empty. It was a bit early for dinner for most Russians. Walking along the dark-wood parquet floor, I could make out several large chandeliers with crystal lights hanging from the richly painted ceiling. Marina Antonovna invited us to sit at a large table in the far corner of the restaurant. The wood lacquered table bore a pristine white tablecloth and was laid out with the hotel's finest cutlery. The chairs were heavy wood and upholstered with dark-red plush cushions and backing. The table's location provided plenty of privacy, but the expansive window provided a new view of Baumann Street lit up for the night. We sat down, and the waitress came over and handed Marina Antonovna a thick beige folder. She sat between Adel and me. The waitress did not give us menus but simply left.

"I have the chef tonight making one of our traditional Tatar dishes." started Marina Antonovna. "In the meantime, I'd like to talk about the hotel."

"OK. Adel told me that you are interested in finding a partner to invest in the hotel."

"Yes. The hotel is beautiful but old. It was built before the Revolution and, as you can see, needs renovation. I thought that a western hotel company might be interested in renovating the hotel."

"More and more foreign businessmen are coming to Kazan," injected Adel. "They need a nice play to stay. You saw what our 'modern' Hotel Tatarstan offers."

The waitress returned with several bottles of vodka, a glass of wine, and some bottles of carbonated water. I asked for water, and Adel opened one of the bottles of vodka. She handed the wineglass to her boss. Marina Antonovna placed the beige folder on the table, putting her glass to the side.

"I brought some information on the hotel and would like to get your thoughts." Marina untied the string and opened the folder. She took out several items. One of which was an architectural schematic of the hotel. She spread it out across the table. "This is one of the old design plans for the hotel. It's not the original, but you can see the hotel's main features."

I had to stand up and crouch over the table to get a good view of the document. The hotel occupied two blocks on Bauman Street and another street. The schematic outlined all the rooms aligned on each floor of the V-shaped wings of the hotel. I could make out the reception area, laundry area, underground facilities for the boiler, etc. A small parking area was in the hotel's courtyard between the V-shaped wings. Marina Antonovna continued to discuss renovations.

"I think that a western partner would want to keep the architectural look of the hotel; perhaps they could attract western stores to occupy the commercial areas along Bauman Street."

"There is plenty of construction work needed to upgrade the rooms." pointed out Adel, standing and crouching around the table.

I recalled that Adel worked at the Tatarstan Construction Ministry and was likely considering opportunities for his ministry. I asked Marina Antonovna if she had a copy of this document, which I could hold on to for further study. She informed me that I could keep this copy. After re-folding the blueprint and handing it to me, our hostess removed several additional sheets of paper from the beige folder. These were handwritten documents that included a schedule of proposed renovations with associated projected costs. She handed the documents to me. More than fifty proposed renovations, from installing modern HVAC in rooms to remodeling, replacing the roof, and repaving the courtyard and parking area. I looked at the total projected cost of several tens of millions of dollars

"I have been looking at a renovation plan for some time," said the hotel manager. "If we use local workers and materials, the renovation costs will be much less for a western investor."

"You have put some serious thought into this project," I said. "I have good contacts with a real estate development firm in Chicago and would be happy to review these plans with them if that is acceptable."

Upon hearing these words, Marina's face brightened. "Oh. That sounds wonderful. Maybe they will want to invest in the hotel or help us get an American hotel to invest."

"My ministry provided the detailed costs for labor and materials," Adel added.

I felt that this meeting was not as random as it first appeared. I stated that the firm in Chicago engaged primarily in design work but had relationships with some of the large western hotel chains. I explained that the big western chains generally do not get involved in construction; they prefer to provide management services to the hotel, which would bear the chain's 'flag' or its brand. Under such an arrangement, the hotel would pay the chain for its brand and management expertise. Having a major flag on the hotel would increase revenue by attracting more customers.

"Yasno. I can give you all the documents in this folder so that you can share them with your contacts in Chicago."

We had seemed to reach a natural pause in the conversation when the waitress returned with our meal. The first course consisted of a broth-based soup with noodles and a piece of fish. Hard-boiled eggs and black rye bread accompanied it. It looked very hearty and likely could be a meal in itself. The waitress carefully placed each bowl in front of her guests. Adel and Marina Antonovna both looked at the dish with broad smiles.

"This is called 'shulpa'," explained Marina. "It is a very traditional Tatar dish."

"My wife makes this regularly at home, but she usually adds mushrooms," said Adel.

"It smells wonderful. I can't wait to taste it."

I was stretching the truth a bit. It did smell fantastic, but I was not passionate about fish. I recalled my time in Siberia, where every other dish contained fish. Although I grew up across the street from an ocean inlet in the suburbs of Boston, I never developed a taste for seafood, except for some shellfish, such as clams. Nevertheless, I grabbed my soup spoon and gulped down a good amount of the broth and noodles. The noodles were delicious, and the broth was not spicy. I noticed that my table companions were waiting to see my impression.

"Well? How do you like it?" inquired Marina.

"Vkusno" (tasty), I replied with a grin. "I like how the noodles take in the broth's flavor."

"The fish is caught fresh from a lake nearby."

To mask the taste of the fish, I steadily ate slices of rye bread after each spoonful of soup. I felt slightly bad about leaving most of the fish untouched. The conversation was less active for the moment as I watched Marina Antonovna sip on her wine and Adel with his mineral water bottle. We had nearly finished our portions of shulpa when the waitress returned to take away the bowls and bread. The waitress returned after several minutes carrying a large cauldron of rice that she placed in the middle of the table. An assistant balanced a plate expertly in front of each guest with a slow and steady hand. The smell was delicious.

"This is another dish you will often see at Tatar dinners: Pilaw." Marina Antonovna described the dish as comprised of rice, vegetables, and boiled meat. In this case, it was lamb. The waitress used a large wooden spoon to scoop up portions of the pilaw and place them on each plate. The dish's aroma extinguished the feeling of fullness I had after the soup.

"This smells excellent." I let out. "I love rice pilaf. I have several Armenian friends, and this was a staple in their cuisine."

"Ah yes, it is common in this region and the Caucuses. Of course, we Tatars feel that we make the best pilaw," our hostess proudly stated.

The taste of the pilaw did not disappoint. The rice was seasoned just right, and the lamb was tender and moist. Raised white bread, looking like a giant bagel topped with oil and seeds, was also placed on the table. Adel filled three shot glasses with vodka and made a toast to our health and friendship. The generous amount of bread and rice had a mitigating effect on the vodka so that after several more toasts, I still felt pretty sober.

"Are you married?" asked our hostess. "You are such a young man to be traveling so far on business trips."

"I have a fiancée in Chicago. We plan to get married when she finishes law school. Aliya was studying in Chicago and became friends with my fiancée, which is how I met Adel."

"Do you have American companies ready to invest in Tatarstan?"

"Perhaps not ready yet to invest in Tatarstan; so few Americans are familiar with the region. I am hoping to bring opportunities here to their attention."

"Well, I hope that the Hotel Kazan will be one of those opportunities," enthusiastically said Marina Antonovna.

"We shall see. I am already a big admirer already of the hotel. I love the old-world charm."

Our waitress had returned to serve tea accompanied by a small plate containing several small balls resembling Rice Krispy treats; pieces of rice and raisins held together by a glazed substance and smelled strongly of honey. I took one of the sticky treats in my hand and nibbled on it. Underneath the rice coating was deep-fried dough similar in texture to a doughnut. It was very sweet-tasting and light.

"I see you enjoy the 'ChakChak'," approvingly stated Marina. "These sweets are trendy nowadays. When I was young, you mainly had them only at weddings."

"They're delicious," I replied, still munching on a piece. "The honey and dried fruit go very well with the tea."

Having finished our dessert and tea, Marina Antonovna announced that she still had some work to do for the evening and rose to leave.

"I enjoyed the conversation this evening very much, and I hope you will seriously consider the opportunities with the hotel. Have a pleasant evening."

She walked out of the dining area and returned to her office. Adel accompanied me back to my room, where we shook hands and bid each other good night. I washed up, changed into my sleepwear, and looked forward to a long night's rest. Slipping under the comforter, I barely remembered feeling my head hit the pillow. Images of Tatar horse riders, with bows drawn, streaming across the Steppe into ranks of medieval Russian soldiers holding long lances and spears were flashing in my mind.

A persistent thumping sound jolted me awake, and I sat up and listened. 'Bang, bang, bang' echoed through the room. My watch on the night table blinked 1:40 in bright green. I climbed out of bed, ventured into the salon, and stood in the middle of the room. I listened. 'Bang, bang, bang' rang out again. The sound was coming from my door. Feeling drowsy and not thinking straight, I opened the door to find out who was keeping me from sleep.

She was standing at the threshold in an elegant blue dress. Dark black hair hung down, covering her bare shoulders. The deep red lipstick on her full lips formed a welcoming smile, with green eyes displaying an almost anxious look. She boldly stepped forward across the threshold into the small foyer and straight into the salon. Bewildered, I closed the door and followed her.

"Excuse me, but who are you?" I blurted out in amazement.

Without a reply, she strolled over to the couch and sat down. Her gaze invited me to join her. I sat on the sofa, wanting to find out who she was and devising the best way to get her to leave. Again, I asked her who she was.

"My name is Tamara."

"How do you know I am here, and why are you here?"

She shuffled closer to me and placed her purse with her small white hands on her lap.

"Kazan is a lonely place at night. We have several new clubs, however, that cater to businessmen."

She moved her hand from her lap and placed it on my thigh.

"Would you like to go to a club with me? I can take you there right now."

I stared at her in disbelief. Sitting in my sleepwear with her hand on my thigh, I was in no condition to just get up and leave with her. I used my hand to remove hers.

"Look. You seem like a nice woman, but I am exhausted. I'm not going out to a club. I just want to go back to sleep."

"Are you sure, my love?" She leaned in closer to me. "You will have a really nice time. There is champagne and dancing and lots of pretty girls."

More awake now, I began to think more clearly.

"I am not going out to a club with you. Thank you for your offer, but I have to ask you to please leave."

She sat there for a few moments while an awkward silence ensued. I was trying to think how I could get her to leave without causing a scene or an incident. She may have a bodyguard or someone nearby. I showed no interest in going with her and sat there quietly while I pondered what to say next. Suddenly, she stood up.

"I need to get some cigarettes. I am going to a store and will come back later."

"OK," I replied.

I saw her depart and quickly closed the door. Relieved, I turned off the lights and returned to bed. Sleep was elusive, expecting to hear another bang on the door. Fortunately, my visitor did not return, and I did not wake up again until morning: another hotel with the same nocturnal interruptions. The more seedy aspects of capitalism were becoming more prevalent. The goal was not to allow the bad to overshadow the positive elements of the new market economy and give ordinary citizens a chance to improve their lives.

# Credits, We Need Credits

I AWOKE TO BRIGHT SUNLIGHT streaming through the lace patterned curtains in the bedroom. While I waited in the salon for Adel to arrive, I turned on the television. There were four stations available; two showed cartoons, and one gave weather updates. The last program was dedicated to local news. A very stern-looking broadcaster talked about a recent speech by Tatarstan's President, Mintimer Shaimiev, who was planning his first official foreign visit to the former Soviet republic of Kazakhstan. Shaimiev, who had been Communist Party boss for the region in Soviet times, pushed for greater autonomy for Tatarstan.

In August 1990, Tatarstan adopted a Declaration on State Sovereignty, reducing control from Moscow. In June 1991, Shaimiev was elected as Tatarstan's first President. However, he supported the planners of the August 1991 coup attempt during which Soviet President Mikhail Gorbachev was briefly arrested. The ultimate failure of the coup hastened the final collapse of the USSR several months later, bringing Boris Yeltsin to power as President of the Russian Federation in which Tatarstan was officially a republic. In spring 1992, Shaimiev held a referendum asking Tatarstan's population whether the republic should be a sovereign entity. Sixty-two percent of citizens voted in favor of sovereignty. As a result, Shaimiev declared Tatarstan a sovereign nation; a new constitution was currently being drafted to reflect the republic's new status. As the summer of 1992 unfolded, the Yelstin government focused on strengthening its position in Moscow and tolerated greater autonomy for regions like Tatarstan. This tolerance would change as time went on, but Tatarstan was enjoying its newfound freedoms for now.

I heard a knock at the door. I turned off the television and walked over to open the door. Adel was standing there in his familiar collared work shirt with rolled-up sleeves, pair of worn jeans, and brown leather shoes. I invited him in as I went into the salon to gather my belongings for the day's trip.

"I was just watching the news. They were talking about Shaimiev's trip to Kazakhstan. Do you think Tatarstan will become a fully independent state?"

"I hope so," Adel answered. "We will maintain strong ties with Russia, of course, but we have had our own state before."

In 1919 during the Russian Civil War, the Bolsheviks created the autonomous Tatar-Bashkir Republic. Bolshevik leader Lenin promoted the idea of independent areas for non-Russian nationalities to garner support for the new Bolshevik state. Stalin, however, did not share Lenin's vision and gradually reasserted central control of autonomous regions such as Tatarstan in the 1920s.

We were heading to a small town called Zelenodolsk, about an hour's drive from Kazan. Passing the White Kremlin on our right, we crossed over the Kazanka River using a bridge built over the inlet from the Volga River on our left. The route Adel decided to follow led us along the Volga River areas. It was a scenic drive, reminding me of the view driving along Highway 1 in California. I peered across the driver-side window to gaze at the deep waters of the Volga. Scattered villages dotted the riverbank, while the other side consisted mainly of forest and plains. We drove through the outskirts of Arakchino, known for its uncompleted Temple of All Religions, a Gothic-style multi-towered structure housing inside spaces devoted to Muslim and Christian faiths. The village also was a familiar spot for ferries crossing the Volga. I wondered whether Arakchino was the inspiration for the famous 'Volga Boatmen' song I had heard so often while learning about Russian history. Continuing our westward journey, we passed smaller villages with names like Dubrovka, Gruzinsky, Safanova, and Aisha, places right out of the novels by Turgenev and Tolstoy. Turning southwest, the car reached the outlying areas of our destination.

Zelenodolsk, with a population of less than one hundred thousand, had been an important city in the USSR for the development of naval warships. As a result, the city's largest enterprise was the shipyard; many of the other town's industries operated to support the shipyard. Grain and food processing were major activities in the city, along with lumber and agricultural machinery. The town also boasted two technical colleges that focused heavily on naval engineering.

"With whom are we meeting?" I asked as we approached the center of the city.

"First, we have a meeting with the director of a lumber factory. After that, there is a machine-building plant I want you to see."

The car pulled into the parking area for a wood processing plant. We walked towards the adjacent two-story grey stone edifice, serving as the main building. What looked like a tool shed turned out to be a guard house. A man dressed in a military-looking uniform looked firmly at the new arrivals. Adel explained that we had an appointment with the plant director. Confirming our story, the guard escorted us through the main entrance. Several minutes later, a tall, thin man with bushy salt and pepper hair wearing a white-striped collared shirt, sleeves up, and a red tie walked briskly toward us.

"Welcome to our factory!" the man proudly stated and shook our hands. "My name is Nikolai Vladimirovich Kuzmin. I am delighted that you have come. Please, follow me."

We followed Nikolai Vladimirovich into a small meeting room off to the right. The plant director invited us to sit down at an oval, wood lacquered conference table. Some cakes and bread and bottles of mineral water lay on the table. The conference room walls were painted in faded green and decorated with pictures of various types of furniture and wood paneling. At the far end of the room hung a portrait of Mitimer Shaimiev. Sitting at the head of the table, Nikolai Vladimirovich smiled and handed us several glossy brochures describing the wood products made at the plant. The plant director gave us a brief factory history as we perused the information.

Founded in the 1920s during Stalin's massive industrialization program, the factory had made a vital contribution to the defeat of the Nazis in the

Great Patriotic War. It continued to thrive post-war by supplying plywood and furniture goods to the region, especially material for the shipyard. Under perestroika, the plant had fallen on hard times, struggling to transition away from the traditional command economy. The situation had become even worse in the last few years after the dissolution of the Soviet Union. The factory was now responsible for finding its suppliers and customers; a central planning ministry no longer told the factory whom to sell to and who would ship their materials. It was a very unnerving environment for management and workers.

"I think Western partners may want to invest in our factory or perhaps buy our wood and furniture," added Nikolai Vladimirovich. "Our prices will be low for them."

"The pictures in the brochures are very impressive," I replied. "Are you still making all of this today?"

"Da. We are not making the volumes in the past, however. We do not have the orders."

"Can we see the plant?" said Adel.

"Da, konechno. I would be proud to show you our facility. I thought we could take a tour, and then I will have my management team meet us here in the conference room to talk about investment possibilities."

"Great," I said. "I am looking forward to it."

We accompanied Nikolai Vladimirovich from the conference room and through a large set of steel double doors leading to a small dirt courtyard connecting the administrative building with an extended, rectangular red brick facility.

"This is our production area. Watch your step as you enter."

A cavernous space covered by an elongated A-framed aluminum roof opened up before us. To the left, several machines and lathes were visible. Many workers attended the machines while others pushed carts through the facility with stacks of wood polls and boards. Finished products were stacked up and awaiting shipment at the far end of the building. The noise level in the building was distracting. We approached several areas where workers were applying a coating to large wood discs spread out on a long steel table. A large machine connected to several exhaust tubes connected to the roof was cutting and grinding large wood sheets into discs. The plant director greeted the machinist and then addressed us.

"Sergei (the machinist) is applying varnish to these chair seats. At full capacity, we can produce two hundred seats per shift."

"What capacity are you at now?" I asked in an elevated tone due to the noise.

"Right now, we are making thirty to forty seats on a good day. Some days when there are no orders, we have to close down the station."

I nodded and asked Nikolai Vladimirovich if I could touch one of the seats. He went over to the end of the table, took one of the discs, and handed it to me, indicating that it was already dry. I ran my hand over the smooth, shining, yellow-tinted wood.

"What type of wood is this?"

"Birch." answered the plant director. "The forests here in the region are mainly birch, so most of our products are cut from birch trees."

In another area, lathes were spinning chair or stool legs into the proper shapes. Nikolai Vladimirovich stopped and explained the process in detail and current production levels. Next, we examined the finished goods inventory. Rows of chairs and stools were stacked two or three high. Behind the stacks, steel-grated doors were visible, which I assumed led to the loading docks for shipment.

"How long do you keep the product here until shipment?"

"We used to ship every other day, but recently we ship maybe once per week. Sometimes it is longer.

We do not have orders for all of the finished goods. We still make goods to keep the workers busy; otherwise, we pay the workers with the goods."

"Really?" I added in astonishment. "So, the workers are then responsible for selling the chairs or stools to get cash?"

"Da. It's unfortunate, but it is better than giving them nothing."

"Have you had to reduce your workforce?"

"Not yet. We do not want to fire workers. Where else will they find a job?"

With the collapse of the old system, payments among companies were inconsistent. Under the former structure, a complex credits system governed payments between the government and companies. Cash was not as crucial as in capitalist economies. Companies in the former USSR were now cash strapped during the transition to a new system. To avoid massive layoffs, many companies paid their employees with payment-in-kind, either with goods, the workers themselves produced or goods the company had received from its customers. Russian banks were in the early development stage of trade-credit rules and business financing, especially for small and medium-sized enterprises.

Back in the administration building, we entered a conference room where a small group was sitting around a wood lacquer table. Everyone stood up when they saw Nikolai Vladimirovich. There were three men and two women. All in their late forties or early fifties, the men wore attire similar to their boss; collared shirts with rolled-up sleeves, and each had a tie. The women appeared to be much younger than the men and wore business suits with a jacket and skirt.

"I would like to introduce my management team," began Nikolai Vladimirovich. "I think that you will find them quite capable."

He introduced each person, starting with the three men responsible for engineering, maintenance, and accounting. Next, he introduced the women. The first woman was in charge of personnel, while the second woman had responsibility for marketing. The plant director then addressed Adel and me.

"You see that we make an excellent quality product. We have much capacity to sell to foreign buyers. But, what we need is credits!"

The rest of the management team simultaneously nodded in agreement. I got the impression that Nikolai Vladimirovich expected me to tell him that I could immediately offer him investors or buyers. Adel seemed to understand this as well. He replied first.

"Nikolai Vladimirovich, your factory has a good reputation here in Tatarstan, and it has a long history of supplying good products. You know that the ministry (Adel's ministry) is working with you on several construction projects."

"Da. I am very interested in this opportunity with the Ministry of Construction. I understood, however, that your colleague is here to help us find western investors or buyers."

"I am here to evaluate *potential* investment opportunities," I added. "I need to understand the opportunity in detail before judging whether my contacts may be interested."

"What did you think of our factory? You saw and felt our products."

"The chairs and stools seemed very nice. However, I cannot evaluate your factory based solely on the plant tour. I would need much more detailed information."

"What type of information?" inquired the plant director.

"Well, for starters, I would want to see your financial information. Do you have accounting records and financial statements to see how you are doing financially? I'd also like to understand your sales and marketing strategy and plan. Can you provide me specifications for your equipment with available and current capacity usage? What is the ownership of the factory?"

"This information I am sure we can provide, but we need customers and credits."

"I understand, but no one will invest in a business without seeing your business plan and understanding how you will sell your products and make money."

"We are waiting for the customers to call us, but very few are calling. You see that we have products ready to ship. We need credits so we can buy materials and pay workers."

"Perhaps, Nikolai Vladimirovich," interjected Adel, "you can have your team explain the sales plan."

"Nina Andreevna," said the plant director, looking at the woman in charge of sales and marketing. "Please describe your sales plan."

Nina Andreevna shifted a little in her seat, pushed the bangs of her dark black hair to the side, and adjusted the flaps on her aqua-colored jacket. She placed her hands on the table and began explaining the plan to attract customers.

"Well, right now, we have three salespeople. They are trained and ready to receive calls from customers interested in buying our products. We receive several calls a week from customers whom we have worked for many years and who know our products."

I was a bit astonished by what I heard. The influence of Soviet thinking still permeated the management of such companies. The managers were intelligent and wanted to do right for the company but lacked an understanding of operating in a market-based economy. The entire economic system had changed rapidly, leaving managers and directors to figure out, without any assistance, how to become effective capitalists. The challenges were evident.

"So," I commented, "How will you inform new customers about your products?"

There was silence in the room. Neither the sales director nor the plant director seemed to grasp the essence of what I was asking.

"OK. For customers with whom you have worked in the past, how do you let them know what inventory is ready?"

"As I said, when customers call us, we let them know what is available," replied Nina.

"So if they don't call, you do not know if they want to buy?"

"Da"

"Have you considered asking your salespeople to call the customers, not waiting for them to call you?"

"Wouldn't they know when they needed to buy our products?"

It was evident that the sales director didn't know modern selling methods. Unfortunately, she and her colleagues were still accustomed to the prior system in which central ministries in Moscow told them whom to sell to and from whom to buy. I furthered my inquiry with her and her colleagues concerning obtaining new customers. The responses were the same. Nikolai Vladimirovich and his team expected me to provide new customers, namely western ones, to his factory. They did not understand how to develop new business. They needed a crash course in market economics to give them a foundation in capitalism, which would empower them to succeed. In the early nineties, this was an area where western governments, organizations, and companies failed to provide adequate assistance to help Russia and its citizens transition from communism to capitalism. Instead, the focus was on macro-economic issues and the natural resource sectors, where large west-ern companies saw considerable opportunities to buy cheap assets leading to big profits. The micro-economic picture at the individual company level was practically ignored, which arrested the country's development of a diverse market economy.

"Nikolai Vladimirovich," I said. "There may be an opportunity here to attract a western partner, but I would like to ask if you would be willing to provide me with some of the information I described earlier, namely financial information and capacity data. I can then review and discuss with my contacts when I return to Chicago."

"I would be happy to have my team pull this information together."

I informed him that the last two years of statements and any statements for this year would be sufficient. I added that any projections he may have would also be of interest. I took a shot and asked for bank records, but Nikolai Vladimirovich refused to agree to that. He agreed to have his engineering director provide me with all the technical specifications concerning the equip-ment and any capacity usage information. I decided to push my luck one more time and requested a description of the factory owners. This request, too, the plant director would not provide. I told him that any potential partners/inves-tors would need to know this information, but it could be dealt with later. He nodded. Adel then thanked Nikolai Vladimirovich for the tour and the time to meet his team and repeated that we would return to the factory later in the afternoon to retrieve the documents. That being said, Adel and I shook the hand of each member of the management team, thanking them for their time and input. Nikolai Vladimirovich accompanied us to the main entrance. Before we left, the accountant met us at the door and handed me a large stack of documents.

"I will thoroughly review the information," I promised the plant director.

I shook hands with the plant director and followed Adel back to the car.

"That was enlightening," I commented as I took my place in the front passenger seat.

"Yes, Nikolai Vladimirovich is a good man. He runs a good factory. He needs guidance and money."

"What he needs is someone to help him build a good business plan. I will think about how we could provide that."

"Ponyatno."

Adel began our journey back to Kazan. We followed the same route back. It was starting to get dark, but I took advantage of my position in the car. The passenger side now faced the river providing a better view of the Volga. It had been a long day, and the ride was generally silent. About halfway back, however, Adel broke the silence.

"What do you think about the factory? Will investors want to work with them?"

"It's hard to say. I will need to look at the information provided. I must say that the lack of a business plan or at least a sales plan will make it difficult. Even if there are no investors, these plants need to learn how to develop sales proactively. They cannot simply sit there waiting for the phone to ring. No one, a company or a bank, will give them 'credits' without proven sales or collateral."

"Yes, I agree. They have no idea how to find customers. I know that there is discussion in the ministry about sending managers to some kind of training, but this has happened only for large enterprises that can afford to send people to Moscow or even abroad."

"Maybe this is an opportunity to think about providing services to these companies to help them develop business plans. Can we speak with your ministry about this?"

"Sure. Maybe the ministry can fund or support this activity somehow, or encourage the factories that it is worth it to spend money on such services."

After that, we both fell back into thinking for the remainder of the journey. About half an hour later, Adel pulled up in front of the Hotel Kazan.

"Did you want to go grab dinner?" asked Adel.

"I don't think so. I am pretty tired. I might just get something in the hotel restaurant or gobble down a couple more nutrition bars."

"I have to try one of those bars sometime since you seem to enjoy them so much."

"Ha. Sure, I'll trade you some for some of Aliya's cooking...."

I grabbed my backpack and headed into the hotel. Inside my room, I got undressed, put on my sleepwear, and sat on the couch with two nutrition bars and a bottle of mineral water. I took out my other book, Dracula, and considered reading, but my eyes were too tired to focus. Instead, I turned on the TV and ate while listening to the evening news program. President Shaimiev's trip to Khazakstan was still the main story, so I finished my bars and dozed a little. Several more plant visits followed, but this day's experience made me question whether Americans and Russians grasped the immense gaps in expectations and realities.

# It's So Sweet

THE WINDOWS IN MY BEDROOM were still dark when the alarm buzzed at 5:00 am. For the next several days, we would stay in Naberezhny Chelny, an industrial city located about a four-hour drive east of Kazan. Before reaching the town, Adel had planned a stop to visit a confectionary plant. Adel arrived punctually as usual. The Hotel Kazan manager kept my room reserved until I returned later in the week, informing me she intended to review the hotel renovation project.

"Packing light?" I inquired mockingly, noticing my companion did not have a suitcase.

"It's only a few days. I do not foresee any problems."

We took a southern route out of Kazan taking the Orenburg Way. Having passed the Kazan Airport on the city's outskirts, the urban landscape quickly transformed into pastures and farmland resembling what one might observe driving through southern Illinois or Iowa. Beyond the vast plains, forest areas were visible, comprised of many birch trees. Scattered villages appeared as we continued south along Federal Highway 239. Barely legible road signs announced places such as Sokouri, Dezhavino, and Chirpovskoe, areas comprising small, mainly wooden dwellings. A few minutes later, we approached a village called Sorochi Gory or Magpie Hills. I gazed at the broad expanse of water directly before us while the car drove over the bridge spanning a large body of water.

"What river is this?"

"This is the Kama River. Our route will take us along the river to Naberezhny Chelny."

"It looks bigger than the Volga!"

"It's only a tributary, but it is the biggest one. It is bigger than the Volga, where it meets the Volga in Kazan."

I rolled down the window and peered into the fast-moving, brownish-colored waters of the river. The width of the crossing brought back memories of trips across the Mississippi River from southern Illinois to St. Louis. An artificial sand barge in the middle of the river connected both banks. he topography on the far riverbank continued to consist of plains and farmland. Villages became scarcer but larger than those closer to Kazan. We drove for roughly thirty minutes while the highway shifted north, following the river's flow. I saw a sign for the town of Chistopol.

"This is our stop," stated Adel. "There is a candy factory in the city, the owner of which I know."

"Candy sounds delicious... I hope they give free samples..." I said jokingly.

"I am sure you can get some free pieces. We will not be here long, just a quick tour."

We entered the outskirts of Chistopol via Engels Street. Chistopol was a quaint little town of fifty thousand inhabitants that ran right up to the bank of the river. Chistoe Pole (Open Field), founded in the late 19th century as a farming area, gradually became a port town in the 20th century. The city's primary industries were ship repair, sawmilling, and metalworking. Like many towns in Russia, a museum to beloved writer Boris Pasternak, whose writings in Russia were now widely available after years of censorship, had recently opened. Engels Street led to the city's main cathedral, Nikolsky Sobor, overlooking the Kama River. It was a beautiful white structure with several blue-domed towers. From there, Adel turned right into the heart of the town. Passing tree-line streets and squares, the vehicle turned left at a small park and headed into the town's eastern outskirts. A small two-story brick building with the sign 'Candy Factory' stood about a mile down the street. There were potholes in the parking lot, and the main building's red brick exterior was faded with noticeable cracks. There was no security guard like at the wood factory, so we simply walked into the main entrance.

"May I help you?" echoed a voice from a small booth just inside the door to our right. A middle-aged woman was seated at the reception desk.

"Da. I have an appointment with Sergei Sergeevich," Adel explained.

Standing in the hallway, I took note of the faded wood paneling on the walls. It took me back to my childhood when my father had installed similar paneling in our house. Several large framed photos adorned the walls showing pretty young women holding trays of various candies. In one of the photos, a woman presented a box of chocolates called 'Tsirk' (Circus). The wrapper depicted a dark-toned mouse, whose face resembled Mickey Mouse, dressed in a white shirt with a short black coat and gold and brown striped shorts. The mouse held a top hat and magic wand in his hands while juggling several balls in the air. "Maybe I will get to try one of these," I thought to myself. Suddenly, I heard a loud voice boom into the hallway.

"Adel, my friend, it's great to see you!"

I watched a thin man in his early fifties stride quickly down the hallway and shake Adel's hand. He wore what seemed the customary dark-colored suit jacket with slightly mismatched pants, brown belt, and maroon tie. In his coat buttonhole shone the red and green Tatarstan flag. His broad smile unveiled several gold-plated teeth, and his dark, busy eyebrows matched his jet black hair, which was slightly graying. Adel returned the warm greeting from his friend and introduced me.

"I am very glad that you have come," Sergei Sergeevich addressed me. "Now is just the right time for foreign investors to put money into our factory."

"I am happy to be here. I was just admiring the photo of one of your candies, the one with the circus mouse."

"Da, da. That is 'Tsirk'. It was very popular."

"Ah. So you are still making the brands used during Soviet times."

"Of course. Parents and children remember the pictures and names of the candies. We would be happy to produce western brands as well," enthusiastically finished Sergei Sergeevich.

"Sergei understands that we are on our way to Naberezhny Chelny but was delighted to have the opportunity to show his factory," added Adel. "Perhaps, there will be interest in producing sweets from your contacts."

"Great. Let's see the operation."

Sergei Sergeevich motioned to follow him back into the plant. We went about fifty yards before ascending to the second floor using a tiled staircase with iron railings. Cracks in several of the steps were easily noticeable. We entered a small concrete landing at the top of the stairs, where two large, heavy metal doors faced us. To the right of the doors hung a number of white lab coats. Sergei Sergeevich offered a coat to Adel and me. He explained that the coats would protect our clothing and the candy from possible impurities. The coat gave me slightly more confidence that the factory observed sanitation standards. Dressed appropriately, we followed our host through the metal doors and onto the production floor.

Several production lines stretched out before me. Although some had plastic shower caps and gloves, workers on the lines were not wearing any other protective attire. The equipment looked well-used and in need of replacement. The most disturbing thing was that the raw material (cocoa powder, sugar, color dyes, etc.) was sitting near the equipment in open bins or containers. Sergei Sergeevich walked over to a sugar-pulling machine and began to explain to us the process. It was hard to hear with the noise of the machines, but I nodded as we moved along the line, making hard candy. Approaching the end of the conveyor belt, I watched the worker operating a shape-forming machine. He cut long multi-colored cords of candy into smaller pillow-shaped pieces. Despite his shower cap, the face seemed familiar. He must have felt my gaze because, at one point, the man looked up from the machine. I recognized the facial features of Alexei, the man with whom I had shared the train ride from Moscow to Kazan. Alexei had told me that he worked in the Kazan region but did not mention working in a candy factory.

"Alexei! Skol'ko let, skol'ko zim!" (Long time, no see!) I shouted over the hum of the machine.

Alexei also recognized me and heartily shook my hand. The impromptu reunion surprised both Sergei Sergeevich and Adel. Alexei seemed hesitant to say more in front of his boss and turned back to his station. I explained to Sergei Sergeevich and Adel my acquaintance with Alexei. Sergei Sergeevich then signaled to Alexei to join our trio. He secured the machine and stepped into our group in the middle of the production floor.

"Alexei helped me survive my first solo train trip in Russia," I began. "He showed me the ropes and even taught me to play cards."

"He learned quickly," added Alexei. "He quit, though, when we started playing for money…"

Everyone laughed. I added that Alexei never mentioned his place of employment. Otherwise, I would have felt less awkward contributing my Snicker candies during our meal. There were smiles all around. Sergei Sergeevich indicated that Alexei had worked at the factory for several years and was one of the most dedicated machine operators. Alexei's facial expression was one of pride, and he stood up straighter.

"Why are you here, if I may ask?" inquired Alexei.

"My colleague Adel and I are examining opportunities for western investment, and Sergei Sergeevich is giving us a tour of the factory."

"That's great news! Everyone will be excited to hear that," responded Alexei.

"Let's not make that too public just yet," jumped in Alexei's boss, not wanting to start rumors.

An awkward silence signaled an end to the conversation, so I shook Alexei's hand and wished him well. The reunion with Alexei was a pleasant distraction from descriptions of production processes. Alexei was an excellent example of how, on a personal basis, Russians and Americans could develop close bonds of friendship. I hoped that I would someday get the chance to see Alexei again.

Next was a station that made milk chocolate candies. Several workers took a large square-shaped object resembling a wafer and placed it into a cutting machine that sliced it into smaller three of four-inch by quarter-inch bars. The bars were then inserted into cardboard boxes and put on a movable cart. A worker pushed the cart of bars towards the back section of the factory floor, where he stacked them on top of similar type boxes. Sergei Sergeevich explained that this was one of the company's newer products.

"Why is the candy just being left out in the open?" I asked. There was no air-conditioning on the floor. "Won't it melt?"

"Well, our temperature-controlled storage room is full," described Sergei Sergeevich. "We do not have enough orders shipping, so we have to stack the next produce over in the back area for now. Without more orders soon, then much of that candy will spoil, yes."

"So, why are you making more candy if you do not have any orders?"

"We need to keep the workers busy. If I don't make more candy, I will have to let them go. I have given them extra holidays, but I have to keep the operation going."

"Have you been calling customers or advertising?"

"Our sales director has her team ready to take any customer calls."

It was the same situation I had witnessed in Zelenodolsk. I didn't even bother to inquire about a sales or business plan. I knew one did not exist. Instead, I asked the plant director whether I could examine some of the candy. Sergei Sergeevich led us to the back of the building, where ten feet tall stacks of various candy products: chocolate bars, wafers, hard candy, etc., stood against the crumbling brick wall. Some of the sweets, such as the hard candy and wafers, had cardboard boxes that offered them some protection. Other products just sat there in the open, unwrapped or unboxed. A slight slant in one of the stacks was noticeable, where the lower levels tilted and slid off to one side due to melting. It was only a matter of time before the whole pile tipped over. Standing in front of one of the stacks, I removed one of the shoebox-sized cardboard containers and examined the sweets. Each piece had a tan-colored wrapper depicting a smiling Matryoshka doll with bold black letters reading 'Shokolad Detskii' (Children's Chocolate). I took a selection from the container. The texture was soft; my thumb and index finger quickly squished the piece. I showed Adel the crushed part and turned to face Sergei Sergeevich.

"This is a real shame," I said. "This candy is already spoiled. Is it possible to rent storage?"

"Nyet. No one has any available in town."

"Is it possible to taste one of the pieces in your storage room?"

"Of course. Follow me."

Adel and I tracked the footsteps of the plant director beyond the production area. We found ourselves on another short landing and descended another staircase to reach a polished concrete floor. Off to the right, I could see another room, the entrance to which was covered by large strips of clear plastic. Our host pointed us toward this area.

"We keep this room cold to prevent spoilage."

My skin reacted immediately to the drop in temperature. I felt scores of tiny goose pimples forming on my arms and neck. Small white puffs of air floated out with each breath. In this area, neat rows of pallets were positioned, comprising several levels of properly closed boxes. A pallet of the 'Shokolad Detskii' packed in tan and red boxes stood just to the right. I gave Sergei Sergeevich a look inquiring whether it was ok to open a box. Having received a look of approval, I carefully pulled back the box's cover. From inside, staring up at me were familiar rows of Matryoski. The texture of this candy was as expected: solid. I nibbled off one corner, tasting a strong sugar aftertaste. This candy was much sweeter than its American counterparts.

"This is good!" I blurted out, exaggerating a bit. "I can see why these were very popular."

"Yes, especially in Kazan," replied the plant director.

"Perhaps you could consider sending your sales team out to cities like Kazan," I suggested, "to build excitement by displaying the chocolate or give away some free in stores."

I asked Sergei Sergeevich for a few more pieces for the car. We navigated our way back to the front part of the building by the main entrance. Our host led us over to the reception area, where the receptionist handed him a thick folder. He turned towards us and gave me the thick grey dossier.

"Here is the information on our products," began our host. "I hope you will find it useful to attract a partner for our factory. As you can see, we make good quality candies."

"I look forward to reviewing it, and thank you so much for the tour and the samples."

"My pleasure. Have a pleasant journey to Naberezhny Chelny!"

Sergei Sergeevich and Adel gave each other a hearty handshake. I, too, shook hands with our host and wished him success. Back in the car, Adel asked me about my impressions of the candy factory.

"It's kind of the same story. The business needs investment, but even more, it needs management assistance. It's like you have changed the rules of a game but didn't explain the changes to the players. They just have to figure it out as they go along. A new rule book needs to be printed, distributed, and support available so that the players can succeed."

"Yes, but what can we do while the book is being printed?"

"I am not sure. Maybe some US companies will bring the management assistance plus the investment. But, it will be difficult to get them interested if all they see is a money pit."

"OK. Seryosha is a friend of mine, so please give his opportunity serious consideration."

"Naturally."

While discussing this, our attention was distracted from the highway. The last thing I remembered was that we recently passed a small village called Aleksandrovka. Suddenly, Adel's face took on a look of irritation while glancing in the rearview mirror. I decided to look at the side mirror to see what was disturbing him. In the reflection, I could make out a yellow automobile rapidly approaching us from behind. A blue light affixed to the car's roof became apparent as it got closer. The car had a blue stripe along the side, which read 'Militsia' (Police). The vehicle continued to accelerate, and the blue light started flashing. Visible on the front license plate were the letters GAI. GAI was the Russian acronym for the Main Directorate for Traffic Safety. GAI police were similar to American state police but reported to the Russian Ministry of Internal Affairs and wielded much broader powers than in the U.S. My companion's apprehension became clear. As a Russian citizen, Adel could be subject to an infraction, real or imagined. At the same time, as an American, I was fearful of being held in the rural region of Tatarstan, far from any American diplomatic representation.

"I have to pull over," dryly stated Adel. "Go find your passport."

Adel's request to locate my passport increased my anxiety. What if they confiscate my passport? How will I let anyone know where I am and what is happening? I followed his instructions and searched my backpack. Adel slowly moved the car over to the shoulder of the road. Holding my passport tightly, I looked again in the side mirror and saw the GAI vehicle pull up behind us. I watched an officer dressed in a dark grey military uniform exit the car. He wore a white belt across the waist of his jacket on which was attached a white holster containing his sidearm. Atop his head was a fur-lined cap with a red GAI badge. The officer walked up to the driver's side window. He bent down and examined Adel and looked across at me. It was evident he could tell that I was a foreigner. He addressed Adel.

"Where are you heading?"

"We just left Chistopol and are heading to Neberezhny Chelny. What did I do, officer?"

"Give me your papers."

Adel turned to me with his hand open, signaling me to give him my passport. Nervously I complied. He handed them to the officer, who took a step back and carefully examined the papers several times, glancing back into the car at Adel and me. I tried to keep a calm demeanor but could feel my stomach churning. Moments later, the officer ordered us to exit the vehicle. Adel stepped out of the car and stood directly in front of the officer. I left the car, walked around the front, and stopped next to Adel.

"What is this American doing here? Why are you escorting him around this region?"

Adel explained the purpose of my presence: I was here at the invitation of the Ministry of Construction for the Republic of Tatarstan and was visiting several factories in the region. The officer seemed unimpressed with the explanation.

"I want you to open up your trunk," the officer demanded.

"There is nothing in there but my colleague's suitcase," responded Adel.

"Open the trunk now!" repeated the officer in a firm tone.

This time Adel did not question the officer's demand. He quickly walked over to the back of the car and raised the trunk hatch. The officer strode over and peered into the trunk. His facial expression displayed concern.

"What is in the bag?" said the officer referring to my suitcase.

Adel looked back at me, still standing by the driver's side door.

"Just my clothes, Sir," I informed him.

He was surprised to hear me address him in Russian. I watched him instruct Adel to step to the side while he leaned into the trunk. The officer slowly stepped back, holding a small black bag. I recognized it immediately as my toiletries travel case containing my razor, toothbrush, etc. He removed a small clear plastic bag filled with multi-colored pills. To save space when I traveled, I would bring only the amount of my medication required for the trip, keeping them in a Ziplock bag for convenience. However, judging by the look on the officer's face, he considered the bag's contents more sinister. He looked up and motioned me to approach.

"Shto eto? (What is this?)" the officer asked me.

"Tabletki (pills)" I began. "They are related to my prescription medications. I did not bring the bottles with me for the trip."

"These are not narkotiki (drugs)?"

"Nyet, nyet. I do not use narkotiki. As my colleague said, I am here to work with local companies."

"Well, I am not sure. I cannot tell if these are narkotiki or not."

"I assure you, officer. They are just aspirin and my prescription pills."

"How can we convince you?" interjected Adel.

Still holding the plastic bag in his hand, the office turned pensive. He turned his face toward Adel.

"Well, I can simply fine you for carrying unidentified medication. We deal with drug traffickers in this area, but I don't yet see a reason to arrest you."

"How much is the fine?"

The officer fell once again into thought. Then, he turned towards me and declared.

"I think that $200 would be sufficient to settle this."

"Khorosho." I heard Adel say.

"Ladno", I replied.

I took out ten twenty-dollar bills from my wallet. Seeing the money in my hand, he returned the plastic bag to the travel case and tossed it into the trunk. I handed him the bills, which he counted. Satisfied, he handed back to Adel and me our identification documents. He instructed Adel to close the trunk. Before leaving, he warned us to be more careful as we might not run into such an understanding officer in the future. We thanked him for his consideration and returned to the car. I didn't even bother to check on the state of my travel bag and suitcase. We could do that when we got to the hotel. We sat silently in the car and waited for the GAI vehicle to drive away back towards Chistopol. Adel cautiously started the car again, put it in drive, and headed back onto the highway towards our next stop. A sense of relief descended on both of us.

"I do not want to go through that again," I finally said.

"Agreed. Usually, that is what these guys are looking for, a payout. It's a way to supplement their pay."

Adel chuckled, and we continued on our way to Neberezhny Chelny, hoping that the rest of the journey would be uneventful.

# Guns and Vodka

Neberezhny Chelny was mainly an industrial town dominated by factories and warehouses. We drove up to a compound protected by a tall gray metal wall with barbed wire along the top near the city's eastern edge. A guard in a military-style uniform stood at the main gate holding an AK-47 assault rifle. The armed man approached the car and asked about the reason for our visit. Having received confirmation of our visit, he waved us to proceed. We entered an expansive parking lot behind a long rectangular building comprised of fabricated steel siding. A sign, in red letters, over the main entrance indicated that the plant made electronic equipment. Adel parked the car close to the main entrance, and we headed towards the plant's main door. I glanced over my shoulder and witnessed a formation of a dozen or so men, dressed in tan military-style uniforms and holding an assault rifle upright in front of their chests, running along the perimeter of the compound. I stopped and watched them until they disappeared behind the building.

"Are they guarding or attacking this place?" I asked half-jokingly.

"They are the private security detail," replied Adel. "Most of them are former soldiers, and many served in Afghanistan. The pay is better than in the army."

"Is crime that bad?"

"The mafiosa is very well armed, and other companies sometimes use their security forces to intimidate rivals. It's necessary if you want to feel safe."

We continued into the main entrance pulling back one of the two heavy steel doors. Just inside the doors, we were met by another guard, also armed, standing by a reception desk. The receptionist greeted us and asked us to wait a few moments for the plant director. At the other end of the reception area, another set of metal-framed glass doors opened, and a sturdy built man stepped toward us. His gait suggested that he had hip or knee trouble with its slightly uneven pace. His hair was pure white but still held its youthful thickness. A pair of glasses hung from the breast pocket of his dark blue suit, which covered a white collared shirt and red tie. His high cheekbones compressed his grey eyes when he smiled, and they became noticeably smaller. A few gold-plated caps shone brightly among his otherwise yellowish teeth. The plant director introduced himself as Anton Borisovich Ivanov and gave us the usual warm welcome. We engaged in small talk and followed the slow walking, white haired Anton Borisovich back through the metal-framed doors, leading to a narrow stone-tiled hallway with conference rooms stationed on either side. At the end of the hallway on the right was a heavy wooden door with our host's name inscribed on a gold plate.

"After the tour, we will meet back in my office with some of my directors," explained Anton Borisovich. "I want you to see my plans for transforming the plant."

"Sounds good," I replied. "What type of products do you make?"

"Dashboard components for vehicles, cabling, and lighting devices"

In my head, I thought that this was the first director to mention having a plan. Leaving the hallway, we continued through another narrow wing built of concrete blocks that connected the administration area with the production area. We exited the connector wing into a large production area. An endless array of cables, wires, and exhaust tubes swept down the ceiling onto the production area like a massive octopus. Several production lines were visible, with workers scurrying between machines. The director handed Adel and me a hard hat and safety glasses and motioned us to follow him. Our first stop was a line that appeared to be making speedometers, which resembled a Frisbee and were larger than those I had seen before.

"These can't be for automobiles," I stated.

"No, we are making the components for the truck dashboards. We have a line for each device, and then we package all the components into the dashboard housing."

"How have your production levels been? Do you see a lot of slowdowns?"

"Nyet. Our largest customer sells its trucks primarily in Russia and the other former Soviet states. We have recently been increasing sales in street buses, so we will likely start making more parts for those."

"Impressive. So, why are you looking for a foreign partner?"

"I don't want to be totally dependent on one big customer that is free to choose new suppliers, and if they decide to work with some other enterprise, we will be finished."

"That makes sense."

"Anton Borisovich," interjected Adel. "Tell him about your idea!"

"I can discuss this in more detail in my office, but I want to find a partner interested in making small consumer goods like toasters and microwave ovens. Russia is in dire need of good quality consumer goods."

"I completely agree," I said. "I would love to hear more about your idea after the tour."

"Of course. Let"s move on to the other production areas."

The plant's equipment was well-maintained and clean. The workers wore immaculate matching uniforms. There were safety placards on equipment and around areas with dangerous materials. At least at first glance, the factory looked and ran like a western operation. I imagined that I might have found a serious candidate for an American partner. Anton Borisovich finished the tour and invited us into his office.

"Please, take a seat, make yourself comfortable."

The office was furnished with several leather chairs arranged around a wood-framed glass table. Off to the right, the plant director's wood desk and executive chair sat in front of walnut wood-paneled walls. Russian and Tatarstan flags stood side by side on the edge of the desk. There was a door just behind the desk also covered with walnut panels. In the back of the office was a large window with white embroidered curtains; next to the window, there was a bookcase and a small round tray table upon which sat several bottles of mineral water and vodka. Adel and I lowered ourselves down into adjacent easy chairs. The back of the chair was firm, but the leather cushion was worn and gave way quickly to my body weight. Anton Borisovich slowly went over to his desk to use the telephone. He made a quick call and returned to the easy chairs, choosing the one facing my colleague and me.

"I just informed a few of my directors to join us. I want you to talk with our sales director and marketing manager."

"May I?" I asked, pointing to one of the bottles of mineral water sitting on the coffee table.

"Please. Would you like some coffee or tea?"

"Spasibo, nyet. I really just need some water."

"I'll have coffee" said Adel.

Anton Borisovich got back up and made another quick call. He returned to his easy chair.

"You speak Russian well. Where did you learn it?"

"Spasibo. I studied Russian at university. I am enjoying getting to use the language. It is not so easy to find a Russian speaker where I live in America."

"Where do you live in America?"

"Chicago. It's in the middle of the ...."

"Chicago! Al Capone!" Exclaimed our host.

I had to laugh, which encouraged my companions to do the same. I was on the cusp of explaining the history of the Chicago mafia when there was a knock at the door. Anton Borisovich's gold teeth caps showed as he shouted to his guests to enter the office. The door opened, and a tall, slender blonde woman in her early thirties stepped into the office, followed by a short, stocky man with thinning brown hair and wide-framed glasses. Dressed in a chic white blouse and black skirt, the woman offered us a smile and moved slowly in her black stilettos across the room. She held her arms up in front of her body, carefully balancing a couple of thick binders, which seemed on the verge of escaping her grasp. I watched her walk behind the chairs opposite me to find a place next to Anton Borisovich. Before taking her seat next to her boss, she leaned over to place her binders on the coffee table. I observed, in astonishment, Anton Borisovich extend his right hand over the woman's back and gently pull on her back bra strap, which was noticeable under her white blouse. The woman's face showed slight embarrassment as she straightened herself back up. Anton Borisovich introduced the woman.

"This is Darina Samirovna Batyrshin. She is our Director of Marketing. She is a graduate of Kazan University and has been here for almost two years."

"Pleased to meet you, Darina Samirovna," I greeted her.

"Likewise," she responded.

All this time, the man, who accompanied Darina Samirovna, flanked his boss to the left. The plant director turned towards him.

"This is Mikhail Ivanovich Potemkin. He runs our sales department. He has some ideas on expanding our sales."

Mikhail Ivanovich bowed slightly and took his seat. We exchanged pleasantries, and Anton Borisovich began again.

"Darina Samirovna has put together some excellent marketing campaigns for us. I want her to show you her materials."

Having received her cue, the marketing director leaned forward and flipped open the top binder on the table. She unsnapped the binder clips and removed several brochures that featured an array of consumer goods such as microwave ovens, washing machines and dryers. She handed the materials to Adel and me.

"These represent the products we can make for Russia and foreign markets such as the Middle East and Asia where we sell parts for our trucks."

"We believe our contacts in these countries will help us find buyers," added the plant director. He turned toward his sales director. "Correct?"

"Da," answered the stocky Mikhail Ivanovich. "I have compiled some preliminary sales estimates."

"I have also prepared an introductory marketing campaign," added Darina Samirovna.

"This is wonderful!" I said. "May I see your projections and campaign plan?"

The sales and marketing directors pulled out some additional items from their binders and passed them along to me. Adel leaned over to look at what I was reviewing. There were multi-year, by-country sales forecasts for new products with prices and volumes. I handed the sales information to Adel to study the numbers more closely. I then turned my attention to the marketing campaign plan. I started to flip through the multi-page program that included proposed slogans and channel plans for each target market. There were timelines for market entry and expected costs for advertising, trade shows and other marketing events. It was a notable plan. I turned my attention back to Darina Samirovna to inquire about the basis for her expense estimates when I noticed that Anton Borisovich had placed the palm of his right hand on her thigh. I paused in my question while his hand moved along the outline of her skirt, almost reaching her waist.

"Where did you come up with your advertising costs?"

She shifted her left leg in an unsuccessful attempt to get her boss to remove his hand. She composed herself despite the situation.

"I called several media providers to inquire about rates, here in Russia and abroad. I used our past trade show expenses as my starting point."

"Good idea," I replied.

Still holding his hand on the thigh of his marketing director, Anton Borisovich added that he thought the plan was sound and was delighted with the work done by Darina Samirovich. He said he thought the plan would attract a foreign partner to invest in the enterprise. I struggled to focus as the plant director continued to touch his marketing director. I thought of mentioning how uncomfortable and unprofessional it was for the leader to harass a female employee. I imagined meeting with foreign investors while Anton Borisovich stroked the thigh of his marketing director. It would be a nightmare. Although Russian women had been full participants in the workforce since early Soviet times, even surpassing some western countries, they still did not generally receive equal respect and treatment from Russian men. It made me question how reliable a partner this man would be. Did he not perceive how western business people would be uncomfortable and unwilling to work in such an environment? His behavior distracted from all the good things he accomplished in his production operation. I returned to the conversation.

"There may be a real opportunity to find a western partner. Your production operation is solid, and you have put some serious time and effort into your planning. Are you looking for a partner to assist with operations or financing?"

"I think we need investment. We need funds to pay for the materials to make the consumer goods. With credits, we can make good profits, which will please any investor."

"The ministry will also help support with transition funds if we find the right partner," added Adel, who had been reviewing the materials.

"OK. Besides these materials, I would need accounting information for the last couple of years. Do you have these available? I would want internal numbers and any audited statements."

"I think we can get that for you. Let me make a quick call to our accountant," said Anton Borisovich as he got up and headed over to his desk. He talked briefly on his desk phone and looked up back at me.

"Can you wait twenty minutes? The accountant said it will take him a little time to print off our internal records."

I looked over at Adel. He indicated that we had enough time to wait for the information. I looked back over at our host.

"Sure. I have to use the restroom, so you'll have to excuse me." I replied as I got up to head into the corridor. Before I could leave, Anton Borisovich smiled at me and pointed to the door stationed behind his desk.

"Please, use my personal washroom."

I walked over to the door, turning the gold-tinted handle to enter. Inside, I closed the door behind me and flicked on the light switch. Following a couple of short flickers of light, the steady current illuminated a small but extravagantly decorated washroom. I found myself standing on white marble flooring interlaced with black lines and copper-plated dots. The lower half of the walls displayed pink marble. Intricate crown molding running about waist height separated the pink marble from vertical rectangles of white marble that reached the ceiling. The ceiling was painted in white stucco with a small but elegant chandelier hanging in the middle of oval-shaped, ivy-patterned crown molding. Standing just inside the threshold, I saw on my left a gold brimmed washbowl supported on a marble column pedestal. The faucet and hot and cold water handles were also gold plated. Standing next to the washbasin was a round, gold-plated end table on which numerous hand soaps and perfumes were displayed. The toilet had an adjacent bidet, with the seating area of both items covered by the same gold plating as the toilet paper holder. A long mirror ran along the wall on the other side of the washroom. Just beneath the mirror stood a marble-coated dispenser for throwing used towels.

The overall ambiance of the space made me feel underdressed. "This must be an executive perk," I thought to myself. Executives received stock options, private jets, and the like in the West. In Russia, I mused, the CEO gets a posh bathroom. This extravagance was a physical manifestation of the inequality between management and workers, albeit excessively. In Soviet times, members of the 'nomenklatura' or high Communist Party officials had access to particular stores, schools, and clubs. It seemed the practice was being adapted to the new market economy. I made sure to leave the washroom looking pristine before exiting.

"That is quite a washroom," I declared, shutting the door.

"It's one of the benefits of being plant director," proudly stated Anton Borisovich.

Adel gave me a strange look while the others seemed to acknowledge the existence of this 'benefit'. Our host is looking for investment, but how much did that washroom cost? Again, I tried to imagine a group of American investors thinking about putting money into a company after seeing that 'benefit'. Adel whispered to me that he wanted to know what was in the washroom. I replied that I would explain it in the car. We sat there chatting for several minutes when another knock at the door occurred. Another shout of 'enter!' and a scrawny, middle-aged man in a blue dress shirt and tan pants cautiously entered the office. He carried a thick white folder and several thin-bound documents, which I assumed were the audited reports. He approached Anton Borisovich.

"Ah, Gregor! There you are at last. Did you manage to get everything I requested?"

"Da," meekly replied the accountant. "It took some time to find last year's audit report."

"Excellent. Hand them to me."

Gregor transferred his burden to his boss, who made a motion like he was checking the weight of the documents. He handed the papers to me across the table. Gregor remained motionless.

"That will be all, Gregor, thank you," dismissed Anton Borisovich.

With a look of relief, the accountant took a rapid pace out of the office and closed the door.

"These documents with the sales and marketing plans should be enough to grab the interest of western investors," stated our host.

"It all looks good. I will review the financial data in more detail later. I look forward to discussing your enterprise with my contacts."

"Molodets (excellent)!"

"Anton Borisovich, I wanted to thank you for your time today," said Adel. "The tour and your presentation were interesting. However, we have to get going as we have another appointment."

Our host nodded and stood up, soon followed by the sales and marketing directors. Adel and I also rose to our feet. I, too, expressed my thanks to the plant director and his directors. The two directors left the office, so Anton Borisovich remained alone with Adel and me. We all shook hands, and our host escorted us back to the main entrance. I laid the documents in the back seat and took my usual place in the front. I peered through the windshield to see whether I could locate any more security force members but only noticed the guard at the gate. We passed through the gate, waved to the guard, and headed back west towards the hotel and park area. The glass factory was located on the western outskirts of the town.

"The plant is impressive, isn't it?" asked Adel as we drove through more industrial neighborhoods.

"Yes. That was the closest operation yet to something you would see in Europe or the US; at least, from a production perspective."

"Anton Borisovich is a smart guy. He is ambitious."

Adel turned onto Machinostroitel'naya Street (Machine Building Street), which ran west back through the middle of the town. I gazed at the rows of fabricated steel warehouses and factories.

"I agree. He has a plan and appears to have some competent directors. I'm sure he will find a partner."

"Do you think that one of your contacts in Chicago will be interested?"

"Perhaps. I do have some concerns with his unprofessional behavior, though."

"What do you mean?" Adel said sincerely.

"Come on. You didn't notice him harassing Darina Samirovna? He fondled her bra and stroked her thigh while we were trying to have a serious conversation. I could tell that she was very uncomfortable."

There was some silence for several moments. I wasn't sure whether my companion was searching for the right words to mitigate the plant director's actions or whether he just didn't consider the behavior to be something problematic. I thought the conduct would also have offended him, given his reaction to the phone call in my hotel room the other morning. I waited for him to respond.

"It is not uncommon for women to put up with these things," he started. "It was like that in the Soviet Union, and directors are used to acting that way. I would never do that to a woman, but it's a part of the culture."

"I understand, but if Anton Borisovich wants to impress and attract western and especially US investors, who act according to different standards, he has to and should display more professionalism and respect for his employees and women, in particular. In the US, he would likely be sued for harassment and maybe lose his position."

"Well, maybe he just needs some training."

"For sure, I would be very hesitant to put together a meeting with my contacts and risk having a scene like today."

"OK. I will follow up with him."

"And, what was with that luxury washroom? Have you ever been in there? That must have cost a fortune! And he wants to ask for investment."

I noticed that the street we were driving on had now become Volga Highway. Another lane expanded the route, and some urban housing developments were visible off the left. "That must be where the plant workers live," I thought to myself. The housing was quite a distance from all the factories and warehouses. I imagined packed busloads of ordinary Russians making their way each morning from these concrete apartment blocks to the numerous production facilities scattered around the town. It brought back my public transport experience in Moscow when I had to fight for a spot on the bus to see Adel at the police station.

"It's a symbol of power and authority," answered Adel, bringing me back into the conversation. "These guys still want to hold on to the privileges they enjoyed as important Party members."

"I can appreciate that, but it says to an American that he is a narcissist and doesn't care much for his employees. I mean, we have the equivalent in the US with big CEOs flying around in private jets."

"Well, you must remember there were a lot of material deprivations in the Soviet Union, even for higher-ups, especially in the last few decades (Adel was referring to the late Brezhnev period and scarcity conditions under perestroika). There is a feeling that if I earn some money now, I want to buy things I couldn't."

The Volga Highway made a sharp turn to the right, and we followed it almost to the bank of the Kama River. We exited at an offramp just before crossing over the river. We continued to head west, hugging the southern bank of the river. A narrow, artificial sandbar to the right ran parallel to the river bank and supported the bridge's columns, allowing the Volga Highway to traverse the river. The western edge of the shoal was undeveloped with clumps of trees and bushes mixed in with sandy terrain and only a couple of hundred yards from the river's shore. As we pulled into the parking lot, the plant came into view. It was a small two-story rectangular edifice constructed of grey concrete bearing a series of windows on each floor and a dark blue 'Glass Fabrik' sign affixed just below its flat roof. The main entrance, covered by a thin metal grey awning, was situated on the narrow side of the building. In front of the main entrance, there was a little grassy area, which contained several short trees. The owner had attempted to create an ascetically pleasing welcome space for visitors. Behind the small administration building was a much taller and longer windowless grey facility, which housed the production operations. This facility must have been at least a thousand yards in length; a smokestack was towered at the far end of the facility. It had a wavy roof spotted with several HVAC and exhaust vents. Adel and I entered the car through the grey steel doors.

"Can I help you?" asked a man wearing a dark blue jacket and matching hat with the words 'Okhronik' (Security) depicted on his jacket lapel. The man was standing to our right behind an enclosed glass partition with a metal desk, two small monitors, and a bank holding three walkie-talkies. I could see that he was wearing a heavy utility belt with a sidearm. Adel approached the glass to explain the reason for our visit. While he was speaking with the okhronik, I studied the design of the tiny administrative area. Professionally done photographs of snow-covered mountain ranges hung on the pea-green concrete walls alongside desert scenes. In the middle of the hallway were several photos of large gatherings of employees, all dressed in similar colors and styles. At the far end of the hallway, I could see a series of wood-framed glass double doors on either side of the walkway, leading to conference rooms. A stairwell rose from the area past the conference rooms.

"OK, we are all set," Adel said. "The plant director should be here momentarily. I have known Razil Damirovich for quite a while. He is a smart guy but a little flashy. What do you say in America, larger than life?"

"Yes. A big personality."

"For sure. He was the director here before Yeltsin, but he has quickly picked up business savvy."

"Yasno"

Right on cue, a dark-haired middle-aged man sporting a shiny silver suit descended the stairwell at the other end of the hallway. A broad smile was already discernible on his somewhat darker complexion. He wore wing-tipped shoes and a maroon handkerchief neatly tucked into his left breast pocket with a matching tie to complete the ensemble. He raised his right hand as he moved closer to our position. Adel returned a wave with his right hand. We stepped forward to meet our host.

"Adel! How have you been? It's so great to see you," said the plant director, almost in a shout.

"Razi! Everything is great," replied Adel, extending his hand to the plant director. "Razi, I'd like you to meet my colleague from America."

"A pleasure to meet you! Razil Damirovich Zaripov."

I returned the greeting and shook our host's hand. He had a tight grip, and the length of the grasp allowed me to observe a glittering gold watch clinging loosely to his wrist. He looked directly in my eye and held his smile, which displayed what I considered to be professionally whitened teeth. The plant director then invited Adel and me to follow him down the hallway, past the conference rooms, and under the stairwell. Behind the stairs along the back wall were several offices. Razil Damirovich led us into the largest one in the right-hand corner. The office was comfortably furnished but not overdone. A sizeable wooded desk sat in the back corner of the office, while an oval conference table stood in the middle of the carpeted space. A sofa boxed in by two end tables was opposite the far wall opposite the desk. More nature scenes and the usual standard photo of Tatarstan's President were displayed on the walls. Before getting comfortable, Razil Damirovich explained he wanted to give us the customary tour.

We exited the administration building from his office through a door on the left, taking us into the beginning of the main production area. The floor was made of polished concrete. A walkway was outlined by yellow lines along the floor to help avoid accidents. Putting on hard hats and protective eyewear, we followed the plant director along this walkway to a station that contained a row of machines resembling long cylinders laid horizontally and supported by block columns. Each machine had an exhaust tube running from the top side all the way up to the flat ceiling about ten yards above. Attached on either side of the cylinders were conveyor belts. I could feel the heat emanating from the conveyor belt strike my face. Opposite the conveyor, a worker sat behind an immense control panel to monitor the process.

"We make flat glass primarily," explained Razil Damirovich. We are standing in front of the cooling area. These cylinders apply cooling to the heated glass, which is fed from that conveyor belt (he pointed to his left). The glass then proceeds here (he pointed to his right), where the cooled glass is smoothed into one continuous sheet. From there, we cut it to the proper size where it is transported to a loading area and lifted onto carriers to be stacked until shipment. It's a pretty simple process."

I looked in the direction of the loading area and saw two large yellow forklifts holding vertically stacked sheets of glass. One backed up cautiously, turned around, and then slowly moved down a long pathway until it disappeared from view. Feeling warm from the continuous heat, I asked our host what the source was.

"Back behind the belt, we have a smelting furnace, which feeds the raw material into the float bath (the conveyor belt giving off heat)."

The plant director then led us toward an area about one hundred fifty yards away. A space jetted out from the walkway, covered by brick walls, and a tarpaulin roof harbored several pallets with stacked sheets of finished glass. Our host informed us that the glass stayed here until shipment, which generally was within a few days; the local construction boom was driving up his business. Admiring the inventory of glass, I noticed an enormous square chunk of glass placed against the far wall. It looked about four or five feet high and must have been several feet thick. Its thickness gave it a yellowish hue. My curiosity got the best of me.

"Razil Damirovich, what is that large piece of glass standing there?

The plant director glanced in the direction of the block. A smirk came over his face as he walked over and lightly caressed the smooth surface. His eyes betrayed a hint of nostalgia when he turned back to look at me.

"This," he said, "...this block is a reminder of from where we have come. This block is what we used to make to satisfy the annual output quotas from the central ministry in Moscow."

The look of confusion on my face must have been unmistakable.

"The chinovniki (bureaucrats) in Moscow would give us a target for how many kilos of glass we needed to produce each year following the Five-Year Plan. There was no concern about the quality of the glass or whether the glass met certain specifications. Therefore, when we found ourselves behind the plan, we would simply make large glass blocks, like this, useless to anyone, but it counted against our quota."

"It caused problems for construction," contributed Adel, "when, for example, windows would arrive for a building site, we were never sure that they would fit or be durable enough."

"So, there were no inspections?" I asked in amazement.

"Of course," replied Razil Damirovich. "The ministry would send inspectors to examine the plant and to review our records, but finding problems would cause more work for them and, on occasions when an inspector did want to report something, a little 'maslo' (bribe, literally: butter/grease) would take care of the issue."

"There are no bribes nowadays?"

"Well, let's just say that our customers now are more demanding. Problems still arise from time to time…but those can also be resolved."

The tour finished, we returned to Razil Damirovich's office to meet his management team and talk about investment over lunch. Place settings were laid out on the oval wood table for five people; baskets of rye bread were lying at each end of the table, and in the middle stood several bottles of vodka. The director quickly called to inform the others that we were ready for lunch. Adel and I took seats at the table adjacent to Razil Damirovich.

"I hope you like Tatar cuisine because I have had some delicious plates prepared for us today."

"I have been getting a crash course during my stay. So far, everything has been wonderful."

"Excellent. Have you had Echpochmak yet?"

"Nyet. What is it?"

"Ah, you are in for a treat!" gaily exclaimed our host. "Adel, would you like to explain to your friend what Echpochmak is?"

"Of course," answered my companion.

But, before he could tell me, there was a knock at the door. Razil Damirovich shouted that the guest could enter. A tall, lanky man with overgrown bushy reddish hair entered the office. He was followed by another man of about equal height, older and much heavier. Both men wore dark grey suits with blue ties, which hung a little too far past the belt buckle. Thick grey file folders were tucked under the arms of both men as they occupied the remaining seats at the table. The man with ginger hair was the sales director, and his colleague was responsible for production operations. Both men appeared slightly nervous; there was noticeable fidgeting with their hands and posture. Smiles replaced the look of uncertainty when the plant director repeated that Echpochmak, apparently a rare treat at the factory, would be served for lunch. There was a knock at the door, and a short, stocky middle-aged woman pushed a cart containing lunch into the office.

"Ah, Masha," began Razil Damirovich, "bring the plates here. Please serve our guests first."

Masha complied with her boss's wishes and served me a white plate with three triangular hand-sized pastries. On the top of the light brown pastries was a thin ridge of crust formed by the folding over of the dough. The pies were warm and had a soft-baked texture. A meaty broth accompanied the pastries.

"This looks wonderful," I commented. "What is inside?"

"The dough is filled with onions, potatoes, and minced meat," Adel said. "Sometimes, a small hole remains on top, and the broth is poured inside. Try it!"

I took my fork and severed off a corner of the first pastry. It was a salty mix of meat and potato and gave me the sensation of eating a potpie. The meat was very tender and moist. Satisfied with my look, Razil Damirovich gave a hearty laugh and invited everyone to enjoy lunch. No one hesitated. After a few moments, our host got up and grabbed one of the bottles of vodka from the middle of the table. He unscrewed the top and freely filled each of our glasses.

"Na zdroviye!" he stated, still standing with arm outstretched.

"Na zdroviye!" everyone responded.

We all drained our glasses. Then, the plant director quickly refilled them. Another toast: To friendship! Again, we drained the glasses. A third toast quickly followed: To Success! A third time I swallowed down the vodka. I still hadn't finished my three pastries, and my head was starting to spin. Lunch continued in this fashion. A few smaller dishes were served: another pastry-like plate called Kystyby filled with potatoes and porridge. More toasts followed each dish. I was having a hard time concentrating on the discussion by this point. I realized that Razil Damirovich had asked his directors to explain their plans to Adel and me, but I could not comprehend them. I consumed an increasing amount of bread and dough to offset the vodka.

At last, the lunch ended and, I hoped, the toasts as well. None of the bottles of vodka remained full. After removing the lunch plates, a type of tea, called sherbet, was served. It was very sweet and tasted of strawberries. After tea, the two managers departed, while Adel, the plant director, and I retired to the couch behind the table. I sunk into the soft cushion and tried to pull my thoughts together, not wanting to make a poor impression on our host. "Perhaps," I thought, "I should apologize and ask Adel to head back to the hotel." Suddenly, Razil Damirovich, who had lit a cigarette and sat next to me on the couch, put his arm around my shoulder and declared:

"Well, my boy, that was a great lunch, no?! This plant has a bright future."

"Da. It all seems wonderful," I replied, hoping he didn't ask for specifics.

"Yes, I agree," added Adel, who had somehow managed to appear to be sober.

"It's such a beautiful day," stated our host, "enough of business! Let's go shooting!"

I thought at first that the vodka had affected me more than I realized. I gazed over at Adel, whose face expressed skepticism.

"Razi, I am not sure that that is a good idea," began Adel. "We finished quite a few bottles over lunch. By the way, where would we get a gun and shoot?"

"We only had three bottles, and I feel fine. I have a rifle here in the office. I got it from the security team. Trust me, you and Ken will love it!"

"But, where can you shoot? We are in an industrial area."

"We'll go to the sandbar under the bridge. I have a small boat by the bank. It's only a five-minute ride to the sandbar."

"Won't the police be concerned?"

"Nah, they know all about it."

I didn't say a word. I wasn't sure that I could walk properly, never mind get in a boat and shooting a rifle. I wondered if we should politely decline and just head back to the hotel. I leaned into my companion and whispered such into his ear. He shook his head gently.

"All right, is everyone ready to go?" asked our host.

He got up from the couch and went to the far corner of the room. I watched him pick up the receiver on his telephone, speak a few words, and then hang up. He approached a green metal cabinet similar to a sports locker. He leaned down and spun the dial on the door lock. He made a few dial spins and then pulled on the door handle, which opened without effort. He reached into the cabinet and withdrew a long rifle. It was easily identifiable as an 'Avtomat Kalashnikova' or AK-47 assault rifle with a brown wooden fixed stock, black metal frame, and banana-curved magazine. The AK-47 rifle was popular in many movies, such as Red Dawn and the First Blood series, but I had only seen one up close that one time at the snow picnic in Khabarovsk.

Dressed in his suit and holding the rifle in one hand, Razil Damirovich waved to Adel and me to follow him. The plant director had also thrown a small gym bag over his shoulder, which I assumed held ammunition. We followed him out of the office to a small gravel clearing, where two men dressed in black fatigues were standing next to a small ATV-like vehicle. Razil Damirovich greeted the men and handed them the rifle and gym bag. The sunlight glared into my eyes, causing me to shield my face. Just before boarding the vehicle, I heard my name pronounced.

"Ken? Eto ty? (Is that you)?"

I raised my head cautiously, placing my right hand just above my forehead. Dressed in black fatigues and wearing a black cap was the smiling face of Sasha, one of my travel companions from that fateful train trip from Moscow to Kazan. His blonde hair was tucked neatly under his headgear, but I recognized those dancing blue eyes and thick red lips. Sasha had been on his way to Tatarstan to find work after leaving the military. Seeing him now reminded me of his desire to obtain employment outside of security work. Alas, it seemed, he was unsuccessful.

"Sasha! Kak dela? (How are things?)," I exclaimed. "I didn't know that you were working here."

Realizing that he might have spoken out of turn, Sasha looked reticent and stood motionless while looking at Razil Damirovich, who had turned his head around upon hearing my name. I turned back to our host.

"Razil Damirovich, I spent an interesting train ride from Moscow to Kazan in the same compartment with Sasha here. Sasha was my partner while we played 'Durak'. He told me that he was returning home after the army, but I didn't know he worked for you."

"Ah, now I understand. Yes, we have hired quite a few former soldiers for our security detail. Plant security is becoming increasingly important against the influence of mafiosa and such."

The plant director let his new security man know it was ok to speak with me before we set off. I listened to Sasha summarize his unfruitful search for a non-military job. He was lucky and thankful (he stressed this) to his boss for the opportunity to work at the factory. I would have liked to have spent more time with him, but our host was anxious to get moving. We said short goodbyes and expressed the hope to see one another again. I waved to Sasha as we pulled out of the gravel clearing and headed toward the river bank. The south side of the river was situated only a few hundred yards from the edge of the factory premises. We drove along a couple of small backroads winding his way to the entrance of a narrow sandy area bordering the river. My companions and I crawled out of the ATV and stood with our dress shoes in the sand. The security guard took the rifle and gym bag and handed them back to his boss. Razil Damirovich led us off several yards to the right to an area covered with bushes.

A short wooden jetty tied to a small pontoon boat was behind the bushes. Our host explained that he had the jetty built to shield it from prying eyes. He instructed us to step into the boat while he prepared for departure. Adel lowered himself down first into the flat-bottomed watercraft. He extended his hand to steady me as I stepped into the gently swaying boat, resting in one of the hard plastic seats in the middle of the craft. The plant director then jumped into the vessel with the rifle and gym bag. The security guard was the last to come in the boat, having leaped onboard shortly after he unmoored it. The guard busied himself with starting the small outboard engine. Razil

Damirovich checked to see that his guests were secure and gave the order to pull away. I felt a slight jerk as the propulsion from the engines broke the boat's inertia. We then moved calmly away from the jetty into the river's current. The shoreline of the sandbar was already visible. Clumps of trees and sand sat several hundred yards opposite our position. I looked to the right and watched cars moving swiftly over the bridge supported by columns constructed on the sandbar. In about five minutes, the boat jerked us forward as it rode up onto the shore of the sandbar since there was no jetty, which might attract too much unwanted attention.

Our destination reached, the man in fatigues turned off the engine and moved to the front of the boat, where he jumped down into wet sand. He extracted a short step ladder that he attached to the bow. We followed Razil Damirovich down this narrow step ladder onto solid but damp sand.

"We have to move about fifty meters into the wood line so that we have some privacy and to muffle the sound," explained our host as he moved off in the direction of a gathering of trees.

The heat of the day was reaching its peak, and I was glad to hear that we would be in a shaded area. A narrow footpath led into the clump of trees. I struggled to maintain my balance as I stepped over rocks and branches. About thirty yards later, we came into a small clearing surrounded by trees and bushes. Razil Damirovich planted his gym bag and rifle next to a worn tree trunk about four feet high. He removed his suit jacket and necktie, laying them carefully on the trunk's flat surface. Adel and I followed suit, hanging our jackets on a couple of thick tree branches to keep them from getting soiled.

Holding a bunch of paper in his hand, the security guard walked past us and headed off to our left. I watched him approach a row of tree trunks about twenty or thirty yards in the distance. The tree bark bore multiple holes, likely wounds from previous shooting outings. This excursion was obviously not the first time our host had come here. The guard walked behind the trees and picked up what looked like plywood sheets, which he attached to thin metal rods that stuck up vertically from each stump. Then he unfolded the pieces of paper and affixed them with tape to the plywood sheets. These were paper targets. A series of concentric circles stared back at us. The sheets were protected from behind by another cluster of trees, although I was sure some rounds would find their way through the trees into the river. Hopefully, no unsuspecting ship would be passing by. His prep-work completed, the guard returned to our position.

"Is everything all set, Maxim?" inquired the plant director.

"Yes, Sir," replied the guard.

"Molodets. You have both fired a weapon before, yes?"

"Razi, you know I did during my army training," retorted Adel.

I had shot a .22 caliber rifle as a Boy Scout, but I had no experience with assault weapons. I thought I had mentioned that before we left the office, but I couldn't remember. I was still feeling tipsy and was in no rush to fire anything that could kill me or anyone else. Adel seemed to understand my hesitancy.

"I have never fired an assault rifle like that," I said. "I am happy to watch you do it."

"Maybe you should shoot a bit, and we can watch," added Adel.

"Nah, I do this all the time. I want Ken to feel the power of the AK-47."

The plant director invited me to come forward to show me how to use the weapon. He held the rifle with both hands with the barrel pointed into the ground. The magazine was attached. He extended his arms upward so that I could take the weapon into my hands. I could feel its weight as I took hold of the assault rifle. The wooden stock was smooth; the metal receiver section felt cool. Razil Damirovich instructed me to keep the barrel downward and turn my body towards the targets.

"Place the stock up into the crux of your shoulder," he continued placing an imaginary weapon into position on his body. I did as instructed.

"Now, bring your head down, so your nose almost touches the stock. Do you see the front sight?"

I placed my nose almost directly behind the rear stock. I stared down the top of the barrel. I saw a small metal post at the end, which I took for the front sight.

"Da." I answered.

"OK, now close your other eye and focus the right eye on the target placing the front sight in the center of the target."

My head had cleared a bit. I was still struggling to focus my thoughts, but I did my best to concentrate my gaze on the distance group of thin circles set on the white background of the target. I let Razil Damirovich know that I was focused on the target.

"Great. Now slowly pull the trigger. Do not jerk it."

I put my index finger into the trigger well and started to exert pressure on the metal latch. Then, I thought for a moment. "What if I shoot wildly? Will I hit someone or something?" I hesitated and lowered the weapon.

"I have never shot before. I don't want to shoot blindly."

"Don't worry, Ken," encouraged our host. "This is just practice. There is not a round in the chamber."

Feeling more reassured, I raised the weapon again and tucked it tightly against my shoulder. I pulled on the trigger until I heard a 'click'. I still half expected a bullet to exit the rifle, but there was no sound or motion from the weapon. I lowered the gun again and extended my arms with the intent to hand it back to my instructor. I received a look of approval from the plant director. Apparently, my practice attempt had met his standards.

"Nyet, nyet, you have to fire a live round," declared Razil Damirovich refusing to accept the rifle.

"Khorosho, how do I load one?"

He explained how to pull back the charging handle to push a round from the magazine into the chamber. Using my left hand to brace the rifle against my shoulder, I gripped the charging handle with my right hand and pulled the lever back towards my face. It required a bit more pressure than I expected, but at last, I felt the round enter the firing chamber. I repeated the steps followed during my practice attempt. With my aim steady on the target, I pulled again on the trigger. I was surprised by the loud crack that burst into the air as the round exited the barrel. I felt the strong impact of the recoil from the buttstock strike against my shoulder. This unexpected force made me stagger a few steps backward and almost knocked me off my feet. Dazed, I did not even notice where my round had landed or whether it had struck the target. The weapon was still in my hands; the barrel pointed towards the target. Razil

Damirovich slowly walked toward me and placed his left hand on the barrel to lower the weapon. He had a broad smile and an air of pride.

"Otlichno (exceptional)!", he started. "Not bad for the first time. I think you even hit the plywood. Maxim, did you see where the round struck?"

"It chipped off a piece of the upper left corner, Sir. He pulled it up because he didn't let out his breath," responded the guard.

"Ah, right. I neglected to tell you not to breathe in when you pulled the trigger," stated Razil Damirovich.

"No problem. Shall I try again?"

"Sure, take as many shots as you want. This time remember to let out your breath and hold it before pulling the trigger."

Having survived the initial experience, I felt my confidence grow. I held the weapon more securely against my shoulder to dampen the recoil effect and bent my knees slightly to help steady myself. I did not feel tipsy anymore and focused my attention on what I was doing. I retook aim and fired several rounds in rapid succession: 'crack, crack, crack' echoed into the air but did not surprise me. I was better able to absorb the recoil, which allowed me to put one of the rounds onto the target. I was starting to feel like I could handle a weapon.

"This is not as hard as I thought," I declared. "It's rather fun."

Our host laughed. "OK, let's see a real expert do it."

Maxim approached me and signaled to me to hand him the weapon. I readily transferred the rifle into his steady hands. He motioned for me to step back. I watched him assume a tactical stance and move towards the targets shooting in automatic mode. The noise was almost deafening as a steady stream of rounds exploded into the targets, shattering pieces of plywood in all directions. Maxim emptied one magazine and had seamlessly ejected it, replacing the empty one as he moved. It was an impressive display of skill and made me realize how amateurish my attempt had been. Maxim ejected the second magazine, cleared the firing chamber to ensure no rounds remained and returned to our position. He presented the weapon to his boss and retook his place off to the side.

"Wow!" I exclaimed, "that was something. Where did Maxim serve?"

"Maxim was a Spetsnaz (Special Forces) member and spent several years in Afghanistan," explained our host.

"These guys are top-notch and not to be messed with," added Adel, who also seemed impressed by the guard's exhibition. "Their training is much more advanced than we received in the regular army."

"I guess you are lucky to have him as part of your security team," I commented to Razil Damirovich. "I sure would feel much safer."

"I have a twenty-man team. Most members, like your friend Sasha, have prior military service, but only a few have Maxim's skill. You have to protect your assets since there are no good legal options."

I recalled America's experience in the 1920s when companies maintained private security forces due to the rising influence of organized crime or to quell unionizing efforts. Russia appeared to be going through a similar experience. It remained to be seen whether the country would take steps to create a society based on the principle of the rule of law or would it fall back on its historical tendencies where a ruling elite remained above the law and corruption flourished. That was a pivotal question for not only the Russian government but also for the Russian people. A spirit of hope continued to exist for now, but for how long would it last.

We continued to take turns shooting for about an hour until the ammunition was exhausted. My accuracy improved with each attempt. By the end, I even felt skillful enough to try fully automatic. Everyone collected the spent shell casings which littered the area. We tossed the carbon-stained metal containers into the gym bag. The day's heat was now passing, but we decided to sling our suit jackets over our arms as we walked back along the path towards the river bank. Maxim held the boat steady when we reached the sandbar's edge, allowing us to safely climb back into the craft. After storing the rifle and gym bag, we took our seats on the board. Maxim then pushed the vessel back into the water, making sure to jump on board before drifting too far out. He glided to the stern and started the engine. Five minutes later, we found ourselves back at the short jetty on the southern bank of the river. Maxim jumped from the boat onto the jetty and secured the vessel. We exited the craft, made our way to the ATV, and returned to the plant. Adel and I thanked Maxim for his services and shooting exhibition. He nodded in acknowledgment and drove off.

"Well, that was fun, wasn't it?, stated Razil Damirovich, sitting again at this desk.

I had to admit that, despite the rocky start aided by too much vodka, the excursion to the sandbar had been an exciting experience. "I enjoyed learning how to shoot!" Yes, thank you for suggesting that, Razil Damirovich."

"While we were gone, I had my team collect the documents for my business that you can review and discuss with your contacts in America."

Our host indicated a tall stack of files lying on the oval conference table. I was glad the plant director provided this information since I had not engaged fully in the discussion over lunch. I thanked him for the information and added that I looked forward to reviewing his investment plans. Adel chimed in that it was getting late, and we needed to head back to the hotel. Razil Damirovich proposed one last toast before our departure. I wanted to refuse, but I remembered Adel's advice not to insult his friend. Thus, we raised our glasses one last time: To the Future! The alcohol stung my throat as it went down, but I managed to keep the smile on my face. At the door, Adel and his friend exchanged hugs and cheek kisses. We exited the building and strolled to the car.

"I didn't think I was going to make it through all that," I blurted out when we regained the main road towards the hotel.

"I tried to tell you that Razi was larger than life."

"I keep trying to limit how much vodka I drink, but it doesn't work. I don't know about you, but I barely remember what we discussed over lunch."

"I understand. It's a cultural thing. It might be best to finish all our business discussions before lunch."

"For sure," I laughed.

Back at the hotel, it was difficult to fall asleep that evening despite my weariness. I felt the lofty expectations weighing heavily on my mind. Perhaps someone more experienced could have contributed more to help sow the seeds of democracy and free markets in Russia. The window of opportunity for Russia and America to forge a lasting partnership was already closing. Both sides' initial euphoria that followed the dissolution of the USSR was beginning to wane. In Russia, the majority in parliament ('the Duma') consisted of anti-liberals with solid representation by communists and nationalists. The harsh economic conditions, brought on by overly ambitious and seemingly corrupt reforms, had tarnished the attractiveness of the western-style market system for many Russians. In America, the 'peace dividend' expected with the end of the Cold War was slow to come or even viewed as declining. New laws and restrictions imposed by the Duma hindered foreign investment through complex property ownership and tax regulations. I desperately wanted to make my mark before it was too late.

# Banya Blues

I MET ADEL IN THE hotel restaurant for breakfast. I sat next to my companion, who was slowly sipping a cup of coffee. A half-eaten croissant lay still on a saucer.

"Have a rough night?" I asked.

Adel turned to me, his eyes still staring into his coffee cup. "After I got home, Razi called me, and we ended up chatting for quite a while. I only slept three or four hours."

He invited us to spend the afternoon at his dacha outside the city. He has a lovely private area about ten kilometers from here. He likes to show off his success, and refusing to come would be an insult."

"OK, fine. Should I go back to my room and pack anything special?"

"Not necessary. I expect Razi wants to show you around his private place, share some drinks and talk."

A young woman in a white blouse with a red and green scarf and sporting a black mini-skirt came to the table to take my order. Needing a caffeine boost, I ordered a cup of coffee and two sweet rolls from the buffet table. I continued to ration my nutrition bars to ensure sufficient supply for the train and plane rides back to Chicago in a few days.

The young woman returned bearing my coffee and pastries. I took a small sip, pleased to see that the sugar cubes helped mask the coffee taste. I ravenously ate the two sweet rolls, washing them down with my sugary coffee, while listening to Adel describe the route toward the dacha. The meal finished, we paid the bill and exited the hotel to Adel's car.

"How long a drive will it be?" I inquired.

"The dacha is in a small community about thirty minutes away. It's a nice place; it backs up directly onto the Kama River."

Adel drove northeast from the city. The paved road eventually gave way to a dirt surface. After the spring rains, grooves formed by dried mud gave the ride an uneven feel.

"This place really is out in the sticks," I observed.

"We Russians like to find solace and isolation after living so close together. The woods here are suitable for hunting. It's not that far from the city but gives a feeling of being far away."

"You said the dacha was part of a community. How big is it?"

"There are maybe forty or forty-five families who have built a dacha in the area. It was common to build a dacha for relaxation and grow food that mitigated scarcities in the towns. Of course, nowadays, the nouveau riche have constructed luxurious dachas, mainly for show."

Exiting the forest, a small cluster of dwellings came into view. These small dark-wood structures with metal roofs protected by rickety wood fences and high grass partially obscured vegetable gardens belonging to ordinary Russians. We continued around a bend that led us along the river bank. Here the dachas were more elaborate. The multi-level palaces, most made of brick, enjoyed a perfect view and easy access to the water. Protected by iron or metal fences, some with barbed wire, the homes had access to private jetties on the shoreline where small pleasure crafts were moored. The car slowed and stopped in front of a three-story structure comprised of birch logs. A large bay window jutted out from the first floor through which a crystal chandelier was visible. The upper floors displayed tall vertical windows, and the flat tiled roof supported several antennae. A green metal gate flanked by an imposing burnt orange brick wall guarded the entrance.

"We're here!" Adel announced.

"Great. It looks impressive and very secure", I added, observing the thin string of razor wire running along the upper edge of the wall.

"Razi completed it last winter. He is only now getting to enjoy the place in nice weather."

We alighted from the vehicle and approached the metal gate. Adel pressed the button on the wall intercom. After several moments, a female voice asked who we were; Adel announced that Razi had invited us to come. I heard a brief popping sound as the metal latch released, and the heavy green door opened slowly. We followed the gravel path up to a white stone staircase with black iron rails, ascended to the top, and rang the bell embedded in a birchwood door, which housed a thick vertical glass decoration in the center. As I stood on the landing, I gazed at the well-manicured hedges on each side of the gravel path. The shrubbery was as tall as a man and provided additional privacy from curious neighbors. Footsteps were heard coming from inside. The door opened, and Razil Damirovich greeted us wearing a light-grey polo shirt and khaki pants, his gold watch even more evident without sleeves.

"My friends! I am so glad that you could come! Welcome to my little private sanctuary."

"Spasibo bolshoe for the invitation," I responded. "This area is quite lovely."

"We took the forest road from the city. I see that the dirt roads have finally hardened," stated Adel.

"Da. I have petitioned the government to extend the paving up to this region. It was difficult to make it up here in the early spring after all the rains", explained our host gazing past us at the river. "Could you help me with that?"

"I can talk to the boss and see what we can do," replied my companion, trying to determine whether his friend was serious or joking.

Razil Damirovich moved off to the side, enabling Adel and me to enter the foyer. The entire interior consisted of birchwood with hardwood floors and walls composed of thick interlocking logs. The ceiling supported dark wooden beams separated by bamboo-tinted screens. A spiraled wooden staircase at the opposite end of the foyer, bearing intricately carved handrails, spun its way up to the upper floors. An inviting living area was situated off to the right. Two large sofas with plush upholstery sat on an expansive Persian rug around a rectangular dark wood coffee table. An elaborately decorated white ceramic stove stood behind the sitting area. The ceramic stove had three layers, with the bottom layer used as a fireplace.

Ceramic stoves were traditional heating and cooking appliances, but this one was extravagant. Its white tiles displayed detailed turquoise-colored reliefs of horse carriages and peasant life. The bay window, covered with lace curtains, extended out from the house's front wall. Two French-style chairs flanked the bay window. The chair on the left blocked access to an oval tray table filled with many expensive-looking liqueur bottles. An additional bay window was situated slightly above the ground floor bay window, and its windows had frosted glass in a floral design. Standing opposite the sofas and coffee table, a modern entertainment center displayed a massive television flanked by two tall speakers. The room had all the comforts one would expect in a manor-style home. Our host proudly invited us to move into the living area.

"Go ahead, make yourselves comfortable. Usually, I would have wood in the fireplace, but the weather is warm today."

Adel and I hesitated for a moment before entering the lavish living space. I still had dirt and gravel on my shoes from the factory tour; my companion seemed to share my feeling.

"Should we take off our shoes?" I inquired.

"Nyet, nyet. It's ok. I will have the cleaning woman take care of anything later on. Please, try one of the sofas. I had them imported from Italy."

I sat on the sofa nearest the entertainment center. I sank into the plush cushions, upholstered in gold and maroon stripes. Razil Damirovich occupied the similarly decorated, easy chair that adjoined the sofa. Several cantors of clear liquid surrounded a crystal candy bowl on the coffee table. Gazing to my right, I could see the dining area with a long oval table with eight chairs, beyond which was a kitchen with all the modern amenities. A sliding glass door offered access to the rear outside space.

"Are you thirsty? I can have Darya bring us some drinks."

Before Adel or I could respond, our host stood up and shouted, "Darya!" A youthful-looking, slender woman with long black hair appeared on the second-floor landing. Her loose-fitted white blouse had a lace pattern along the sleeves. A thick red belt and light tan pants completed her ensemble. She stared down at the man, who had summoned her, with expectant eyes.

"Darya, please bring us three new glasses. My friends and I have some business to discuss."

"Of course, Razi," answered the woman, whose voice I recognized from the intercom. "Do you want the brandy glasses or…"

"Da. That will be perfect, thank you."

I watched the woman gracefully descend the elaborate staircase. She was aware of the audience, measuring each step to put her in the best light. Reaching the bottom, she stopped briefly in front of us.

"Hello, my name is Darya. I am Razi's girlfriend. I am delighted to meet you."

"My apologies. I have completely forgotten my manners," Razil Damirovich said. "This is my girlfriend, Darya Ahmedovna. She works as an accountant. We met at a business conference a few months ago. She is a wonderful cook and often stays here with me on weekends."

The niceties observed, Darya proceeded into the kitchen, returning a few moments later carrying three heavy crystal cognac decanters. She placed them on the coffee table next to the carafes.

"Is there anything else?" she asked her boyfriend. Having received a negative response, the lovely young woman again took to the stairs, ascending as gracefully as she descended, and disappeared into the hallway on the second floor. The scent of her eau de parfum still lingered in air. Our host reached over the coffee table and grabbed one of the clear liquid carafes. He popped off the round crystal stopper using his free hand, making a loud thud upon striking the table. I watched him pour a generous amount of liquid into each glass.

"To good beginnings!" announced Razil Damirovich. We replied in kind and quickly drained our glasses. The memory of yesterday's drinking bout was still fresh, and I did not want to repeat my mistake. I was intent on pacing myself, ensuring my capacity to focus. Finding my glass soon refilled, I did my best to ration the amount I drank with each toast. I peered through the bay window and regarded the wind gusting, which brought a mass of clouds across the river, extinguishing the warm rays of sunlight that bathed the room. The lacquered wood on the walls and floors lost its bright reflection.

"That's disappointing," reflected Razil Damirovich. "I was hoping we could take the boat out for a spin, but the water will be too choppy with all that wind."

"That's a shame," I replied, feinting dissatisfaction. I was not overly keen to be in a vehicle on the water driven by our host, who had finished all his glasses of vodka.

Adel seemed to share my concern. "Maybe next time, Razi," he added.

"Since we can't go out on the water, I say let's take advantage of the banya."

I thought that I had misheard Razil Damirovich. Adel raised an eyebrow.

"Banya?" I asked, looking to confirm what I had heard.

"Da. I had a banya (sauna) built on the lower level. I've only gotten to use it a couple of times so far. It'll be great for relaxing before dinner."

I had read stories in Russian literature about banyas but had never been in one. Images of old, heavy-set men wrapped in towels, sitting on tiled steps, rushed into my imagination. Not once had I entered the sauna offered by my health club back in Chicago. I was not sure that I wanted to have this experience now.

"I didn't bring a bathing suit or change of clothes," I explained.

"Don't worry about that. Clothing is not worn in the banya. You can put your clothes back on after."

"Perhaps, we can just eat and drink and chat some more in the backyard," interjected Adel in a blatant attempt to come to my assistance.

"Nyet, I don't like to sit out in the wind. The steam will be more relaxing. Anyways, Ken should experience authentic Russian culture...."

Razil Damirovich got up and invited us to follow him towards the kitchen. We walked past a large rectangular island that allowed ample food preparation space. The sliding glass door to the backyard came into view. A stone patio supported a large iron table with several chairs, and a fifteen-foot umbrella provided shade to guests. The burnt orange brick wall enclosed the backyard and prevented prying eyes from neighboring dachas. It looked like an enjoyable spot to spend an afternoon. Our path, however, led past the sliding door and onward to the left, where a shiny birchwood door stood open, revealing a staircase leading downward. I followed Razil Damirovich and Adel down the narrow wooden staircase inserted between cut log walls. I could feel the dampness in the air as we descended. It reminded me of walking along a waterfront pier on a foggy evening, not stuffy but relatively cool and wet.

A wood plank floor covered the lower level. Built below the dacha's foundation, the banya's walls consisted of similar birchwood logs. Wood beams crisscrossed the ceiling supporting the underground space from the weight of the house. There were no windows, but various clusters of leaves and grains hung on a string along the top of the walls. A few paces to the right of the stairs sat a wooden bathtub filled with water. An opaque changing screen stood next to the bathtub. Opposite me, a door leading to a small closet-looking room unveiled an inlaid bench of dark wood planks. The back of the bench was topped by a flat area covered with what looked like green bushels. From my position, I could see about one-quarter of the sauna. A short stone-tiled table flanked the door and contained a copper metal water bucket and wooden ladle.

"You can remove your clothes over there," instructed our host, pointing to hooks attached to the wall on the left. A low stool offered a stack of towels. "Or, if you prefer, you can change behind the screen for more privacy."

I started towards the screen but saw my companions remove their clothing in front of the hooks. Not wanting to make a poor impression, I turned back and joined the others. Adel and Razil Damirovich chatted as they undressed. As an athlete in my youth, I had showered with teammates many times; bantering was customary and accepted. Now, however, I remained silent, feeling self-conscious and unaware of the rituals associated with the banya.

Naked, I stacked my clothes on top of my shoes, took hold of one of the white towels, and followed Adel into the banya. Our host remained standing by the tiled table near the entrance. He filled the bucket with water from the bathtub and joined us in the banya. Adel and I sat on the wooden pew while the proprietor strode past us and set the bucket and ladle on a small table opposite the bench. The interior was more expansive than it appeared from the outside. Adjacent to where we sat, a rocking chair was covered with bamboo.

On the opposite side of the room was a square-shaped wood-framed pit filled with stones. Piled several feet high, the rocks reminded me of something used in building a rock wall. An old-style thermometer hung on a nail over the pit. The sauna walls and ceiling consisted of thick planks of birchwood, while stone tiles covered the floor. A cylindrical wooden pail on the floor by the table contained a gathering of tree branches. A single bulb in the middle of the back wall provided all the light for the space. The air, at the moment, was humid but comfortable.

I was seated closest to the door; Adel occupied the middle position. The two Russians placed their towels on small hooks attached to the opposite wall. My towel remained in my lap. There was a brief awkward silence, or so it seemed to me. Razil Damirovich broke the quiet.

"Well, this is more relaxing, isn't it?"

I looked over and smiled. "This is a nice setup you have. How hot does it get in here?"

"It depends on the amount of water thrown on the stones. The heat isn't the main factor. It's the humidity. That is what opens the pores and lets the skin breathe."

"We have used the banya for centuries. It has good health properties. Many Russians still prefer the banya to modern baths and showers," explained Adel.

"Sounds good. This experience will be another first for me…."

"Nu, davai (well, come on)!" exclaimed our host. "I started heating the rocks this morning, so they should be ready."

He approached the metal bucket, used the spoon to scoop up some water, turned towards the stone pit, and tossed the water onto the hot, dry rocks. A loud "hissing" sound reached my ears. The thermal reaction of the cool water striking the hot stones caused a plume of steam to rise from the pit. A wave of moisture, like an avalanche, quickly spread and engulfed the confined space. The hot gas attacked my lungs as I drew in my first breaths; my chest constricted, blocking further onslaught of stinging air. I let out a succession of short rapid coughs and was unsure how long I could sustain this spasm. I noticed my companions, somewhat perplexed, staring at me.

"Are you OK, Ken?" asked Adel. He had a concerned look on his face and placed his hand gently on my back.

"Don't worry, my friend. The first blast of steam always feels strong. You will adjust in a few moments," added Razil Damirovich, his facial expression betraying a slight smirk.

Still unable to speak, I gave them a hand sign that I was working through the adjustment process. Gradually, the tightness in my chest slackened, allowing me to clear my throat. I slowly inhaled another breath, cautious for another assault of scorching steam. My lungs accepted the subsequent air more readily. I sat back up straight.

"Wow," I began, "that was unexpected. I felt like my lungs had collapsed. I didn't know if I would be able to take another breath."

Seeing that I had recovered, Adel and our host laughed. Adel seemed relieved. However, I got the impression that the proprietor had looked forward to such a reaction. I would not have been surprised if he had thrown on more water than usual to produce such an effect. The first wave of steam was still floating in the air. The droplets of sweat that blanketed all our bodies reflected the sharp rise in humidity. I removed the towel from my lap and attempted to wipe off droplets sprinting down my face.

"Ready for the next round?" playfully announced Razil Damirovich.

Without waiting for a response, he got up again and poured another spoonful of water onto the still steaming stones. Another eruption of steam wafted through the space. Scarred by my previous experience, I did not breathe deeply when the moist mass of hot air infiltrated my lungs. This tempered approach helped me adjust more quickly, enabling me to remain talkative.

"You were right. I tolerated that second wave better."

"See, you will be a real Russian by the time we're done today...."

Feeling more confident, I eased my posture and relaxed. The three of us, sitting naked on the hard wooden pew, discussed various topics of the day. Several times, the conversation was interrupted by other waves of fresh steam emanating from the stone pit. Each new surge of hot gas, however, reduced visibility in the banya, further distorting our facial features. Suddenly, Razil Damirovich rose and brushed away a path for himself in the heavy air. I saw his outline move over the opposite side of the room, where he bent over and grabbed the cluster of leafy branches sitting in the wood pail. He remained standing as he returned to the bench.

"Now, it's time to open up those pores and get all the impurities out," he announced through the fog. "Let's have our American friend go first."

Basked in sweat, I imagined that my pores were already sufficiently open. I was not sure what our host had in mind. Adel tapped me on the shoulder, indicating that I should stand up. I got to my feet.

"What do I need to do?" I inquired hesitantly.

"You need to lay flat on your stomach," said Adel.

"Where and why?" I did not see a place for one to lie in such a position.

Adel pointed to the narrow area located just above the bench. Through the thick mist, I discerned an area roughly two planks wide. Bushels of leaves covered the space, which I thought were for decoration.

"There?" It hardly looked wide enough to fit my body.

"Yes, just hop up there and lie down," instructed Adel.

"Ok, but why?"

"The birch twigs will help open up the pores. The steam has softened up the skin."

"You are going to hit me with the branches?" I asked in amazement.

"Razi is going to tap you along the skin. It is the traditional method."

The fog had dissipated somewhat, and I could see our host holding the gathering of branches. Again, he appeared to have an expression of delight on his face. Not wanting to be rude, I managed to make my way up onto the leafy area and positioned myself on my stomach. The unsmooth texture of the bushels irritated my bare skin. I hoped that this "cleansing" would be brief and painless.

"Are you ready?" I heard our host ask as he positioned himself slightly off to my side.

"Da," I responded and lowered my head onto my crossed forearms.

I heard the 'whoosh' of the branches cutting into the air, followed by a sharp sting. The first strike landed on my upper back. Involuntarily, I raised my head and felt my eyes begin to water.

"What the hell was that!?" I let out. "I thought this was supposed to be tapping. That was hard."

"My apologies. Your skin must be softer than I expected. I will go easier."

I considered calling an end to this cleansing but thought my refusal might reflect poorly on Adel and me. I decided to stick it out and 'take one for the team'. I repositioned myself and got ready for the next blow. Razil Damirovich struck me more gently but still with more force than a tap. Blows landed all along my torso, leaving pieces of leaves, which had ripped off the branch, attached to my skin. Feeling tenderized, I refused our host's request to turn over and have him 'tap' me on the front side; there were too many sensitive areas. I crawled down from the space and sat back on the pew while I covered the seat and backrest with my towel to cushion my back and underside, which were still sore to the touch.

Adel replaced me on the bed of leaves and received similar treatment. Apparently, his skin was better conditioned, and he seemed to enjoy the cleansing, permitting his friend to 'tap' his back and front sides. I dodged a few leaves that flew off the branches as Razil Damirovich assailed Adel. His cure finished, Adel rejoined me on the bench. I watched as Razil Damirovich prepared to take his turn. Hoping to get a chance to 'cleanse' our host and exact a certain degree of revenge, I inquired whether I might, to have the complete experience, try my hand at tapping him.

"May I take a turn? To be a 'real' Russian, I should know how to do this."

Razil Damirovich appeared hesitant to relinquish the cluster of branches held in his hand.

"I think it would be better if Adel gave me the cleansing. He has done this before."

I thought I noticed a mischievous grin slowly come over my companion's face. Adel understood what my intention was and seemed willing to play along.

"It's OK, Razi. I'll lead him through it."

"Alright," our host finally acquiesced. He handed Adel the handful of branches and, with a concerned look, assumed the position on the bed of leaves. Delighted, I stood up next to Adel.

"OK," he stated, "I'll start, and then you can take over for me. Observe how much pressure I use."

"Ponyatno," I replied, assuming that this detailed instruction was intended to relax our host. I watched as Adel began to strike lightly on the upper shoulders and arms. There were no strong 'whooshes' of air or pieces of leaves jumping off the body. I was observant and waited patiently for my turn.

"You see. You want to awaken the pores to allow more air to enter," continued Adel as he flipped the branches. I nodded and extended my hand.

"I think I got the hang of it, Adel. Let me have a go."

He ceased his motion, lifted the cluster, and transferred the branches to my awaiting hand. The texture of the white birchwood bark was rough in my hand. Many of the leaves had fallen off during the previous sessions, exposing more branch wood. This fact tempered somewhat my desire to exact revenge, not wanting to inflict real pain. I firmly gripped the bushel and lowered it onto his calves with sufficient force to make an impression. I saw a weak grimace expressed on our host's face.

"How was that?" I asked.

"Fine, fine," responded Razil Damirovich.

"Shall I continue?"

Having heard a grunt of approval, I wielded the bushel up and down the body, rattling my patient with equal strikes. I relented as the flesh turned pinkish and stepped back to give the proprietor a reprieve. I looked to my right at Adel. His facial expression indicated that I had taught his friend his lesson.

"Spasibo," I said, "for the opportunity to practice on you. I'll let Adel finish."

I returned the cluster of branches to Adel and sat back on the bench. I heard Razil Damirovich flip himself over to allow Adel to administer the front-side cleansing. Our host then managed his way down from the leaf bed. I figured that the ritual had ended and expected to depart from the sauna. The proprietor, however, moved over to the water bucket and scooped one more spoonful of water, which he tossed on the heated stones. A fresh wave of steam invaded the space, which had cooled down considerably during the cleansing activities. My lungs absorbed the hot air well, and I found myself covered in a pool of sweat once again.

"Are we going to repeat the whole process?" I was a little anxious to give Razil Damirovich another round on me with the branches. "I assumed the cleansing was the final step."

"Not quite yet," answered our host. "Now that the pores are open and we've had another steam, we can plunge into the bathtub."

I followed Razil Damirovich's instructions to open the door. A tremendous rush of cool air struck me, and I began to shiver. I quickly threw my towel over my shoulder and quit the steam room.

"Nyet, nyet," cried our host. "Don't dry off yet."

I watched as Razil Damirovich, still completely nude, strode over to the wooden bathtub and climbed in. Adel followed behind him and, picking up a bucket lying next to the bathtub, scooped up some tub water and poured it onto his friend's head. Steam drifted away from the exposed body area. The water was, it seemed, quite chilly.

"Whew!" exclaimed our host. "That brings you back to your senses!"

He shook his head to remove excess water before emerging from the tub. A broad smile covered his face.

"OK, my friend. It's your turn. Take the plunge!"

I reluctantly removed my towel, handed it to Adel, and dipped my left foot into the tub water. My big toe felt the sharp sting of icy water, which traveled rapidly up my leg. Instinctively, I pull back my foot from the water.

"Bozhe Moi! (My Goodness), that water is freezing!"

"Da, this is the final stage of the banya experience," explained Adel.

"The cold water removes the last of the impurities," added Razil Damirovich.

He made a motion with his hand encouraging me to re-enter the tub. I inhaled deeply and slowly submerged my left foot and leg into the tub. My skin took a few seconds to adjust to the temperature, then I swung my other leg over the side of the tub and dropped seated into the cold pool. The rush of cold made me shudder, and I could feel my teeth chatter. Preoccupied with controlling the shivering, the sudden onslaught of cold water falling over my head shocked me. A second wave of chills gushed over my body. I sat in the tub, shaking, reminiscing fondly of the searing steam of the banya. I looked at Adel to gauge whether I had soaked in the icy tub long enough. Having observed a glance of approval, I raised myself out of the tub like a gymnast on the uneven bars. I placed my feet back on the stone tile floor, desperate for warmth. My travel companion took pity on me and flung the towel around my shoulders. The soft, cottony feel of the towel rejuvenated my senses. My teeth stopped grinding, but scores of tiny pimples still covered my body as my flesh tried to raise my thermal temperature.

"Refreshing, no?" interjected our host.

"I am not sure 'refreshing' is the word I would use, but it was an experience." I retorted. I began to stomp my feet in place to create more heat. The expression on my face must have betrayed my craving to dry off and change back into clothing.

However, we were not yet done. I followed the Russians back into the banya. The worried look on my face must have betrayed my thoughts. I fully expected another thrashing at the hands of our host. Fortunately, Adel informed me that we were simply going to sit in the steam for a few minutes to bring out temperatures back up. I leaned back on the bench, relieved that I had seemingly survived the experience. About ten minutes later, Adel turned to his friend.

"Razi, it must be getting close to dinner. Let's finish up and head back upstairs," stated Adel.

"Of course. You are right."

The three of us again exited the sauna and moved to where we had left our clothes. I won the race to get redressed. Even after the short second steam and wearing my clothes, I still felt a chill. A warm meal, I hoped, would be the cure to mitigate the lingering effects of the ice bath. Before leaving the lower level, Razil Damirovich entered the banya to extinguish the fire. I followed my Russian companions back up the wooden staircase, where we re-entered the kitchen area.

"Hi guys! How was the banya?" Darya was standing in front of the black marble island in the middle of the kitchen, chopping up vegetables on a thick, flat cutting board. Several large pots were simmering on the stove behind her. There was a delicious aroma of meat and spices, which enveloped the entire area. The scent filled my nostrils and made my mouth water in anticipation. I had not realized how hungry I was.

"Everything smells so good", I blurted out unexpectedly.

A broad smile appeared on Darya's face, "Spasibo bol'shoe" was the reply.

"I told you she is an amazing cook," our host added. "Wait till you taste the main course."

"The meal should be ready in about fifteen minutes," announced our cook. "I am just finishing the soup vegetables."

"Excellent, let's head into the dining room," suggested Razil Damirovich.

The dacha did not have a separate formal dining room. It would be more accurate to describe it as a dining area. The open design of the ground floor did not separate the different spaces with walls. Instead, a long oval-shaped dining table was visible in the distance between the living room and the kitchen. A weaved basket containing various bushels of grains, mushrooms, and flowers stood in the middle of the table. Two large glass carafes filled with clear liquid flanked the centerpiece. We took places at the table. Then, our host stood up, reached over the table, and grabbed one of the glass carafes. He walked over to Adel's and my seat, filled the tall glasses, and then returned to his place at the head of the table.

"To a wonderful dinner!" toasted the proprietor with hand raised.

"To a wonderful dinner!" repeated Adel and I.

I put the glass to my lips, expecting to taste the bitter sensation of vodka. I was surprised, instead, to have the tasteless feel of cool water splashing in my mouth. The water was refreshing after the sauna session. I had lost a large volume of liquid through perspiration and felt a bit dehydrated. Razil Damirovich caught my eye. He seemed amused by my reaction to the water.

"You thought it was vodka, yes?"

"Da. The carafes are identical to the ones in the living one, so I assumed they contained vodka."

"We all do not drink vodka all the time, my friend. You can become drunk very quickly if you consume vodka soon after banya."

"I can understand that."

"I bet Adel can tell you some stories of us in our youth when we made the mistake of drinking right after banya. Right, Adel?"

My travel companion appeared reticent to discuss his youthful adventures. He just smiled and nodded. I decided to try to change the topic.

"Razil Damirovich, I wanted to thank you again for your invitation today. I have enjoyed the experience of a real dacha and banya."

"My friend, you are most welcome. And please call me 'Razi'. You don't need to be so formal anymore. We have shared a banya and 'cleansed' each other." Spending time naked while beating each other with twigs broke down barriers.

Darya brought in a metal tray with soup bowls containing dumplings of meat and rice set in vegetable broth. While we ate, I asked Darya what companies she supported as an accountant to broaden the conversation. She discussed her work with the various industrial enterprises in the region, aiding them in preparing their financial reports. I went on to ask her opinion on the reliability of such financial reporting.

"Well," she began, "one must understand that proper accounting was never a priority in the USSR. The goal was to satisfy the Plan, and the numbers were often 'adjusted' to show that a particular factory met the expectations of the government. There were procedures to be followed, but there was no central regulatory body to enforce accounting rules like in the West."

"So, how credible are the financial results I received from the plants we have visited?"

"Larger enterprises have better resources to keep track of actual sales and expenses. They work more with foreign partners, who require compliance with western standards, so I have more confidence in their numbers. It is more difficult to validate the accuracy with smaller enterprises."

"That makes sense. I should be highly skeptical of the financial information."

"I would agree, yes."

I observed the facial expressions of Razi and Adel. They had not expected Darya to be so forthright in her explanation. Razi cleared his throat noticeably and stated that perhaps it was time for the main course, signaling an end to the conversation. Darya got up, collected the soup bowls, and returned to the kitchen.

"Is this something discussed at the ministry?" I asked, looking at Adel.

"We are aware of the issue but feel Western partners can introduce modern standards after investing."

"I see. But, it might be challenging to get American investors interested in the first place without reliable financial information. Would the government consider bringing in western consultants to improve accounting systems and processes?"

"That would be expensive. We would prefer investors pay for the assistance."

The government and enterprises in Russia wanted western investment but did not want to incur expenses to attract this investment. In the west, American companies sought opportunities in Russia but were hesitant to invest without financial and legal reliability. It was a quandary that I was not in the position to solve as a twenty-four-year-old. I turned my attention to Razi.

"Razi, would you be willing to pay for assistance to make your business more attractive to western investors?"

He looked a little uncomfortable with the question but reflected for a moment.

"We are fortunate to have an accountant who had studied in Europe. But, there are areas where expert help would benefit the factory. I would be willing, for a reasonable price, to pay for help. I think, however, that the government should provide such resources."

I looked at Adel to gauge his reaction. His friend was shrewd and gave an answer which played both sides of the fence. I expressed that this could be another potential area to explore: providing affordable advisory services to smaller companies ignored by the big international firms. We discussed how this might work in a region like Tatarstan, having independence from Moscow but needing the national government's financial resources. Adel indicated a willingness to discuss the idea at his ministry.

Darya arrived, bringing in the main course. As a foreign guest, I had the honor of being served first. The multi-talented accountant placed a shallow bowl of what appeared to be a meat stew before me. Chopped pieces of beef and potatoes, as well as pickles, sat in a tomatoey broth. There was a strong aroma of onions and garlic.

"This is 'Azu,'" explained Darya while serving the others around the table. "It's a popular Tatar folk dish."

"It smells amazing," I commented.

"My wife prepares Azu with the pickles served as a side dish," added Adel, never missing a chance to brag about his wife's cooking.

It tasted similar to beef stew and was not as spicy as expected. The meat was incredibly tender and almost melted on the spoon. I used several slices of rye bread to mop up the remaining broth in the bowl. Eating her Azu, Darya chimed in on our discussion concerning the need for advisory help for smaller enterprises. Her opinion was that many plant directors were either too ignorant or too proud to realize they needed assistance. She agreed western firms would find plenty of opportunities but could not extract the exorbitant fees that the well-known firms charged. It seemed evident that improving the management of these smaller enterprises could significantly impact the success of the market economy in Russia. In the US, small and medium-sized businesses formed the core of a diversified economy, which had never existed in Russia's history. It was exciting to imagine myself having the possibility of contributing to this development.

I began to feel a bit feverish and had a slight headache, so I drank more water. The conversation was less serious over dessert, revolving around the season's promising start for the city's football team, Rubin Kazan. I noted how Adel and I had driven by the stadium on our way out of Kazan. Both men shared that the team had a great chance to win Russia's Premier League this year. Darya, who had grown up in Pervouralsk in the southern Urals, expressed her hope that Ural Yekaterinburg would make a strong showing for the title. I knew little to nothing about non-American football and listened with curiosity to the passionate arguments in support of each team. However, all sides agreed that Spartak Moscow was the team to beat as they had the money to attract the best players, some of whom came from western Europe.

Darya served tea from an elaborate Samovar to finish the evening. Each 'stakan' (tea glass) bore a metal covering with intricately designed images of swans. My temperature seemed to be rising as I slowly stirred the sugar cubes into my tea. I placed the back of my hand on my forehead to check my warmth. Our hostess noticed my movement.

"Are you feeling alright, Ken?" she asked in concern.

"I'm not sure. I feel warm, and my head aches. I thought it might be from eating hot food, but it's getting worse. I think I'm sick."

Darya got up and put her hand on my forehead like my mother had done when I was little. Her soft hands measured my temperature for what felt like several minutes. Eventually, she let out a "tsk-tsk" sound, a good indication that something was not right.

"You do seem to have a temperature," the accountant-cook-physician declared after completing her examination. "Perhaps you should get some rest."

"You are welcome to use one of the sofas here," sincerely offered our host.

My thoughts immediately centered on returning to the hotel. The last thing I wanted was to be ill in a remote area of Russia. I envisioned myself languishing in a small, decrepit facility reminiscent of Ward Number Six by Chekhov and subject to the suspect care of a modern-day Dr. Andrey Yefimitch. The terrifying descriptions of hospital stays depicted throughout Russian literature rushed into my mind. If I jumped into bed soon, I might be able to fight off whatever this illness was and be recuperated by tomorrow. I thankfully declined Razi's offer, stating that returning to the hotel would be the best option. Our host and hostess did not object to our departure, likely relishing the idea of several unexpected additional hours of privacy. We exchanged well-wishes, handshakes, and hugs and then exited the dacha via the gravel pathway to the awaiting car.

The wind had calmed as the storm had moved away. The lingering clouds obscured the dying rays of sunlight, low thrusts of red and orange foretold of tomorrow's heat. Retaking the dirt road back towards the forest, Adel turned with a look of skepticism.

"Are you actually feeling ill, or was that a clever excuse to return to the hotel?"

I returned an expression of feigned disbelief.

"You think I would lie to get out of staying at the dacha?" I responded with a wink. " I really do not feel well. I was warm at the table; now I am starting to feel chills."

We drove in silence through the darkened forest road towards the city. The symptoms worsened, leading to uncontrolled trembling as I struggled to regulate my body heat. Arriving at the hotel, I said goodnight to Adel and trudged into the hotel to my room. I slung the backpack off my shoulder and tossed it in the corner of the room before tearing off the covers on the bed and jumping in, fully clothed. I enveloped myself in the blankets to generate heat but to no avail. Frustrated, I threw off the covers, leaped out of bed, and headed into the bathroom.

"Direct heat is what I need," I thought. I turned on the hot water spigot in the shower. I began to undress as I waited for the water to turn hot. The shivering intensified as I stood naked on the cold tiled floor. "This is unbelievable," I said to myself. "The banya must have given me a nasty cold." Seeing steam begin to rise into the bathroom, I poked my hand into the shower to test the temperature of the water. I stepped into the shower, and a flood of hot water pelted my skin, causing me to jump back. My back leaning against the shower tile, I contemplated which was worse, the chills or the hot water. I took a deep breath and advanced, step by step, like a fencer, back towards the stream of hot water, enduring the discomfort until my skin adjusted to the drastic change in temperature. Several minutes spent under the steam cured my chills. Wanting to keep warm, I opened the shower door and grabbed one of the towels, quickly wrapping it around as much of my body as possible. I stepped onto the carpet in the living area to warm up my feet.

I dressed in my sleepwear and returned to the bathroom, rummaging through my travel kit to find aspirin and NyQuil gel tablets to make me drowsy. In bed but not yet ready for sleep, I began reading the next chapter of Dracula. I gazed out of the hotel window into the dark cloudy night from time to time. The reflection of my face in the glass recalled Jonathan Harker's description of his journey into the imposing Carpathian mountains toward Dracula's castle. I imagined myself seated in a similar plush train compartment, looking into the vastness of an unknown world, with a mixed feeling of anxiety and excitement. I hoped that my experience would end more favorably than Mr. Harker's. My eyes became heavy as Mr. Harker accepted Count Dracula's invitation to enter the castle 'of his own free will', a crucial decision that sealed the Englishman's fate. I, too, had freely accepted an invitation to come to Russia and now, feeling ill and alone, dreamt about my destiny as I drifted off to sleep.

# An Emergency Stop

A FEW DAYS LATER, I left Kazan and returned to Chicago. I arrived at The Pyramid Group to discuss the hotel renovation opportunity. Don and Jim remained interested in the project and agreed to bring me back on as a consultant, using the firm's office for meetings, etc. I stayed in contact with Adel, mainly via phone and fax. Our estimated cost to perform the renovations was much higher than the one proposed by the Russians. We would have to modernize most sewage, water pipes, and electrical wiring. There was also a concern about the hotel's structural integrity, given its age and assumed lack of regular maintenance. A closer inspection was required to determine accurate renovation costs. A two-person team would return to Kazan to examine the building firsthand. The firm was willing to donate the development hours incurred so far but expected, from now on, compensation for its time and resources.

I helped draft a proposal by which the Hotel Kazan was required to pay for the Pyramid Group's development services. In return, the firm would present a complete renovation plan, including costs for construction. It would partner with the hotel to find an American operator that would invest in building and provide management services. The proposal included expected costs for development, which ran into the tens of thousands of dollars and included the return trip to Kazan.

I faxed the proposal to Adel, expecting a quick turnaround given Marina Atonovna's stated urgency. After a week without response, I contacted Adel to inquire about the delay. The message received from Kazan was that the hotel manager would not agree to the Pyramid Group's terms, describing them as exorbitant. After several more exchanges, we reached a compromise. The Russians agreed to pay for the trip to Kazan, albeit for only one person, and Pyramid Group's architectural work up to a maximum amount of $30,000. The firm agreed to partner with a local Kazan firm to perform some of the drafting, drawings, etc., under the supervision of our architect to manage costs. The agreement was not ideal but allowed the project to move forward. Since I was already familiar with the hotel, it was decided that I would return to Kazan. I was to spend several days taking videos and photographing much of the interior and certain exterior features so that the architect in Chicago could make a more detailed review of the structural needs of the building. A local Russian architect would assist me in obtaining permits and other plans needed to bring back to Chicago.

I arrived at Sheremetyevo and stayed overnight in a hotel near the Golden Ring, the major circular route around downtown Moscow. The following day, I took a taxi to the Kazanskii Vokzal and boarded the train to the capital city of Tatarstan. I sat in the second class compartment and occupied my time during the twelve-hour ride by reading and learning to use the video camera. When I set foot off the train later that night, Adel greeted me with a warm smile.

"Did you have a pleasant journey?" he asked, shaking my hand and taking hold of my larger suitcase.

"Everything went well. The food was passable, and I am now an expert with my video camera."

"Khorosho. Let's get you settled in. I am sure you are tired."

We started walking through the dimly lit station. The repetitive sound of passengers' feet striking the concrete floor echoed throughout the deserted space.

"Am I staying at the Hotel Kazan?"

"Where else?"

I laughed. "I thought so but didn't want to assume. How have you been? Is Aliya well?"

"I am fine, thank you. Very busy at the ministry. We have many new construction projects underway. Aliya is also well. She is busy working on a case defending a group of small businessmen targeted by the tax authorities."

"Is Marina Antonovna still unhappy about the cost of the project?"

Adel pushed open the glass doors of the main entrance, and we walked out in the chilly night air. There were already several inches of snow on the ground, a fast start to the upcoming Russian winter. I had made sure to bring my heavy winter coat. I wore my authentic fur hat, a gift on my earlier trip to Siberia, making me look like a true Russian traveler. Adel was now dragging my suitcase through the unshoveled snow.

"She still does not want to spend the money on the design work feeling that the hotel management company should pay for that as part of managing the hotel."

When we reached the hotel, the receptionist recognized me and greeted me with an enthusiastic, "Dobry vyechor!". "It's nice to see you again." She gave me the key to the same room as before.

"This is the same room I had last time," I told her with a smile.

"Marina Antonovna directed me to keep it reserved for you," responded the receptionist.

I inserted my key and jerked at the door, forgetting how heavy it was. I pulled harder, and it swung open, permitting us to walk into the foyer. Stepping into the salon, I flicked on the closest table lamp, splashing light on the sofas and chairs. Nothing had changed in the room. My companion dropped my suitcase by one of the sofas. Surprisingly warm, I removed my fur hat and coat.

"Well, everything seems in order," Adel said. "I am going back home given the hour."

"Of course, thanks so much for picking me up. What is the schedule for tomorrow?"

"We have a meeting with Marina at 10:00 am to discuss the inspection plan. I will come by at 9:30 am."

"OK. I will see you then. Have a good night."

I was ready to go when I heard the knock at my door the following morning. Adel escorted me along the corridor leading to the reception desk.

"Did you sleep well," inquired my companion.

"Yes, thanks. It took me a little while to fall asleep, but I slept like a rock once I did."

"Did you have breakfast in the restaurant?"

"Nyet. You know me. I brought along a sufficient number of nutrition bars. I ate a couple in the room before I got dressed."

Adel grinned and shook his head. He would never become accustomed to my strange eating habits. My complete non-interest in coffee and a hot meal baffled him. We reached the reception desk, and the woman on duty knocked on the manager's door.

"Yes, what is it?" emanated from behind the door.

The receptionist cracked open the door and poked her head inside.

"Marina Antonovna, Adel Mateevich, and the American are here."

"Excellent, show them in, Razina."

Razina opened the door wide and stepped aside to allow us to enter. Our hostess was seated at her desk, flanked by several tall piles of folders. The portrait of Tatarstan's President hung proudly behind her on the cream-colored wall. On either side of the picture were the flags of her native land and Russia. This morning, Marina Antonovna had her thick black hair set up high on her head, fastened in the back with a jade barrette. A gray vest covered a well-fitted white blouse, and a rose scarf wrapped loosely around her neck from which a pair of reading glasses dangled attached to beads. She seemed genuinely glad to see us.

"Dobry den! It's so nice to see you again. Please take a seat. How was your trip?"

I returned the greeting and lowered myself into one of the two chairs facing her desk. Adel occupied the other chair. I briefly summarized my journey to Kazan and expressed my thanks for the invitation and the same accommodations. The hotel manager politely listened and then inquired if I had brought the necessary documents and equipment related to the renovation project. I confirmed that I had a video recorder, camera, and inspection checklist.

"Wonderful! I am looking forward to our partnership. I have asked Ahmed Bolotov to accompany you during the inspection. He has a great reputation, and I believe he can perform much of your firm's drafting and drawing work at a lower cost."

"OK, when will I get to meet him?" I asked.

"I've asked him to join us this afternoon so we can begin the inspection after lunch. I wanted to go over the process for your stay."

"Ponyatno."

Marina Antonovna explained that the architect would work with me while I took video and photos of the building, which should take one and one half to two days to complete. She would then review the materials before allowing me to bring the information to Chicago. Based on my findings, Ahmed Bolotov would begin work on initial drawings of changes and request required permits related to expected construction needs. While I listened attentively to our hostess describe the course of events, I realized that the accelerated path envisioned by the Russians might cause concerns for my firm. The renovation drawings could be completed relatively soon, but attracting and negotiating with a hotel company to invest and manage the project would take much more time. I was not sure the hotel manager fully appreciated the challenge.

"Well," I said after she had finished outlining the itinerary. "It will be a hectic few days."

"I wanted to invite you both to dinner tonight. I have made a reservation at an excellent local restaurant called Dom Chaya (Tea House). It opened in the '70s and has become very popular with people of your age, Ken. It is close to the university. It is not as elegant as our restaurant, but it will give you a good idea of what local cuisine is like for everyday people. Dmitri Pavlovich from the city planning commission will also be joining us."

I peered at Adel to gauge his reaction. He smiled and nodded in approval. That settled, we got up again and returned to my room. There were several hours before the first inspection appointment. Adel remained in my room, and I reviewed the initial development work done in Chicago with him. I also showed him the video recorder and demonstrated the device's basic features so that he could operate the camera if necessary. While Adel practiced with the video recorder, I brought up the subject of Marina Atonovna's expectations for the project.

"Marina Antonovna seems to think that actual renovation work will begin quickly. You are a member of the construction ministry. You understand the timing associated with such a project. Don't you feel her timeline is a bit aggressive?"

My companion halted his scan of the salon and raised his head from behind the rear lens. His face took on a pensive expression.

"Perhaps. I know she has been pushing for this project for quite a while. Once we have some revised drawings, it will be easy to get the permits for construction."

"I understand, but it will take time and some luck to convince a hotel operator that Kazan is the place to invest for this renovation and offer management services. With the limited budget, I am afraid we will struggle to develop a professional project plan convincing enough to show to large American hotel chains. I don't want Marina to become frustrated with the process."

Adel placed the recorder on the coffee table and sat on the sofa.

"I think that she will comprehend better once we finish the inspection. We will likely discover so many structural issues that they will see the scope of the renovation and its complexity. Then, the new projected costs and time to complete will become more apparent; she will have to acknowledge that their original estimate was understated and accept your firm's timeline."

"So, we should wait until later this week to address these concerns?"

"That is my recommendation. Marina Antonovna wants to review the findings. Let's talk to her after we have the review."

"Agreed."

We arrived back at the hotel manager's office in the early afternoon. We again found our hostess seated at her desk. A tall, slender man, sitting in one of the chairs across from Marina Antonovna, rose to greet me. He appeared close to Adel's height, making him slightly over six feet. The front and top of his head were clean-shaven, with well-groomed traces of the former bushy salt and pepper hair in the back. A thin, partially graying beard surrounded his face. Dark-rimmed glasses shielded deep-set brown eyes. Tucked into the collar of his black tunic was a gray and white striped ascot. Grasping my hand firmly, the architect introduced himself.

"Bolotov, Ahmed Ramilovich. I am pleased to meet you."

"Pleased to meet you," I replied. "I look forward to working with you."

"Me too. This structure has so many possibilities to highlight its past and bring it into the present."

"Ahmed Ramilovich has renovated several buildings in the city over the past three years," chimed in Marina Antonovna. "I am sure your firm will find his thoughts very appropriate."

The hotel manager summarized her expectations for the next several days. According to her version of events, Ahmed Ramilovich's role would be as the inspection leader instead of supporting my assignment. I looked at Adel and then addressed our hostess.

"Per the agreement, Ahmed Ramilovich will assist me in performing the inspection. I have a checklist of critical areas that the firm wants to understand concerning essential structural issues."

The architect's jovial expression waned a bit. I got the impression that Marina Antonovna had explained our agreement in different terms.

"Da, konechno," stated the hotel manager, "But we will count on Ahmed Ramilovich to provide drafting documents for the proposed changes."

"I am sure that The Pyramid Group will consider employing Mr. Bolotov's services. In any event, we will function as one team."

I asked the local architect to review the checklist and give me his opinion of where we should start. The architect indicated that the foundation and lower level would likely represent the most prominent trouble areas. Picking up our equipment, we walked out of the office and, followed by the architect, made our way to the stairwell leading to the basement level. Ahmed Ramilovich walked briskly, reaching the basement level first. The damage was apparent to any novice, but I thought it wise to allow the architect to act as our guide.

Adel and I took photographs and videos of the affected areas. Numerous cracks in the foundation walls and the stone floor likely resulted from poor construction and the lack of maintenance over many years. The architect explained that the fissures risked the collapse of the upper floors. The boiler room was the nerve center for the heating and plumbing systems. Stepping through a low brick entranceway, I cautiously walked on the dust-covered stone floor, avoiding random wood planks and shards of metal. To my front stood two enormous metal cylinders fixed side by side. Age and neglect had left a thick coat of rust on the exteriors of both objects, while a vast network of metal pipes, carrying heat to far regions of the hotel, extended from the cylinders into the ceiling. The architect approached the cylinder to examine it in more detail. He looked at the various gauges and scratched the surface in several places.

"This looks like the original equipment," loudly stated our partner over the humming of the device. "The gauges are from the early twentieth century, and the state of rust indicates iron as the material, which is typical for that period. The efficiency of these boilers is not great. Replacement would be the recommended option."

"What about the pipes running from the boilers? Would they also need replacement?" I inquired as I photographed the space. "Do they give us any indication of the state of the plumbing?"

Ahmed Razilovich looked more closely at the piping. He reached up and tapped one of the pipes causing flakes of rusted metal to peel off and crash to the floor. He shook his head.

"I wouldn't rely on these pipes. Some of them may still be serviceable, but the level of rust concerns me. Rust particles are likely traveling through the heating system into the rooms. As far as the plumbing, that is a different system. We can find the drainage and sewage pipes down here too."

The blueprints indicated the central sewage depository was roughly twenty yards away. We stopped several paces before three large circular-shaped metal covers set a few feet apart on the concrete floor. Thick copper-colored pipes ran into each of the covers. The solid pungent odor also confirmed the sewage site.

"The septic tanks for the hotel are buried under the foundation," explained the architect. "The copper pipes carry the waste from all sections of the hotel and deposit it here."

"Is this system modern enough?" I asked.

After recording a video of the treatment area, Adel lowered the device and shook his head. The architect's facial expression displayed agreement. I let out a loud sigh and started to take photographs of the space. After a few minutes, I let the camera hang down by my waist.

" I do not remember the original cost estimate assuming replacing the boilers and septic tank, not to mention the foundation issues."

"Well, the good news may be," added Ahmed Razilovich, "that the plumbing piping could be copper, which is resilient. You may not need to replace it if it is still in good condition."

"We can examine the plumbing in a sample of rooms throughout the hotel to get an idea of the quality," interjected Adel.

"That can be on the agenda for tomorrow," I said, looking at my watch.

It was getting late in the afternoon, and I wanted to ensure we would not be late for dinner. Like my companions, I was covered with dust and dirt and needed a shower and fresh clothes. Everyone agreed to start again in the morning. Ahmen Razilovich requested a copy of the checklist to review that evening. I handed the architect the clipboard and wished him good luck. We shook hands and parted ways. Adel and I returned to my room.

"I'll be back around 7:00 pm," stated Adel. I need to see Aliya and get some new clothes."

"Yasno. I'll be ready at seven."

I was sitting on the couch in casual attire when I heard the familiar sound of Adel's fist against the door. I found my colleague dressed in his usual jeans and leather shoes. Under his coat, I could see a white collared shirt peeking over a dark blue sweater. I grabbed my jacket and shapka and accompanied him back to his car. It was a brief ride; we likely would have walked in better weather. We parked the car on a side street and strolled in the snow about fifty yards up Bauman Street. Off to my right, I noticed a series of bright red Cyrillic letters. The words 'Dom Chaya' were prominently displayed alongside the word 'Café' and two other words, which I did not understand and assumed to be these exact words in the local Tatar language. Behind the entrance sat two mannequins, a man and a woman, outfitted in traditional Tatar costumes. A variety of sunflowers and other plants surrounded the couple. Adel approached the door marked 'Vkhod' (entrance) on the right and held it open for me to pass through. I stepped up over the threshold and walked into a cafeteria-style eating area. Small groups of young people, most likely students, occupied many of the tables, covered with small pastries and teacups. A queue shuffled along a buffet line to the rear of the space, offering soups, bottled drinks and tea, and a variety of local favorites. With a look of indifference, an imposing babushka waited for the customers to finish their selections at the cash register.

"This floor is typical of many eateries in Soviet times," explained Adel. "The food is good and cheap. The service is another matter, but since most customers are students and pensioners, it is not the main concern."

My companion guided me past the buffet line and towards a stone staircase. White iron balustrades decorated the marble stairs. Some potted plants lay in the stairwell, and the walls displayed framed paintings of Mediterranean beach scenes. As I ascended the stairs, a tall mirror decorated with red and yellow painted flowers wished me "Bon Appetit!" in Russian. A more formal dining area spread out before me on the second-story landing. There was no hostess to guide us, but we recognized Marina Antonovna and Dmitri Pavlovich seated at a table in the far corner of the dining area.

"Dobry vyechor," I said, greeting our host and hostess. "I hope that you have not been waiting long."

"Nyet. Only a few minutes," replied Marina Antonovna.

She motioned for us to sit. I removed my coat and hat and placed them on a white iron portmanteau standing in the corner. I sat in one of the small wooden chairs. A waitress arrived and handed us menus. I placed the menu on the table while observing that the others appeared eager to converse. The hotel manager was the first to speak.

"So, how did the inspection go today?"

I summarized the examination of the basement, stressing several areas of concern with the foundation, boilers, and septic tanks. Adel provided some detail from his knowledge of construction, describing some potential challenges, and mentioned that Ahmed Razilovich was very helpful in identifying the issues. I explained that the plan for tomorrow focused on the plumbing and load-bearing supports for damage, which would increase the renovation cost. It was clear that this news was not what she expected to hear.

"The hotel has run just fine with the boilers," stated Marina Antonovna. "Can't we simply continue to use them? The guests do not see them. We should focus on the rooms and dining area."

"I understand. But, no western investor will pour money into renovating a hotel that relies on antiquated heating and sewage, not to mention potential foundation issues. From my point of view, the essential thing is to show investors that we fully understand the problems and that, even with higher expenses for renovation, the hotel will make money."

A moment of silence ensued. The Russians did not appear won over by my argument. Adel explained that we needed to identify all the actual construction costs to avoid surprises. I explained that a large American hotel chain would be more interested in the reliability and quality of the systems for the guests than its cost. The hotel chains care about cost, but it lessens the concern if we can show the hotel profitable with these costs.

"Will these extra changes increase your firm's expenses?" asked the hotel manager.

I could see the anxiety on Marina Antonovna's face. She was worried about going over the budget limit in the contract.

"I don't think so. Our architect factored into the budget possible changes such as this. I am confident we will stay within budget."

The waitress returned and served tea. Her return prompted everyone to pick up their menus. The restaurant offered an extensive selection of hot and cold dishes and drinks, traditional Tatar and Russian. I chose a soup with dumplings that I had eaten on my last trip here and was delighted to see that I could get a chicken cutlet Kiev-style, one of my favorites. We all placed our orders, and the waitress left. The conversation turned to the search for potential hotel partners in the US to take on the construction work. As expected, I explained the process and likely timeframe, which was longer than what my Russian partners wanted. During dessert, the hotel manager informed me that she wanted to meet with me the day after tomorrow to review the inspection information. Following the meeting, she invited me to join her and Dmitri Pavlovich on an excursion to experience some of the area's natural beauty.

We had a final round of coffee, and I thanked our hostess for a delightful evening; the food had been excellent. Adel and I said our goodbyes, descended the stairs, and exited the restaurant. It had started snowing, so we hurriedly shuffled across the street and down the small alleyway to Adel's vehicle. We drove back to the hotel in silence, the rhythmic swishing of the wiper blades providing the only sound. The city appeared peaceful and bright, holiday lighting accenting the falling flakes. I watched couples walking hand in hand along the sidewalks. I imagined my girlfriend and I enjoying the upcoming festivities back in Chicago. Her exams would be over by the time I returned, and we would stroll along Michigan Avenue, gazing at the beautiful holiday decorations.

Adel and Ahmed Razilovich were waiting for me in the lobby the next morning. The plumbing inspection lasted most of the morning and encompassed most areas of the hotel. We looked at single rooms and large suites, verifying the status of the piping in the bathroom spaces. Adel and I took videos and photographs of cracked piping. Around noon, we went to the hotel restaurant to have lunch and discuss the findings of the morning's inspection.

"So, Ahmed Razilovich, what is your conclusion on the state of plumbing?" I asked while eating some soup with dumplings.

The architect put down his spoon. "The overall network functions but, based on the sample, the piping is too antiquated for a modern hotel. It really should be replaced."

This finding was more bad news since the original renovation costs did not include plumbing replacements. The problems understated in the original plan continued to grow and, with them, the expenses. After lunch, we examined the roof, parking areas, and the electrical grid, uncovering further serious issues. Back in the hotel restaurant, we ended the afternoon in a somewhat depressed mood, sitting at the bar nursing a round of drinks.

"Well, that didn't go as well as I had hoped," I stated, swirling my cognac in the glass.

"Da. The only good thing is that we might acquire all these materials and labor locally to keep the cost down." Adel was staring into his decanter as he spoke.

Ahmed Razilovich tried to sound encouraging. "I agree. It might be financially achievable if funded as a local project."

"Perhaps," I replied, "but the best option is to work with an American hotel chain, which will manage the hotel under its flag. These rising costs will deter many companies from an interest in the project."

"I will mention the local funding in my comments to Marina Antonovna," said the architect.

"OK, sure. At least you don't have to deliver the bad news to her." I looked at Adel. "I might need a place to sleep tomorrow night after this meeting."

My companion laughed. "I am sure Aliya could fix the sofa up."

We ordered one more round of drinks. To lighten the mood, we chatted about sports and the upcoming holidays. As early evening set in, Ahmed Razilovich bade us farewell. We thanked him for his time and expertise and expressed our hope to work with him again as the project progressed. Adel accompanied me back down the corridor to my room. At the door, we parted ways for the evening, agreeing to meet at Marina's office the following morning.

In the morning, I met Adel standing by the reception desk. He was dressed in his formal sports coat and dress pants. I entered the office and found Marina Antonovna seated behind her desk. I greeted the hotel manager and explained that we had a video presentation concerning inspection results. Before showing the video, I summarized the inspection findings, stressing the need to reconsider the original timeline and costs. Adel supported me with his comments. Marina Antonovna looked stern but added that our summary matched what she heard from Ahmed Razilovich.

Marina Antonovna challenged the recommendation to replace the plumbing, sewage, boilers, and roof. She insisted she could attract a western partner based on the aggressive guest projections alone. Given this opportunity, an American hotel chain would be so eager to invest that it would initially overlook these structural concerns. She confirmed her belief that the project could start within six months. Sensing my frustration, Marina Antonovna expressed her profound gratitude for all the work put into the inspection and presentation.

"I believe you have compiled enough information to satisfy your firm's demands," stated Marina Antonovna. "You can begin revising the drawings, hopefully with Ahmed Razilovich's assistance."

"We will do our best," I replied, realizing the meeting was over.

At that point, the door opened, and the deputy planning minister walked in. He greeted us and stood next to the hotel manager.

"Excellent. Now, Dmitri Pavlovich and I are leaving to tour the forest preserve. Are you ready to go?"

At that moment, I was not really in the mood, preferring to return to my room and deal with the frustration I was experiencing. However, I felt compelled to join them.

"Sure, I brought my backpack. Can I leave the equipment here in the office?"

"Of course," responded my hostess. "Adel, would you like to come along?"

"Thank you, but no. I have ministry work this afternoon, so I have to decline. I wish you all a fun excursion."

Bundled up in my fur hat and coat, I followed the couple out the front entrance, where a black and grey Mercedes sedan stood idling. The driver, a burly-looking man with a military-style haircut and sporting a dark suit, exited the vehicle and opened the rear door for the hotel manager. Dmitri Pavlovich took the middle space next to her, leaving me near the passenger side door. The vehicle was spacious and comfortable; it still had a new car smell. From the back, the deputy ministry ordered the driver to head northwest. With a reply of "Yes, Sir.", the imposing man drove off from the hotel.

"Where are we going?" I inquired, hoping to break the awkward silence in the vehicle. The journey was my first time without Adel.

"Our destination is the national park about an hour from here," explained Dmitri Pavlovich. "There are forests, trails for hiking, lakes, and areas for picnics."

"We go there often. One can enjoy the pristine nature even in winter," added Marina Antonovna. "I wanted to show you some of our region's beauty, not just factories and plants."

"Wonderful. I love walking in the forest."

We crossed over the Kirov Street Dam Bridge, leaving the city and heading into the countryside. I recalled some of the scenery along the bank of the Volga from my first trip several months earlier, but soon we sharply turned north away from the river. Idle farm equipment lay neglected in the snow-covered fields and pastures. I gazed out of the window but noticed, from time to time, intimate interactions between the Russians. The deputy minister placed his hand on Marina Antonovna's leg or held her hand, which she freely gave to him. I sensed that they had made this trip together in the past.

"I see the sign for Pomary," I asked. "It looks like a fairly large village. What do they make there?"

My question grabbed their attention. Dmitri Pavlovich straightened up in his seat while the hotel manager fixed her skirt.

"Pomary is not an industrial area," stated the deputy minister. "There is some farming and woodcutting. Why do you ask? Do you want to stop and visit?"

"Nyet. I was just curious. It has been the largest village I've seen since we passed Zelenodolsk."

"Andrei, when we reach the park, pull into the main trail area," ordered the deputy minister.

The countryside transformed from fields to forests shortly after leaving Pomary. Tall birch trees flanked the unplowed road. It was a bumpy ride over the uneven road surface for the final twenty minutes. I imagined a gentle stroll in the forest. We turned off the main road and headed slightly east onto an icy gravel path. Off to my right, I saw a sizeable wooded sign welcoming visitors to 'Mariy Chodra National Park'. Several administrative buildings were visible in the distance. The vehicle parked in a small deserted clearing, blanketed by snow.

"OK, we are here!" exclaimed Dmitri Pavlovich. "Let's get out."

The snow was an inch or two deep, just low enough for my leather shoes not to get too wet. Standing by the passenger door, I surveilled the area more closely. Fir and white birch trees intertwined, forming a protective semi-circle around the parking area. Clumps of snow hung precariously on the fir tree branches, and a slight breeze knocked the white powder into the frigid air. The white birch trees stood tall and proud, their naked limbs piercing the winter sky. Off to the right was a gap about wide enough for two small vehicles leading into the forest, which marked the entrance to the hiking trails. I heard the trunk open and observed the deputy minister lean in and pull out a bottle and three glasses.

"Time for a little celebration!" announced Dmitri Pavlovich, motioning to Marina Antonovna and me to approach. He handed both of us a tall glass and proceeded to unscrew the bottle of vodka. Marina Antonovna smiled as she held out her glass, which her partner filled to the brim. I followed suit and received a hefty amount of liquor.

"To a successful partnership!" toasted our host, his glass raised high.

"To a successful partnership!" replied the hotel manager and I.

We all clinked glasses. The temperature in the trunk had chilled the vodka. A cold sensation flowed into my throat and chest upon the first intake, causing me to shiver a little. The amount in the glass was too much to consume in one shot. I drank about a third of the vodka and noticed that Marina Antonovna did the same. Dmitri Pavlovich, in contrast, had downed the entire flute. He grasped the bottle again and refilled all the glasses.

"Easy, Mitya," chided the hotel manager, "we still have a long way to go."

"Agh, one more toast," replied the deputy minister, ignoring the admonishment. "This time, Ken, you do the honors."

I stood pensive for a moment. I looked around at the vast surrounding forest and the smiling Russians next to me. I raised my glass.

"To Russian-American cooperation and friendship!"

"Mitya, let's stroll into the woods," stated Marina Antonovna. "It's so peaceful."

"Fine, we'll fill up the glasses and take them with us."

Armed with a full glass of vodka, I made my way onto the trail path. My Russian partners were in front, strolling arm in arm. The snow on the trail was not deep, having been patted down by hikers and horses. The air was cold, and the intermittent wind was sharp. However, my fur hat kept my ears and head toasty, and I sipped on my vodka while gazing upwards at the trees along the trail. The towering fir trees watched over us, threatening to drop their snow burdens on these unsuspecting intruders. I inwardly wished I had snow boots to explore deeper into the forest. After traveling for a quarter of an hour, we came upon a small lake.

Not yet frozen, the lake offered refuge to several birds swimming in the crystal blue water. I walked closer to the water's edge, careful not to slip on the icy sandy ground. When I turned away from the lake, I noticed that the Russians were far ahead of me. I picked up my pace, spilling some of the liquid as I went. The two figures appeared very close together, and as I got nearer, I could see that they were kissing. Marina Antonovna, her back against a tree close to the path, embraced Dmitri Pavlovich. Faint giggling-like sounds reached my ears. These two middle-aged professionals acted out a scene from any local high school. I halted my progress, unsure whether to interrupt their liaison. I took a long draught of the vodka, which spread warmth into my body. The wind picked up its intensity, forcing me to shut my eyes against the piercing cold. The wind must have interrupted the passionate embrace since, when I reopened my eyes, I found my partners heading towards me.

"Hey, where did you go?" inquired Marina Antonovna as she fixed her dangling hair. "We were waiting for you to show you something interesting."

"I stopped at the small lake back there. It was so calm."

We continued the stroll, and behind a bend in the path, a wooden sign appeared, supported by log poles and covered by a small slanted roof. The sign read: Zelyonyi Klyuch (Green Key).

"This is one of the most popular trails in the park," explained the deputy minister. "One can see all types of flora and small streams with fish. Of course, it is harder in winter with all the snow."

Beyond the sign, a narrow stream flowed along the snow-laden path. We descended a short log staircase and followed the trail keeping left of the river bank. The gurgling sounds of the water mixed in with the blowing wind. The footing was treacherous, especially with the glasses, but the views were marvelous. The deputy minister told us to stop and be quiet at one point. We stood fixed to our spot, and an enormous creature appeared on a small hill in the distance. Too big to be a deer, it reminded me of a moose from my experiences in northern New England.

"It's an elk," whispered Dmitri Pavlovich, not wanting to alert the animal to our presence. "It is rare to see one at this time of day."

"Do they roam free in the park, or is hunting allowed?" I asked in a murmur.

"Hunting is limited, but the desire to mount those antlers on the wall drives some to ignore the rules."

"Who would want to harm one of those beautiful animals?" added Marina Antonovna in exasperation.

We observed the magnificent creature move off farther beyond the hill and out of our sightline. It was an exhilarating experience, and our little group continued along the trail. A wooden footbridge crossed the stream. The forest appeared endless, the serenity of the moment broken solely by the crunching of the snow under our feet. As daylight faded, we retraced our path back toward the parking area. A final toast was drunk "to safe journeys!" I tucked the empty glass inside my coat pocket to free my hands, improving my balance, which was affected by the alcohol. I paid closer attention to my steps but did not overlook my partners walking arm and arm on the trail again. The nature walk also served as a romantic excursion for the pair; the wild forest provided necessary privacy. As we neared our starting point, the amount of vodka and the cold temperature began to give me the urge to relieve myself. Trailing the Russians by several yards, I considered moving into the woodline, where I could take care of the situation. However, I hesitated, thinking that doing so could be rude. I decided, therefore, to wait until we returned to the hotel, making a calculated risk that I could hold out during the hour's drive back.

"That was a fun adventure," stated the deputy minister as we pulled out of the clearing on our way back to Kazan. Marina Antonovna, fatigued from the long walk, rested her head on his shoulder.

"Da," I said. "The wintery scene was breathtaking, and I especially enjoyed seeing the elk. This park must be just as wonderful in the summer."

"Oh yes, you can come camping and horse riding the next time you are back."

The warmth of the vehicle made everyone feel drowsy. We rode in silence, the only sound being the rhythm of the tires on the snow-covered road. I rested my head against the window. Marina Antonovna leaned back against the headrest, her eyes squinting in a futile effort to remain open. I, too, desired to sleep, but the growing sensation of the need to urinate thwarted any attempts to doze off. The coolness of the window glass against my cheek only accelerated this urge. In an effort of self-distraction, I tried to focus my thoughts on my trip back to Chicago and the holiday festivities that awaited me. Distracting worked for a while, but eventually, my bodily needs tore away my thoughts from those pleasant images. More and more, my thoughts concentrated solely on the increasing strong desire to use a restroom. My watch indicated that the journey would last another half an hour. I crossed one leg over the other to bolster my control, but my change of position had only a temporary effect. As I squirmed in my seat, my behavior resembled a small child, desperately needing to go to the bathroom, placing his hand over his crotch, and shifting to and fro. My movements must have roused my companions.

"Is something wrong?" asked Dmitri Pavlovich. I turned my head to see both him and Marina Antonovna gazing at me with looks of concern. The hotel manager had shifted forward in her seat, keeping her hands on her lap.

"Are you hurt?" she asked in a motherly tone.

I remained reticent. I was embarrassed, but my confidence in controlling my situation was rapidly waning. I took a deep breath.

"I must have drunk too much vodka back there. I *really* need to find a bathroom."

Upon hearing my words, the looks of concern changed to ones of relief and amusement. A wide grin appeared on the deputy minister's face, and even the hotel manager's expression was slightly comical. She relaxed back in her place.

"Andrei, how long 'till we're back in Kazan?" questioned Dmitri Pavlovich.

"About twenty-five minutes, Sir," responded the driver in a gruff voice. He had heard the conversation but remained emotionless.

"Well, can you wait that long?"

The look on my face gave away my answer, but I stated, "I don't think so." In addition to having crossed my legs, I had also placed my left hand over my crotch, hoping the applied pressure would stave off an accident.

Still smiling, my host addressed our driver again.

"Pull in at the next village and head to the police station. We'll have to assist our American friend here before he bursts."

A few minutes later, the car left the highway and took the offramp for a small village. We drove swiftly by the welcome sign, taking the main road into the town. Passing a hardware store and several small hotels, we approached a blue and white square building off to the right. The word 'Militsia' hung over the entrance to the building. The car jolted to a halt as our driver stopped the vehicle. He parked in between a row of police wagons to the side of the staircase. Ignoring the niceties, I leaped from the car and dashed up the stone stairs towards the glass doors. The deputy minister was close at my heels. I brushed hard against a man exiting the station but continued to shuffle quickly down the tiled hallway, searching for the restroom. I attracted the attention of several officers who were perplexed to see this stranger sprinting into their station. Up ahead, an officer with a stern look was making the hand signal to stop.

"Stoi (stop)!" I heard him shout, but I continued to move forward, fearing the consequences if I halted. Seeing me advance, he placed his hand on his holster.

"It's ok; he's cleared! This is an emergency. He has to use the restroom," shouted Dmitri Pavlovich, still trying to catch up with me.

Luckily, the officer recognized the deputy minister and withdrew his hand from his holster. The policeman guided me toward the restroom just around the corner. I rushed into the lavatory, my wet shoes almost causing me to slip on the concrete floor. Finding my objective, I quickly took care of business. Finished, I breathed deeply and calmly washed my hands and face. I exited the bathroom to find Dmitri Pavlovich standing at the entrance, accompanied by several officers. They were all smiling, amused by the sight of an American barely avoiding pissing himself. I could hear jokes exchanged at my expense.

"Feeling better?" asked the deputy minister, trying to contain his laughter.

I wanted to keep the mood upbeat after creating a scene in the station.

"And lighter," I replied.

This comment caused another round of laughter from the policemen and more quips concerning Americans' lack of bladder control. Dmitri Pavlovich patted me on the shoulder.

"Shall we head back to Kazan now?"

"Da. I think I'm good to go."

I thanked everyone for their understanding, and the officers escorted us out of the station. We pulled away from the station and regained the highway, arriving at the hotel twenty minutes later. Before returning to my room, I received a warm embrace from Marina Antnovna and a hearty handshake from Dmitri Petrovich. My departure to Chicago was set for tomorrow, and Adel would arrive early the following day. There were no snowflakes to watch that evening, only the sound of the wind howling against my window. My mind started to wander, preventing the onset of sleep, but fatigue soon became insistent, and I gently drifted off to thoughts of home.

My companion was punctual as usual; there were no delays in making the train to Moscow. This time, I did not remain in Moscow overnight but went direct to the airport, where I caught the last flight headed to Chicago. The non-stop journey meant that I traveled continuously for more than a day, but seeing my fiancée's happy expression upon my arrival erased any tiredness. The holidays were splendid. There was ample time to overcome the jetlag from my travels, and my recollections became the subject of interesting conversations at the dinner table with family and friends. I also took the time to rest and reflect. I had been through quite a few exciting experiences, but, realizing that time was short, I wanted to seize the opportunity to contribute to building a brighter future between Russia and America.

# Cooperation and Disillusionment

As the new year rolled around, design work continued on the hotel renovation project in Kazan, but given its low budget, the project was no longer a top priority. In contrast, pressure increased from Marina Antonovna to accelerate the progress. As the plan dragged on, the frustration in the fax messages and phone calls with Adel grew. I did what I could to promote the project among the architects. The renovation of a nineteenth-century hotel in Russia paled in comparison to the multi-million dollar fees earned from office buildings and golf courses. I strained to keep the design work going while convincing my Russian partners not to cancel the project.

I partnered with the local chamber of commerce to promote those Russian enterprises with a realistic chance of finding an American investor. One program director, in particular, was very excited about marketing prospects for Chicago area businesses to invest in Russia. Following several meetings with this director, during which I presented the business plans for select companies, we identified chamber members interested in doing business in Russia. We drafted and sent marketing brochures, accompanied by an official letter of support from the Chamber of Commerce, to those targeted companies. The response to our marketing campaign was higher than expected. Roughly a dozen businesses in the Chicago area indicated an interest in exploring further the idea of a possible partnership with one or more of the Russian companies in the brochure. After a few rounds of talks, about half of the businesses expressed a desire to contact one of the Russian enterprises to begin negotiations concerning a potential relationship. During these early exploratory talks, Adel and I served as intermediaries, supported by the chamber, coordinating calls and translating to both parties.

These were exciting times. All indications pointed to the real possibility of attracting investment for these Russian companies. Several American companies proposed trips to Tatarstan to visit their potential partners. Adel led the effort to coordinate such a trip with his local government. I stayed in contact with the American companies, advising them on the local business environment and my experiences with their potential partners.

While planning these trips, the program director notified me about a week-long international investment conference hosted by the chamber in Chicago in mid-summer. Smaller companies from many countries would arrive in Chicago to exhibit their products. The program director proposed that the Russian companies should attend the conference, where they would receive individual exhibit booths. It was an intriguing idea. I discussed the proposal with Adel, who thought that the enterprise directors would jump at the chance. The American companies agreed with the concept, which would save time and money on travel. Thus, we adjusted the plan. The Russian directors would arrive in Chicago to exhibit their products and, more importantly, finalize investment agreements with the American companies.

Adel was correct that many Russian directors wanted the chance to fly to the United States. The final list I received from him consisted of ten enterprises, almost twice as many as initially expected. Some directors, who I had met in Tatarstan but did not have an identified American partner, wanted to display their wares. However, the most surprising attendee was the Hotel Kazan manager. Marina Antonovna communicated via fax that she intended to come to Chicago to accelerate the renovation project. The delegation comprised more than twenty persons, including Adel, who was to act as the delegation leader. Given the group size, I requested assistance from the chamber of commerce, which the program manager graciously offered. The chamber would help arrange transportation and interpreting services during the delegation's stay.

My excitement grew when the week of the conference arrived. "By this time next year," I thought to myself, "some of these businesses will have started selling goods or making products in Russia. The night before the delegation's arrival, I told Deb that this twenty-four-year-old recent graduate student was about to help break down Cold War barriers and support, in a small way, the creation of a new lasting friendship between old rivals. She smiled, allowing me the moment to enjoy my anticipated success. I went to sleep that night dreaming of how the world was changing from containment to cooperation with Russia and how lucky I was to participate in this new world. I pondered all the future trips I would undertake, becoming a prominent international business executive. After years of struggling, my decision to study Russian and its history, politics, and culture would finally pay off.

The following day, I arrived at O'Hare International Airport. I exited the chartered bus, which the chamber of commerce had arranged, and headed into the international terminal to meet the delegation. Waiting at the Arrivals welcome area, I noticed Adel's six-foot-four frame from among the sea of passengers. I held up my large sign, "Tatarstan Delegation" in bold Russian letters. He moved past the barrier gate and walked briskly towards me, his hand outstretched.

"It's so nice to see you again!" exclaimed Adel. "The rest of the group is right behind me."

"Great to see you as well!" I said, giving him a firm handshake. "Did the trip go well?"

"Da. Normalno. A couple of directors were upset that there was not enough alcohol on the flight, but apart from that, everything went fine."

"Of course. When everyone arrives, I have a chartered bus waiting to take us to the hotel."

I recognized most of the Russians as they emerged from the exit gate. However, there were several new faces. I observed one walking arm-in-arm with Marina Antonovna as she approached my position. The hotel manager was dressed, as usual, in elegant business attire, in a sleek black vest and gray skirt, which must have made sleep during the long flight challenging. Holding her elbow was a blonde woman of approximately the same age. The woman's blue dress appeared slightly wrinkled, likely due to attempted sleep on the plane. With a light mauve scarf around her neck, she giggled alongside her companion. The pair were the only female members of the delegation.

"Marina Antonovna, how wonderful that you have come! We are looking forward to working with you this week."

"Spasibo, Ken. I am interested in seeing Chicago and moving our project along."

We shook hands, and she introduced me to her companion.

"I'd like you to meet Vera Maksimovna. We are old friends, and she will be helping me this week."

I greeted Marina's friend, who added that her last name was Petrova. When everyone had arrived, I led the group out of the terminal and towards the bus. Adel stayed by the back to corral any stragglers who fell behind or had trouble with their baggage. The drive to the hotel was relatively quiet. Most guests occupied themselves by gazing out the windows. Adel sat with me, discussing the first night's hotel logistics and dinner plans. There was a burst of excitement among the delegation when the impressive Chicago skyline came into view. I pointed out some key landmarks, such as the Sears Tower and Hancock Building. As we entered the downtown area, silence again reigned with everyone's attention fixed on peering skyward. No city in Tatarstan, not to mention Moscow, had, at that time, such tall structures. The bus stopped at the back entrance to the hotel to avoid parking trouble due to the heavy traffic. Located in the South Loop area, the hotel displayed its sandy stone façade trimmed with gold metal. Adel and I herded the group into the hotel to the reception desk, serving as guides and interpreters, and helping each guest checkin. Before leaving the group to find their rooms, I informed everyone that dinner was in the hotel restaurant and to meet back in the lobby in an hour.

While the delegation was busy settling in, I stayed in the lobby. I reviewed the schedule for the next several days. Engrossed in my reading, I failed to notice the man standing in front of my chair.

"Evening. Did the delegation get in OK?"

I raised my eyes and saw my colleague from The Pyramid Group, who had arrived to join us for dinner.

"Hey there, Jim," I responded. "Yeah, everything went well. Everyone is up in their rooms unpacking."

Jim Mazuros was one of the architects at the firm. Jim was supposed to have gone to Khabarovsk with me, but an urgent client project scuttled those plans. He now expressed interest in the hotel renovation project. Jim was an eloquent speaker who would keep the conversation interesting over dinner. My colleague wore his typical tan sports coat with padded sleeves, covering a white and blue striped dress shirt, accenting blue trousers. His naturally curly brown hair had lost some of its thickness over the years, but he kept it well coiffured; only small traces of grey were discernible. Jim had worked in Chicago for decades but retained a slight drawl from his youth in the south. Reading spectacles, which completed the ensemble, were neatly placed in his breast pocket.

"Can you make sure that I meet the hotel manager?" Jim asked. "I would love to discuss the hotel plans with her."

"Sure, I'll introduce you when she comes down. Be warned. She brought a girlfriend with her."

"Even better, I can sit between them at dinner," added Jim with a playful wink.

Our chat was interrupted by the arrival of the chamber's program director. Because of the size of the group, I had also invited her to dinner. She trod carefully across the carpeted lobby, dressed in a blue business suit and stilettos. Emblazoned on her lapel was the chamber of commerce logo with her name inscribed underneath. I got up from my chair to greet her. Jim quickly followed suit.

"Good evening, Sarah. I'm so glad that you were able to come. Your presence will make this evening manageable."

"My pleasure, Ken. Happy to do it. I am looking forward to meeting everyone. The chamber is so excited to have this delegation participate in the conference."

I introduced Sarah to Jim, and we huddled around one of the small coffee tables in the lobby. We discussed the transportation options for the delegation. It was impractical to have many large group events, so we split the delegation into a few smaller teams that would visit various city sites. At the end of the week, a farewell dinner was reserved at the newly opened restaurant atop the Hancock Building, where the city views would be spectacular. While we were talking, I saw Adel exit the elevator. My Tatar companion was sporting his suit jacket and dress slacks. I excused myself for the moment and went to speak with him.

"Any problems with the rooms?" I inquired.

"No, I didn't check on everyone, but no one called me to complain."

"OK, good. I'm sure something will come up later."

I introduced Adel to my colleagues. Adel spoke passable English, although with a thick accent. I could see that Jim and Sarah had to listen closely to understand what he said. Before the rest of the delegation started returning to the lobby, I told Adel about the logistics plans for the week that Jim, Sarah, and I had just formulated. He agreed with the program but asked who would translate for the teams. Sarah added that several interpreters would be available through the chamber to accompany the groups. The tall Russian nodded and moved back towards the elevators to meet the directors as they came down for dinner. I suggested to my two American colleagues to wait by the elevators.

Adel and I introduced Sarah and Jim to each member as they strolled into the lobby. Making a special effort to ensure Jim and Marina Antonovna became acquainted, I brought my colleague straight to the hotel manager. I introduced Jim, adding that he was working on her renovation project. Marina Antonovna was decked out in a lovely black cocktail dress and a heavy pearl necklace. Her girlfriend also wore formal evening attire, her blonde hair laying loosely over her bare shoulders. After about fifteen minutes, the entire delegation had gathered in the lobby. We noisily shuffled past the reception area, finally arriving at the restaurant.

The hostess initially appeared intimidated by the size of the invasion force at her door. She quickly adapted and adeptly guided the troupe through the main dining area into a spacious private room with oak-framed glass doors. The table was elegantly set with a white cloth that stretched its full length. Wine and water glasses sparkled, reflecting the light emanating from the crystal chandeliers. Dark red carpeting covered the floor up to the pinewood walls. Each wooden chair bore upholstery similar to the carpet. The overall ambiance of the space was old-world luxury. I watched the impressed facial expressions of the visitors as they entered the room. After everyone was seated, I rose from my seat and formally welcomed the delegation to Chicago. I expressed how excited my colleagues and I were to have them at the conference and briefly explained the itinerary for the next several days. While speaking, servers had begun to fill the wine glasses, so I ended with a toast.

"To friendship and success!" I declared, my arm raised.

"To friendship and success!" resounded the group, followed by a very loud clinking of glasses.

The conversation over dinner was lively. Due to the group size, the menu was limited to two options, both Chicago favorites: prime steak and freshly caught halibut. The wine flowed freely, breaking down the language barrier for most guests. I ate little that evening, preferring to frequently move around the table to listen to the discussions and keep the mood light. Jim Mazuros stayed permanently engaged with Marina Antonovna and Vera Maksimovna. They peppered him with questions about the renovation plans and, from time to time, suggestions for popular nightclubs in the city. Seated opposite Jim, Sarah spent her evening enlightening her interlocutors about her organization's work and the advantages of partnering with her member companies. Another Chicago favorite, Eli's Cheesecake, was served for dessert. I could see that the long journey and the cheesecake weighed heavily on our guests. I announced that the bus would arrive at 7:00 am the following morning to take everyone to the conference center. Adel took command of gathering everyone to return upstairs for the night. I, along with Jim and Sarah, bade everyone a good evening.

"Well, I think that went well," I said to my colleagues as we prepared to exit the hotel.

"Yes," replied Sarah. "The Russians seem very eager to meet with my members. It should be an exciting week."

The next morning, I arrived at the hotel just before seven. Adel was already standing by the elevators, collecting the delegation members. We slowly made our way outside the hotel, where the bus was waiting for us. The hotel manager and her girlfriend boarded first, followed by their male counterparts, many of whom appeared to be suffering from jetlag. Once everyone was settled, we departed. Traffic was heavy, causing the one-mile trip to the conference center to take nearly twenty minutes. The slowness of the drive did not seem to bother the Russians, who busied themselves by peering at the numerous storefronts along the city's most famous thoroughfare, the Magnificent Mile. When we pulled up at the conference center, it took a few minutes for everyone to navigate the busy sidewalk crowded with pedestrians on their way to work. A concierge directed us to the registration desk inside the conference center, located off to the right. While the Russians took turns completing registration materials and receiving their credentials, Jim Mazuros arrived.

"Hey, Jim, can you go find Sarah? Last night, she mentioned she wanted to come and greet the delegation when we arrived."

"Sure. No problem."

Jim moved off towards the wide staircase at the end of the reception hall, where he ascended and disappeared behind large double doors. Every exhibitor received a map of the exhibition hall indicating the layout of the booths. The map contained information in English, Spanish, Polish, and Japanese, but not Russian. I was explaining the booth diagram to several Russians when I heard Sarah's voice. I looked up and saw her approaching the delegation. Jim was following close behind.

"Dobry den!" she exclaimed. "Welcome. I am so happy to see everyone this morning. Is everyone registered?"

There were a few nods, and several directors held up their laminated credential cards.

"Wonderful. I apologize that the maps are not in Russian but let me show you personally to your booths."

The program manager pushed in the collapsible door bars and held the door open to allow the guests to proceed into the exhibition hall. The area contained tens of thousands of square feet covered by a thirty-foot high ceiling supporting metal beams and exhaust ducts. The booths were all the same size, approximately ten feet by ten feet, and decorated with the particular company's home flag colors. I passed by booths for two firms from El Salvador framed in blue and white flanked by the red-colored booth of a Japanese auto supplier.

Sarah guided the delegation to their booths near the back left of the hall. The booths faced outward along a narrow footpath and included a long table to exhibit goods or marketing brochures. Several chairs sat next to the table for the exhibitors to entertain visitors. Many of the booths were still empty or in various stages of setup. Walking past stalls from Polish, Mexican, and Filipino companies, we reached the far left corner of the hall. Standing in front of a row of blue, white, and red booths, Sarah explained that this was the Russian section. Boxes or cases shipped from Russia containing product samples and marketing materials sat in the back of each booth. A white sign with thick black letters in English hung from each booth identifying the particular enterprise. Adel and I assisted those with poor command of English to find their stall.

After finding their respective space, the delegation members set to work removing their materials from the boxes and organizing their booths. I walked along the row and noticed Marina Antonovna, accompanied by Vera Maksimovna, sitting quietly in her booth chair. Her booth did not have any boxes to unpack. She had a look of mild boredom.

"You didn't bring any brochures for the hotel?" I asked.

It took her a moment to acknowledge my question. She turned her head, but her eyes were looking past me. Meanwhile, Vera Maksimovna was busying herself with something in her handbag.

"Da. I have some in my purse," replied the hotel manager. She unzipped the tan leather pouch sitting on her lap and pulled out a stack of glossy materials displaying the familiar façade of the hotel. She placed the pile on the table and, like a card dealer, spread them out in a neat row.

"I am not really here for the conference," she added. "Jim and I had a good conversation last evening, and I want to see when I can go over the renovation plans."

"Well, the plan is to meet at the Pyramid Group in two days. I know you do not have a product to exhibit, but you can still perhaps create interest in the hotel."

She sighed and fanned herself with one of the brochures.

"I suppose. Perhaps Jim can come over and talk with me."

I looked towards the aisle and waved to my colleague to join me. A big grin on his face, Jim greeted Marina Antonovna warmly and took a seat next to the two ladies. I whispered to Jim that his role was to keep the ladies occupied while also discussing the hotel. He nodded, and I moved off.

"When will the other translators arrive?" I asked Sarah, who was helping one of the directors empty a crate.

"They should be here shortly."

I took over for Sarah, who needed to go and assist other delegations. After having arranged automobile dashboards components, I went to find Adel. My Tatar colleague was placing some resin samples at another stall. I tapped him on the shoulder.

"We need to discuss tonight's dinner plans," I stated. "The group is to be split into two parties. Do you have any suggestions on how best to divide the delegation?"

Adel motioned me to move away from the exhibit. "I think it best to keep the industrial guys together to have common themes to discuss. I wrote down a list of the groups last evening." He handed me a folded sheet of paper from his pocket.

"This is great! I'll let Sarah know, so the drivers are aware. I think we will spend most of the day helping bring visitors to this area. We are pretty isolated back here."

"Soglasno (agreed). If they get too bored, they are likely to wander off."

"Well, I have the two ladies set for the day."

The two translators appeared about thirty minutes after the start of the exhibition. The Russians were delighted to meet Irina and Sasha, who explained to the delegation that they lived in a western neighborhood of Chicago called the Ukrainian Village. Many immigrants from the former USSR lived in the area, which was home to many Russian/Ukrainian themed restaurants and stores. There were many visitors that first day and Irina and Sasha were instrumental in helping the Russian exhibitors manage the inquiries and discussions about Russia and Tatarstan. Jim did a miraculous job keeping Marina Antonovna and her girlfriend engaged. I saw lots of smiles and laughing during the day. Adel and I escorted small groups of the delegation to visit the other booths. The Russians were curious to experience the products from Mexico, Poland, Japan, and other countries. I gathered the group in the early evening to head back to the hotel. Once everyone returned to their rooms, Jim and I ordered a drink in the bar and relaxed in the lobby.

"How long until we need to leave?" inquired Jim.

"About forty-five minutes. The chamber is sending over two shuttle buses."

"I assume that I will be going with Marina and Vera?"

Jim and I were still chatting when, about thirty minutes later, I noticed Adel enter the bar. He looked a bit disturbed.

"Dobry vyechor," I said as he approached. "What's wrong? Is everyone almost ready to go?"

He remained standing and placed his hands on the back of the stool next to me.

"Everything is OK. Well, except for Marina Antonovna. She said she and her friend will not join us for dinner."

I left the bar with Adel, telling Jim that I would be back shortly. Marina Antonovna opened her door in response to my knock, still dressed in her bathrobe.

"Good evening, Marina Antonovna. I heard that you and Vera would not be going to dinner tonight. The restaurant is a classic Chicago one."

"Ken, call me Marina, please. I think we have known each other long enough."

"Spasibo, Marina."

She smiled and nodded. "I am sure that the restaurant will be fantastic, but Vera and I are planning to experience one of the nightclubs in the city. Jim told us about several last night, and we don't want to miss all the fun."

My jaw must have dropped because both ladies broke out laughing.

"Marina, are you sure that is a good idea. We have a set schedule with the delegation. Do you both feel confident enough to travel alone using limited English?"

"We will be fine. Anyway, the guys are so boring, and they just want to drink and smoke or talk about business or their mistresses."

I began to think about what I would tell the rest of the members. I couldn't force them to attend the events, but I was afraid that I would lose more people going off on their own. It could cause quite a few problems. Pondering how to convince the women to stay, I heard a slight knock at the door. Marina motioned to me to open the door, and when I did, I found a cleaning woman standing outside holding a small hand iron.

"Here is an iron from the supply room," meekly stated the woman, clearly wanting to complete her task quickly. "The guest can keep it until she checks out. Simply call the reception desk to return the iron."

Iron in hand, I closed the door and faced the Russian women. Marina Antonovna almost leaped up in joy at seeing the small device. She grabbed the iron from me and placed the shimmering blue dress on the bed onto the ironing board. She performed several passes with the iron, moving it back and forth over the garment. I stated that I needed to return to the lobby to board the buses for dinner.

"Jim is really looking forward to discussing the renovation plan's details over dinner tonight. He came especially for this opportunity."

Continuing to hold the iron and smooth out the dress, the hotel manager replied that she had enjoyed Jim's company today and would be happy to talk again tomorrow. Vera Maksimovna remained silent and stared intently into the small mirror of her makeup case.

"Well, OK then. Please be careful this evening, and I will see you again tomorrow."

I exited the room and heard the door close as I stepped along the corridor towards the elevators. When I alighted from the elevator, I saw the rest of the delegation standing in the lobby. The mingling of the voices created a loud, incoherent buzz. Adel informed me that he had already told everyone which bus they were taking, so we were ready to depart. I told my colleague about Marina's plans for the evening in a low voice. He did not appear surprised by the news. During the plane ride from Russia, the two women had made no secret of their intention to sample the nightlife in Chicago. I also discreetly let Jim know of the change in plans to which he responded with disappointment.

"Great, I could've stayed home," said Jim, having heard of the change in plans, "but now I'll have to entertain all evening."

We herded the two groups onto the buses, waiting outside the back entrance. To my surprise, none of the men inquired about the women. Adel guided his group to a popular Italian restaurant on the Gold Coast area of the city, while Jim and I escorted our guests to one of the many sports bars on the city's north side. The Italian restaurant promoted its historical connection with the Al Capone era, which I thought would interest the Russians who associated Chicago with this notorious time. The sports bar impressed the Russians in our group. They were taken aback by the scores of large-screen TVs hanging on the walls, each displaying a different event. Several of the Russians bought Cubs hats in the bar, which they proudly wore while taking turns playing the numerous sports video games. There was a lot of beer, nachos, and vodka; everyone had a good time. The festivities ended at a reasonable hour, in time for the visitors to catch a few hours of sleep. Before heading home, I asked Adel if he had heard or seen the two ladies. He had not and did not dare to knock on their door. I assumed we would learn about their adventure tomorrow.

The women showed up in the lobby early the following day, looking none the worse for wear. I did not inquire about their evening, assuming that Jim would learn enough during the day since he planned to join the ladies in their booth once again. The main event for the afternoon was the meeting at Pyramid Group to discuss the hotel renovation plans. Shortly after lunch, Jim and I escorted Marina Antonovna via taxi to the firm's office on Michigan

Avenue. The sidewalk was filled with tourists and business people peering into the many high-end fashion stores that lined the street. When we exited the elevator, the architect, who was leading the project, greeted us.

"Welcome to The Pyramid Group," announced a tall, slender man with thick sandy hair and large octagonal spectacles. "I am Mark Morrison." Dressed in a tan sports coat and blue shirt with no tie, the architect smiled, causing the sharp lines around his eyes to become more prominent. "Please follow me. I have a conference room prepared for our meeting."

Marina Antonovna proceeded first and gazed with interest at the metal-framed photos of office buildings and golf courses hanging along the wood-paneled corridor wall. I followed our guest into the space along with Jim and Mark. A series of blueprints were spread across the table, and the familiar schematics of the Hotel Kazan were clearly discernible. Marina Antonovna took a seat nearest to the entrance. My colleagues and I occupied the few remaining chairs on either side.

"Well," began Mark, "how is the exhibition going? Are you enjoying your time in Chicago?"

Marina Antonovna replied, "Very well, thank you," in her thickly accented English. "Chicago is beautiful city."

"I saw you admiring some of our projects on the walls outside."

"Yes, you have big projects. Perhaps my hotel is big project for you."

I was somewhat surprised by her English comprehension level. Mark then dove into his presentation. The technical details were beyond Marina's English ability; we took frequent pauses so I could translate. Using the overhead projector, Mark contrasted images of the current hotel, taken from the videos and photos shot in Kazan, with digital representations of his proposed changes. The plan envisioned upgrading many vital systems in the hotel, such as plumbing, heating, and the foundation. The proposal was impressive in its design and scale. These changes would transform the aging structure into a modern hotel capable of servicing a significant increase in guests.

"Plan is nice, but what is cost to build?" asked Marina Antonovna flatly.

Mark explained that the proposed changes' estimated costs were more than ten million dollars. "Of course," he added, "You may be able to lower the price with local workers."

"Would American company be ok pay this? I do not have money for that level. Maybe we not do plumbing or heating and lower cost make more companies interested."

"If we can attract a chain to manage the hotel, they likely would be willing to work on the financing," I added. "Remember, that is part of the fees for our service."

"We have already put together a list of potential hotel companies to approach," interjected Jim. "I have many contacts in the Midwest region. We would just need your approval to move forward."

In Russian, the hotel manager repeated to me the option of using the Kazan architectural firm to finish the drawing work and employing local construction firms. I summarized her discourse for my colleagues.

"The local architect would save some cost," I replied, "but I am not sure he can produce materials as Mark has prepared. These documents will be crucial to convincing a hotel chain to invest. And, if a chain invests, it will want to direct who does the construction work."

Marina Antonovna nodded but did not appear satisfied with the response. She thanked Mark for all the work and approved contacting hotel chains about potential investment. Jim explained that the firm was ready to begin that process as soon as she wired over the second half of the fee payment. Our guest stated that she would take care of this the following week when she returned to Kazan. Mark gave her a thumb drive containing a copy of the renovation presentation and the blueprints. The meeting over, Mark escorted us back to the elevators, where we shook hands. The taxi ride back to the center was silent; Marina Antonovna seemed lost in thought. Upon arrival, we found the rest of the delegation preparing to leave for the day. I told Adel about the presentation and Marina's reaction on the bus ride to the hotel. He shared my concern that the hotel manager's unrealistic expectations might negatively impact the project.

I felt excited when I arrived at the hotel the following morning. If all went as planned, there would be much to celebrate. This was the day to finalize joint venture agreements with the American companies. And finally, to give the delegation an impressive send-off, a dinner was planned at the recently opened Signature Room restaurant located on the 95th floor of the Hancock Tower building. The restaurant's floor-to-ceiling glass windows furnished breathtaking nighttime views of the city.

The bus dropped us off at the exhibition center at the regular time. While the Russians got settled into the morning routine of arranging the booths, I went to find Sarah to verify the joint-venture meetings and confirm her attendance for dinner. I ran into her by the reception area.

"Hi, Sarah. I just wanted to see if the rooms are all set for this afternoon. Adel and I are planning on bringing the five directors over shortly after lunch."

"Yes, everything is ready. The companies are excited to finish the agreements. I already have a press release ready to post later this evening."

"Excellent. You are still coming to the Hancock Tower tonight, right? I want to show my appreciation for all your help."

"Aww, that's very nice of you. Yes, I do plan on attending. The dinner starts at 8:00 pm, correct?"

"Yes, you can meet us up on the 95th floor. We will be the large, noisy table."

Feeling confident about the day's outcome, I returned to the row of booths. To my surprise, most of the stalls were empty. Only the Hotel Kazan was manned, where Jim was conversing with the two Russian women. I walked over to the booth.

"Dobry yutro. Where is everyone? There is no one at any of the other stalls. Even Adel is missing."

Jim gave me a perplexed look. Apparently, he had been so engrossed in conversation that he hadn't noticed the exodus of the delegation. Vera Maksimovna wore a feigned look of ignorance. Marina Antonovna's smile resembled the Cheshire Cat's devilish grin upon seeing Alice stumble into Wonderland; her expression masked knowledge of some nefarious event. I remained silent for a moment, waiting for her to unveil what had happened.

"My dear Ken. A man called Igor Sadyuk arrived this morning, claiming to be from Ukraine but living now in Chicago. He told Adel and some directors about his very successful business here in America. According to him, Russians do not need to give up control over their companies to receive investment. He invited all the men to come and discuss with him their plans."

I was flabbergastered. Competing thoughts began to rush around in my head. Instead of preparing for meetings with American investors, the entire delegation had disappeared to talk with this mysterious Ukrainian. I needed to find out who this man was and what he was trying to do.

"Marina, do you know where this Mr. Sadyuk is?"

Still smiling, she responded, "He mentioned that there was space on the other side of the hall where the men could talk privately."

"Ken," said Jim, "Do you want me to go with you?"

"No, I'll find them and see what the hell is happening."

I walked off at a rapid pace, in the direction indicated by the hotel manager. I turned at a bend across the central section of the hall and saw, seated in a close semi-circular formation, the male members of my delegation. Huddled together in chairs, they were listening intently to a man sitting in the center. He was speaking in a low voice and gesturing frequently. In his greyish blue business suit with no tie, this middle-aged man, with wavy grey hair parted to one side, gave the impression of a salesman desperately aiming to close a deal with skeptical customers. Like traders in the pit at the Chicago Mercantile Exchange, the man and the Russians swapped questions and answers at a hectic pace. Still unable to hear the content of the discussion, I moved in closer to the gathering. Adel, located on the outer edge of the semi-circle, must have heard my footsteps. He turned around and, upon seeing me, quickly rose from his chair. He walked over to where I was standing.

"Hi, Adel, what's going on?"

"Ken," he stated, "This Ukrainian guy, Igor, who lives here in Chicago, has been telling us that we do not need joint ventures to get investment. We (Russians) can control our businesses, have foreign partners invest, and receive a piece of the profits in return. Igor says he works with Americans based solely on 'cooperation'. We want *cooperation*."

My Tatar colleague pronounced this last word slowly and with emphasis. I didn't know how to respond and remained silent for several moments. It was hard to accept that an unknown guy could convince Adel to change his mind so quickly about a process he and I had built for more than a year.

"Cooperation? You now want cooperation. That is what you are telling me," I retorted. I had to admit that I was more than a little upset. "We have meetings this afternoon to sign several joint venture agreements. Do you even understand what 'cooperation' entails?"

Adel could see the frustration on my face. "Well, we can explain to the Americans that we want to change the agreements to cooperation."

"Which means what, exactly?"

"They (the Americans) will invest in the enterprises but will receive an amount of profits without any ownership."

"And if the enterprises do not make any profits?"

"Well, then they don't receive any until we make profits."

I shook my head in disbelief. "You met this guy an hour ago, and now you are ready to throw away the work we have done since last year? Can you even trust this Igor?"

My contact seemed a bit insulted by my accusation. "He says he has done this many times and is very successful. He is one of us. He understands how things work. We feel we can trust him more than the Americans."

I wanted to go and speak with this Igor myself. However, I noticed that the Russians were dispersing and that Igor had vanished. I stood silently as the directors walked past me. This guy had come and gone like a ghost, his presence leaving a devasting impact. I turned back to Adel.

"Unbelievable. If we tell the American executives that the Russians want to change the terms of the agreements at this point, there will be no agreements. The executives are not going to accept 'cooperation'."

My earlier enthusiasm was gone. I felt unenergetic and unmotivated. Jim reacted likewise when informed of the events with the mysterious Ukrainian. He described his discussion with Marina Antonovna as more subdued following the prior afternoon's contentious presentation. I feared that the success of the trip was in serious jeopardy. Later that morning, I bumped into Sarah and let her know about the Russians' change in approach. She, too, expressed doubt that her members would agree to 'cooperation', given their goals and the time and cost already incurred. She suggested alerting the American companies to avoid surprises. I thought it prudent and left her to take care of it.

I invited Jim to lunch in a small outdoor café, hoping to brainstorm strategies to rescue the conference. We discussed various options, but none seemed capable of preventing a collapse of the agreements. When we arrived back at the exhibition hall, we found the Russians excited; they looked forward to completing 'cooperation agreements'. I told Adel the American executives were notified about the expected request to establish 'cooperation' instead of a joint venture. I gathered the Russians onto the awaiting shuttle, and we arrived at the chamber of commerce building a few minutes later. Sarah greeted us in the reception area, dominated by a sizeable triangular-shaped wood desk. Behind the desk affixed to the wall was the organization's circular seal. The Russians shuffled around while Sarah registered the group. After a few moments, she turned around and faced her guests.

"OK, everyone," she said in her pleasant voice, " I have reserved five separate conference rooms, one for each of your companies. Your American partner is already waiting in the room for you. I will lead each director to his room, one at a time, and we have reserved two hours for the meeting. If you have any questions, you can contact me via a phone in the room."

"What about translators?" I asked, observing some nervousness on the Russians' faces.

"Yes, of course. There is a translator in each room. I wish you all great success!"

Sarah invited the first director to walk with her down the adjoining hallway. While she was gone, Adel tapped my shoulder.

"Are we going into the meetings?"

"No. These are private sessions. You and I will wait here."

The program manager reappeared after a few minutes and called the next pair of directors. Ten minutes later, Adel and I remained alone in the white-tiled area.

"Ken, how soon do you think the investment will begin? The ministry is eager to see foreign money start flowing."

I responded, "I am not sure. Let's see if there will be investment first."

Adel seemed confident in the advice of Igor Sadyuk. I knew the government had put a lot of pressure on Adel to secure concrete investment, which likely influenced his quick support for 'cooperation'. Perhaps, he thought if he could bring in investment without ceding any Russian ownership, his superiors would be doubly impressed. He was taking a considerable risk and would soon find out whether it paid off. I saw Sarah emerge from the hallway more than an hour later. She came over and sat beside me.

"How's it going?" I inquired.

"Well, I peeked into a couple of the rooms, and the discussions seemed sober."

"Kinda how I expected. Do you think we'll conclude any agreements?"

She gave me a non-committal shrug. Adel was trying to hear the conversation, leaning far forward in his seat. I gazed at my colleague and gave him my best 'I don't know' sign. He slid back into the chair, an anxious expression on his face. Sarah got back up and disappeared once again down the corridor.

At last, Sarah reappeared, accompanied by the Russians. None were smiling, a somber look on their faces. They explained that the Americans would not agree to partner based on cooperation, instead insisting on joint ventures with management influence. Now enamored by cooperation, the Russians stated they would search for a different partner willing to embrace this concept. Adel looked perplexed.

"What is so confusing?" I asked him. "I told you that this would happen."

"I can't believe the Americans don't want to work with us," was his reply. "They don't want to be partners but want to control us." It was stunning how quickly my colleague had discarded all of our joint work. He did not blame the failure on the Russians' abrupt about-face regarding joint ventures.

Traditional biases between our two countries continued to influence how we regarded each other's intentions. American governmental and commercial policies to promote US investment were perceived by many in Russia as an attempt to take advantage of the country's present weak economic and military position. The loss of prestige as one of the world's two superpowers also negatively affected the psyche of many Russians. American companies, most making a good faith effort to work with Russians, found it challenging to overcome these obstacles. The Russian parliament, generally resistant to broad democratic reforms, was passing more and more restrictive laws, especially in the economic sphere. President Boris Yeltsin, an early promoter of rapid market reforms, was battling poor approval ratings due to financial hardships, which prompted him to bring more conservative elements into the government. The initial euphoria surrounding the opportunity for a non-authoritarian system to take root in Russia was rapidly waning.

The final send-off dinner was planned for that evening. While the Russians were preparing in their rooms, Jim and I waited in the hotel bar. Nursing a glass of cognac, I detailed the failures of the meetings with the American executives. He nodded in agreement but seemed focused on the status of the renovation project.

"Do you think Marina will move forward with the project?" he asked.

"After today, I am not sure of anything. Let's see if she pays the rest of our fee first."

"I'll hold off then contacting any of the hotel chains."

"Yes. I almost feel like Marina came here to try the clubs and shop. She has collected quite the collection of Neiman Marcus and Macy bags."

Jim laughed. "Yeah, she took several 'breaks' each day and disappeared for a few hours, returning with the bags. I can't blame her. I bet you can't find those items in Russia."

"I am still shocked that Adel was so easily persuaded by that Ukrainian guy. We had so many conversations in Russia, and I thought he understood and supported our work."

"Well, he is a product of his environment," said Jim. "Never having to think like a western businessman, he is more comfortable falling back on what he knows."

The Russians' mood on the bus was festive despite the day's disappointment. Marina Antonovna and Vera Maksimovna were decked out in elegant cocktail dresses. The hotel manager's black shimmering outfit complimented her girlfriend's red and gold striped evening garb. Both ladies sported long sparkling earrings, which almost touched their bare shoulders. The men kept the suits worn during the day, although a few had added a tie or handkerchief for the occasion. The conversation was lively; no one could imagine a restaurant at such a height.

There was a collective gasp as the bus approached the Hancock Tower. The black steel frame of the almost 1,200-foot high building, with its famous criss-cross support girders, stood imposingly while the delegation exited the bus. The lower floors of the building housed many high-end retail shops, while its upper floors were home to numerous wealthy Chicagoans, including Oprah Winfrey. An observation deck giving 360-degree views of the city occupied the 94th floor. Two giant white communication spires rose from the roof of the hundred-story building.

In less than one minute, the ultra-high-speed elevator whisked us up to the 95th floor. We stepped off the elevator and saw a large acrylic wall sign welcoming arrivals to 'The Signature Room'. The hallway to the right led to a set of glass double doors denoting the entrance to the restaurant. A hostess, stationed at a dark wood podium just inside the glass doors, stood ready to greet us. To the left was an elongated bar, also in wood. A vast array of bottles containing top label brands of bourbon, vodka, and other spirits were placed along the sides and top of the bar. My steps echoed off the dark brown stained parquet floor. Jim and Adel held open the glass doors allowing the rest of the guests to file into the restaurant.

"Good evening," I stated. "We are the Russian delegation associated with the chamber of commerce. We have a reservation."

The hostess, Alicia, a young woman in her early twenties, wore a black vest over her white long-sleeve blouse and was grinning broadly. Her jet black hair put up in a ponytail matched her eyes. Her caramel-toned skin hinted at a Latin or Middle Eastern ancestry.

"Yes, welcome!" she exclaimed. "We are very excited to have you here with us tonight. We have reserved the VIP section of the restaurant for your party. Would you like to follow me?"

She moved away from the podium. I traced her steps and turned my head, ensuring the other guests stayed behind me. A narrow passageway led from the reception area to the main dining room. The view that emerged was impressive. The corridor gave way to a massive two-story space bearing the same dark brown parquet floor. Floor-to-ceiling windows surrounded the entire area, interrupted halfway by a border containing painted panels depicting specific city scenes. Rounds tables covered in white linen and flanked by wooden chairs occupied the middle of the space. Square-shaped tables set for four sat adjacent to the windows where the beaming lights of Chicago's skyline reflected proudly. A twelve-foot high wine rack off to the right displayed an immense collection of bottles stacked inside glass honeycomb cubes. Behind the wine rack, we entered an expansive private space. The room offered floor-to-ceiling windows, separated by glass walls from the main dining area. Two long rectangular tables were arranged side-by-side, giving guests incredible views of the city lights.

"Please make yourselves comfortable," said the hostess as we filed into the room. "The servers will be in shortly."

The hostess departed, but no one had taken a seat. The Russians were all standing against the windows, peering into the Chicago night. A cloudless night allowed the visitors spectacular views of Lake Michigan to the east and the Loop, Grant Park, and Soldier Field to the south. I moved from one side of the room to the other, poking my head in between my guests to point out important landmarks. Everyone was still enjoying the views when the first servers arrived and placed the first course on the table.

"Hi, Ken." I heard Sarah's voice and saw the program director approach. She had replaced the blue dress shirt and khakis worn earlier in the day with a fitted, dark blue skirt and matching jacket covering a shiny silver blouse. A diamond pendant sat in her jacket buttonhole while grey stilettos adorned her feet, complimenting the small grey purse carried under her arm. I commented on her stunning transformation and jokingly added that the women made me feel somewhat underdressed for dinner. She smiled and said that she hoped tonight's event would help ease some of the day's frustration.

"Can I have your attention, please," I declared loudly. "I know the city looks amazing, but I'd like to ask everyone to take a seat so we can start dinner. There will be plenty of time to do more gazing."

Reluctantly, the guests stepped away from the windows and started to find chairs. I made sure to sit in the middle of my table while Sarah sat more off to the left. Jim and Adel took up similar positions at the other table. The first course of vegetable soup was still warm, and I observed that the servers had had time to fill the wine glasses, so I decided to make a quick toast. I rose from my seat, drink in hand.

"I wanted to thank everyone," I said, "for coming to Chicago this week. Seeing you make new contacts and even sign a few sales contracts was exciting. Although not everything was accomplished, I hope you see your visit as a success. To Success!"

"To Success!" rang out in the room. However, I noticed that several of the Russians, namely the ones who failed to secure an agreement that afternoon, stood but did not repeat the toast. The conversation over dinner was polite. My colleagues and I moved around the tables, listening and suggesting topics to keep the discussion going. Most discussed the desire to return to their homeland; this was their most extended trip to the West. During dessert, pairs of guests began to leave their seats to continue observing the city under its magnificent lights. At one point, Marina Antonovna got up and stood, arms crossed, at one of the windows. I left my place and stood next to her.

"Marina, what are you thinking about?"

Her pensive expression reflected in the dark glass. Her eyes stared straight into the night. She said, "We can't rely on the West to help us. Your way is not our way. It may work for you but will only cause trouble for my country. Our history has shown this. We will need to follow our own path."

"I am not sure what you mean, exactly," I replied. I wanted her to explain further.

"It means, Ken," she continued, "that I appreciate all the work you and your firm have done, but it will be better to move forward with Russian architects and builders to complete the hotel."

"Where will you find the investment without an American chain?"

"See, that is why we must do this the Russian way. We know to work around the system. I am sure I will find enough money, even if not in a traditional way."

She said nothing more. When the silence became awkward, I returned to my chair. The tables were now mostly empty. Alone at the table, I reflected upon my experiences over the last two years. At only twenty-four-year-old, my journeys had taken me from Moscow to the Volga region to Siberia. Despite having no formal business education, I played a small part in expanding Russian commercial relations with America. The window of opportunity created by Russia's emergence from communism presented me with a unique chance to contribute to friendlier ties between Cold War foes. However, as I stared out at the empty chairs, I realized that this window was rapidly closing. The whirlwind of hope for a better future that had blown so strongly just a few years ago had already begun to shift. I took a final drink from my wine glass, got up, and headed toward the exit. Jim noticed my departure and caught up with me as I headed to the elevator bank.

"Where are you going?" he asked. "We have to finish the evening."

"I can't tonight, Jim. I need to go home."

"What about tomorrow? Will you be there for the ride to the airport?"

"Maybe, I don't know. I just need to get some sleep."

I entered the elevator and waved goodbye to my colleague, whose face still bore a look of astonishment.

I woke up the next morning still suffering from depression and disillusionment. I hid under the covers with no motivation to start the day. Thankfully, Deb entered the bedroom and informed me that one of her best friends had invited us to a comedy show that afternoon. The thought of spending a day with friends seemed to be the perfect remedy for my current state. I poked my head from under the comforter and told her we would go. A few minutes later, she returned to tell me that I had a phone call. I knew who was calling and why. For a moment, I considered asking Deb to say that I was not available but instead dragged myself out of bed. The floor was freezing on my bare feet. I stumbled a little into the kitchen, where she handed me the receiver.

"Hello, this is Ken."

"Ken, it's Jim. I am at the hotel. Are you coming? We are leaving for the airport in an hour or so."

I took a deep breath before speaking into the receiver. "Jim, I am sorry, but I cannot make it. I'm just not feeling up to it."

All I heard for a few moments was a crackling sound on the line. "What? So, I have to get the group back to the airport by myself? I can't believe this!"

"I know it sucks. You have Adel there, and the bus is reserved. I simply can't do it."

"I'll take care of it, but don't expect future support," shouted Jim.

He hung up the phone.

That call marked the end of the journey that began with such promise almost two years before. My initial enthusiasm had transformed into disappointment and skepticism. Harsh reality pierced my naïve romantic notions that bitter adversaries could overcome historical distrust and fear to form a lasting friendship. Despite the desire for change from many Russians and Americans, these obstacles proved irreconcilable. This window of opportunity had indeed been brief.

Within a few short years, facing economic collapse due to poorly managed reforms and skeptical western support, Russia gradually returned to its traditional authoritarian path. Russian presidents Boris Yeltsin and Vladimir Putin steadily regained state control over key economic assets. A state-sponsored economy, dominated by cronyism and corruption, replaced Western-style market capitalism. This environment impeded the development of a modern, diversified economy driven by innovative small and medium-sized companies. Russia became again dependent on its energy sector. Political and social freedoms championed after the fall of communism have also been drastically curtailed. Putin's policies over the last decade had reconstituted Russia's customary totalitarian police state. Many of the conversations and experiences I engaged in during my travels to Khabarovsk, Kazan, and Moscow could not happen today.

Nevertheless, I learned much from my time in Russia. It shaped me in many ways, which has carried through my life over the past thirty years. I often think about what my impact might have been had I possessed the knowledge I have today. The opportunity to engage in intricate business affairs in Russia prompted me to attend business school, after which I spent the next twenty-five years as a finance and operations executive. Perhaps the current me could have helped some Russian companies successfully transition to capitalism. In the subsequent years, I have not returned to Russia; given recent events, I am unlikely to do so anytime soon. I feel I missed a chance, in some small way, to make the world better. But who knows what the future holds. The wind of change is still blowing.

# AFTERWORD

FOR A FEW YEARS FOLLOWING my journey, I stayed in contact with Adel and several of the Americans who accompanied me to Khabarovsk. Adel continued to work at the Tatarstan Construction Ministry and eventually did attract foreign investment, mainly from European companies. To my knowledge, none of the businesses I engaged with in Tatarstan concluded a partnership with an American company. The idea of 'cooperation' was not successful. The Hotel Kazan did not find a western investor and eventually closed in the early 2000s. The structure was demolished sometime in 2008/2009. As expected, I lost contact with Jim Mazuros and The Pyramid Group following the departure of the Russian delegation from Chicago. Makoto and I spoke on a consistent basis for a time after the trip to Khabarovsk, meeting for lunch to discuss business opportunities. Robert contacted me about a year after the Siberian trip about a potential partnership to explore more energy deals. Nothing came from these discussions as Robert seemed constantly hesitant about moving forward. Scott's supply and quality obstacles were too great; he never returned to Khabarovsk to open his restaurant. I suppose The Golden Fish remained the top burger place for several years. As far as I know, Igor Petrovich continued to 'acquire' businesses in Khabarovsk, but I am unsure whether he ever completed his casino.

In the mid-1990s, the economic situation in Russia steadily worsened, leading to a full-blown financial crisis in 1998. The Russian government defaulted on its debt and devalued the rouble. Hyperinflation wiped out the savings of most Russian citizens. Foreign investors lost confidence in Russia, drying up a vital source of capital for Yeltsin's government. To help stave off disaster, the International Monetary Fund and World Bank stepped in with a multi-billion dollar support package. The crisis had a devasting impact on Russians' confidence in the free-market economy. An unpopular and unsuccessful war in Chechnya combined with the economic collapse increased many Russians' desire to end the instability or 'khaos' (chaos).

Facing meager popularity ratings, Boris Yeltsin announced that on December 31, 1999, he would resign from the presidency. His successor was a little-known former KBG official, Vladimir Putin, who had only become Prime Minister in May, and enjoyed growing popularity due to his perceived toughness in the war in Chechnya. Many Russians believed Putin could end the 'khaos' and restore stability and national pride. Putin initially presented himself as a liberal, appearing to court closer relations with the West. Putin leveraged the West's eagerness to incorporate Russia into the international economic and security system to obtain Russia's entry into the G-7 (renamed the G-8), promote foreign investment, and create European energy dependency. Putin's criticism of NATO's involvement in Bosnia and expansion of former Warsaw Pact countries was under-appreciated by western governments. Putin nevertheless allowed the US military to use a Russian air for supply operations at the start of the Afghan War. As Russia's economy improved, bolstered by strong energy prices, and revamped its military, Putin's tone began to change.

In the mid-2000s, Putin's actions and words began to resemble more traditional Russian leaders. Putin emphasized more and more his country's 'special mission', which historically meant opposition to western culture and values. The critical role of Russia as a great power also became a more frequent theme. In 2007, the Russian president delivered a speech in Munich that sharply criticized the United States' monopolistic position in global affairs, describing it as 'unacceptable' and 'impossible'. Georgia's desire for closer ties to the European Union and NATO played a key role in Putin's decision to use military force against the former Soviet republic in August 2008. This action reminded the United States and its western allies of the potential limits of Putin's commitment to cooperation with the West and foreshadowed events in Ukraine.

The Russian president gradually but consistently introduced measures restricting the free press and opposition political parties. He created a new oligarch class entirely dependent on the president's whims. During the 2008 global financial crisis, Putin maintained economic stability by utilizing a special fund created with energy earnings. Many Russians appeared willing to accept the restrictions in exchange for a better standard of living. Putin's attempt to run for a third presidential term in 2012 was marred by allegations of vote-rigging and sparked massive street demonstrations in many Russian cities. The scale of the protests shocked Putin, who feared a popular uprising that might lead to a 'color revolution' similar to what had occurred in nearby Georgia and Ukraine. The experience was a wake-up call for Putin. The Russian president intended to avoid future challenges to his authority and began to enact more draconian policies. Over the subsequent decade, more far-reaching restrictions were placed on journalists and political activists. Violence became more commonplace. Several prominent journalists and political opponents were killed, the most notorious of which was the brazen assassination of Putin critic Boris Nemtsov in 2015. In 2020, Alexei Navalny, widely considered Putin's primary rival, was poisoned by FSB agents while on a flight in Siberia. Navalny barely survived and is currently imprisoned in Russia. Putin has also not been afraid to go after critics outside Russia. Assassination attempts have occurred in the U.K. and Germany against several Russians seen as Putin's foes.

Perhaps in response to a declining economy and falling approval ratings in the early 2010s, Putin took steps to re-establish Russia as a global power on par with the U.S. and China. Officially part of Ukraine since the late 1950s, Crimea, Putin argued, historically belonged to Russia. Using the pretext of protecting the peninsula's Russian-speaking population, Putin sent unmarked troops into Crimea in 2014. The 'little green men' met no resistance and were welcomed by much of the local population. The Russian president wagered that Ukraine's military was too weak to resist and that the US and NATO would not risk direct war with Russia. Putin won the gamble. Russia added further instability in Ukraine by supporting separatists in two eastern regions, thereby giving Putin continued leverage against Ukraine's government. The Russian president acted more like a Russian Tsar, trying to expand Russia's empire. The move bolstered Putin's popularity at home, allowing him to consolidate his power further.

Putin was recreating the traditional totalitarian police state that existed in Russia under the Tsars and Communists. The state legislature, or Duma now firmly under Putin's control, passed new laws further restricting speech critical of the government, rights to assemble and protest, and the ability of foreign organizations to operate within Russia. Many of these measures harked back to Soviet and even pre-Soviet times. As a result, most independent media and social organizations have been suppressed or forced to close, with certain members facing potential imprisonment. In Summer 2020, the Russian people approved a national referendum approving a constitutional change that allowed Vladimir Putin to remain in office beyond his current term ending in 2024. The referendum, heavily backed by the Kremlin, enables Putin to run for two additional terms extending his time as president until 2036. The move effectively gives the Russian leader a life term in office.

Secure in his political position at home, Putin turned his attention to establishing his legacy. A fundamental tenet was restoring Russia's status as a global superpower. Russian forces' unprovoked invasion of Ukraine in February 2022 aligned with Putin's desire to see himself as the leader who reconstructed the Russian Empire. He has even compared his actions to those of Peter the Great. Tsar Peter, noted for modernizing Russia's army and bureaucracy to European standards, led military conquests for over twenty years to expand Russia's empire in the 18th century. Many of these wars occurred in countries currently members of NATO.

Viewing NATO as weak and heavily dependent on Russian energy, Putin was surprised by the strong reaction to his aggression. The effective defense by Ukrainian forces, modernized and trained by NATO advisors since 2014, contradicted Putin's expectation of a quick victory. Russian intelligence reports predicting a warm welcome from Ukrainians were grossly inaccurate; this was not to be a repeat of Crimea. Russia's initial blitzkrieg strategy of taking the entire country failed, compelling Putin to reorient his attack in the Donbas region. Instead of dividing NATO, the invasion reinvigorated the alliance. For the first time since WWII, Germany announced it would drastically increase its defense spending to modernize its armed forces. Sweden and Finland, whose populations were shocked by Russia's overt aggression, reversed their decades-old policies against joining NATO and applied for membership. The United States announced an increase of its forces in Europe, with permanent deployments eastward into Poland.

The scope and swiftness of sanctions imposed on Russia by western governments have immediate and lasting effects on the Russian economy. Restrictions on trade and financing have had a crippling impact on Russia's ability to import needed goods. Russian manufacturers are scrambling to source materials. Automakers, for example, are building cars without airbags. The country defaulted on its foreign debt for the first time since the Russian Revolution. Most western companies have permanently left or have frozen operations in Russia, including McDonald's, whose entry into the USSR in the late 80s signaled hope for better relations. Official state propaganda blaming the U.S. and NATO for causing the invasion has so far been effective. Opinion polls show that a majority of Russians support Putin, and anti-western sentiment is rising. Likewise, anti-Russian feeling has grown dramatically in Europe and America. The war in Ukraine may drag on for months and years as Putin looks to cement his legacy and fears what a failure may mean for his rule. The U.S. and NATO cannot allow major territorial changes in Europe, which would endanger the entire post-WWII international order.

Thirty years later, the enthusiasm shared by Russians and Americans after the end of the Cold War seems a distant memory. Misperceptions on both sides regarding the expected 'peace dividend' contributed heavily to a sense of disillusionment. For Russians, the promise of democracy and free markets did not instantaneously lead to prosperity and happiness for all. Russia's adoption of 'shock therapy', strongly supported by the West, in the early 1990s quickly created large disparities in wealth. Many ordinary Russians, struggling to make ends meet, resented the incredible wealth of the small class of super-rich 'oligarchs', whose wealth was attained by questionable means and who provided invaluable financial support to President Yeltsin. The 1998 economic collapse broke the promise of anticipated prosperity and made many Russians clamor for a traditional strongman leader.

For Americans, Russia did not quickly become a western-style democracy with associated market structures and values. Visions of a US (and implied NATO) partnership with a democratic Russia that would share the same world view never materialized. Yeltsin's war against Chechnya reminded the West that the new Russia might still have similar interests to historical Russia. American business hoped to find (and dominate) a vast untapped market for its products and services. Russians were eager to obtain better quality American goods but, in disappointment to US CEOs, were not as willing to hand over total control of assets. Russian governmental regulations on foreign ownership, taxes, and property protection created frustration and hindered investment.

A slower, more managed approach to democracy and free markets might have given Russians and Americans more time to digest and adjust to this enormous undertaking. A phased economic transition accompanied by a gradual development of democratic institutions and processes would have allowed Russians time to learn how to function within this new society. Russia historically lacked an active and informed citizenry that participated in governance. Expecting most Russians to suddenly manage in a modern liberal democracy was unrealistic. Time and assistance were needed to educate Russians on the duties of citizens in a democracy. A measured economic transition may also have prevented the rise of the oligarchs and permitted the government to direct the market introduction in a more equitable manner. Greater American patience and guidance (financial and knowledge) could have helped Russia build a more stable foundation and allowed democracy to become more deeply rooted. Instead, the emphasis on a hasty and sizeable return on investment (ROI) from the peace dividend was perhaps short-sighted. This ROI ignored the long-term potential of a Russia that would be a full member of the democratic order.

Looking back, I feel that there was an immense missed opportunity. The experiences described in this book appear to me today as almost impossible to imagine. The atmosphere of mutual hope and goodwill has been squandered. The images of a young American working with a former KGB official have been replaced by arrests of Americans on trumped-up charges. Russia has justifiably become a pariah for American business, with US companies all but deserting the country in the wake of the invasion of Ukraine. Any future anticipation of a renewed US – Russia partnership will likely require a post-Putin government. When that occurs, I hope we will have learned the lessons of the past and be able to build a lasting friendship.

Lightning Source UK Ltd.
Milton Keynes UK
UKHW021047060223
416538UK00017B/2197